DRUG WARS

NEIL WOODS

& J.S. RAFAELI

DRUG
WARS

EBURY
PRESS

1 3 5 7 9 10 8 6 4 2

Ebury Press, an imprint of Ebury Publishing
20 Vauxhall Bridge Road
London SW1V 2SA

Ebury Press is part of the Penguin Random House group of companies whose
addresses can be found at global.penguinrandomhouse.com

Penguin
Random House
UK

First published by Ebury Press in 2018

www.penguin.co.uk

A CIP catalogue record for this book is available from the British Library

ISBN 9781785037443
TPB ISBN 9781785037450

This book is a work of non-fiction based on the experiences,
interviews and recollections of the authors and their contributors.
In some cases names of people and places have been changed.

Typeset in 9/11 pt New Century Schoolbook LT Std
by Integra Software Services Pvt. Ltd, Pondicherry

Printed and bound in Great Britain by Clays Ltd, Elcograf S.p.A.

Penguin Random House is committed to a sustainable
future for our business, our readers and our planet.
This book is made from Forest Stewardship Council®
certified paper.

Dedicated to all those around the world
who fight against unjust laws.

Contents

Preface

– by Neil Woods

The observation van is parked on a rough, dead-end street in Leeds, running surveillance on a high-level Bradford drug dealer. Suddenly, the van is surrounded by men in balaclavas. It is tied shut, doused in petrol and set on fire. The two cops inside barely get out alive.

It was no accident that the gangsters knew there was an obs van outside their safe house that night. They had moles inside the police feeding them information.

That incident was never reported in the press, but I remember the operation well. The thought of those two officers trapped inside the burning vehicle stuck with me – it forced me to once again ask myself a gnawing question. How has it come to this? How has it got to the point where the police come under attack because their own systems have been corrupted?

This wasn't the first time on the force I'd experienced high-level corruption. When I was working under cover in Nottingham, my own unit had been infiltrated by the sociopathic drugs kingpin, Colin Gunn.

Gunn had hired a 19-year-old kid named Charles Fletcher to join the police – with specific instructions to get into

CID. For years, Gunn paid Fletcher £2,000 a month on top of his police salary to pass on intelligence about ongoing investigations.

When I confronted my superiors about this I was met with a shrug. 'With so much money in the drugs game, how can corruption not happen?' It had got to the point that with drug investigations, police corruption had just become an accepted part of the game. How has it come to this?

On another major operation, the first lawful order we received was that under no circumstances were we to speak to anyone from Greater Manchester Police – and that if anyone from GMP approached us, we were to immediately report it. We were forced to work under the assumption that a major British police force was so riddled with moles and informants that any contact with them whatsoever was suspect. How has it come to this?

That question stuck with me throughout my final years on the force. It continued to trouble me even after I had left the police and tried to dedicate my life to undoing some of the harm that I had caused. Then we published the book *Good Cop, Bad War*.

The response to *Good Cop* hit me for six. We started receiving letters and emails from all over the country – and from around the world. There were messages from cops and ex-cops; addicts and family members of addicts; drug dealers and serving prisoners who had read the book in the prison library. These were all people who had experienced the War on Drugs at first hand – from both sides of the battle line.

Somehow, what we had written in *Good Cop* resonated with their experience. This outpouring of support and encouragement was both humbling and profoundly inspiring. Then, one letter came through that stopped me in my tracks.

It was from a young man named Adam, whose parents had both been intravenous heroin users. Adam spent his childhood caught in the chaotic mess of overdoses and arrests that often define the life of drug users under a system of prohibition. He spoke of witnessing the beatings his parents received at the hands of ruthless gangsters. He remembered seeing the desperation and shame in their eyes, and of knowing, even as a child, that what they needed was 'help, support, and understanding, not prison and judgement'.

Adam wrote of how he watched the arms race of the War on Drugs unfold – how it got 'more and more violent, more and more difficult'. He wrote of how 'this war wasn't going to be won with force, arrests, prison and isolation'.

He wrote of having to watch his own mother being forced to drink petrol over a £20 drug debt.

Once again, that question – how has it come to this?

In the face of Adam's letter, and hundreds more like it, I decided I would finally try to answer that question.

We didn't get here by accident. The situation Adam, myself and thousands of others caught up in the War on Drugs have found ourselves in, is the result of very specific decisions, taken over decades. These decisions need to be looked at.

The British War on Drugs is almost 60 years old. To explain how it functions, you need to look back into its roots. This is a story that has never been told – until now.

On *Good Cop, Bad War*, I worked closely with the writer J.S. Rafaeli. Throughout that process, we had begun to ask questions about the wider meaning of the personal story we were telling. How did the War on Drugs develop? What impact has it had on British policing and law enforcement? What can this tell us about the relationship between the individual and the state? On a personal level, considering these questions turned out to be invaluable in helping me begin to understand and process the PTSD from which I had suffered since leaving the police.

So, we decided to take on this new project together. By combining my inside perspective of the police with J.S.'s skills as a historian and journalist, we could confidently approach this hugely complex story. This book is a completely equal, joint effort between us – and has been an incredibly challenging, but rewarding, process for us both.

The first thing we decided was that we needed to talk about people. All too often when discussing drug policy, the conversation gets caught up in statistics and vague political ideas. It's academics arguing with politicians arguing with cops – and everyone loses sight of the fact that behind the numbers lie real people, with real stories.

We wanted these voices to be heard. We wanted them brought back into the conversation. So, we spent months going up and down the country interviewing drug dealers, cops, addicts, health workers, activists and politicians – getting to the truth of what the British War on Drugs has meant to the people who actually fought it.

We met some extraordinary people. We cannot thank each and every one of them enough for their courage and generosity in sharing their experiences with us. By necessity, we have had to edit these interviews for flow and brevity, but this is absolutely *their* story.

Each chapter of this book, from the 1960s to the present day, covers themes that have been written about in depth by specialists and academics. We are building on their efforts, and could not have begun to put this story together without the work they have done.

However, this discussion too often happens only in academic circles. This book is meant for everyone – because this is a history that everyone should know. The War on Drugs happens on the street. It's time to take its story out there too.

* * *

The most successful drug cartel in history was not run by a Colombian cocaine baron, a Mexican trafficking gang or an Afghan warlord. It was run by the British state.

Throughout the nineteenth century, the East India Company – backed by British military power – ran simultaneous monopolies on opium in China and hashish in India. In his wildest dreams, Pablo Escobar never got anywhere close. In 1997, when Tony Blair handed Hong Kong back to China, she was handing back the spoils of a nineteenth-century drug war.

At home it was a different story. The original substance-based moral panics in Britain were probably the Gin Crazes that intermittently rocked the country throughout the eighteenth and nineteenth centuries. Each of these crises produced a tabloid outcry, and calls for gin to be banned outright.

Each time, however, those calls were resisted. That was not the British way. Successive governments – including those led by conservative icons like the Duke of Wellington – chose to deal with the gin problem through regulation and licensing, not through law enforcement. This fitted within a deep-rooted British tradition of liberal pragmatism – and, by and large, it worked.

In terms of the modern War on Drugs, Britain has never matched the violence of the United States or Latin America. Yet, the UK occupies a unique and crucial place in the history of this global conflict. Britain is historically the country that has offered the most consistent and coherent alternative to the American-led War on Drugs. If there's one essential discovery we made in trying to answer the question 'How has it come to this?', it's that the drug war is a fundamentally un-British idea.

This is very much a lost history. Most people in Britain aren't even aware of it. They should be. This book is an attempt to reclaim this vital thread in our national story.

The War on Drugs has caused chaos and suffering across the globe. This is the story of its British front – how, from tiny beginnings, it has grown and metastasised into a terrifying force that corrupts the very heart of criminal justice.

We believe this is a story that every British person should know. It speaks to many aspects of who we are as a country. But beyond that, our hope and belief in writing this book is that the story of the British experience of the War on Drugs can offer insight to all those who have been affected by it, throughout the world.

Neil Woods, 2018

1

Soho's Pep Pill Craze!

Setting a Pattern in 1964

Lee Harris never meant to start the British War on Drugs.

Sitting across from us today, Lee comes off as the archetypal sweet old hippy. He's 81 years old, with three grandchildren, and talks nostalgically about the past with Buddhist beads around his neck and a mischievous twinkle in his eye. All in all, he seems a very unlikely starting point for a set of policies that has transformed the entire structure of the criminality, policing and culture of this country. But, as that generation never tires of reminding us, things were different back in the sixties.

'I first came to Britain in 1956, at 19 years old,' Lee begins. 'I had to escape South Africa – on the run from the apartheid police. I had joined the Congress Movement as a white teenager, which was very rare back then – but I was a young socialist and truly believed in the cause.

'I took part in a few underground actions, which got a lot of attention and the police came after us hard – so I had to leave the country. But I hated it anyway. I utterly despised apartheid – I couldn't stand books being banned and having to hide what I was reading. It's funny really – when I came to Britain I had never even drunk alcohol before, let alone smoked grass or anything. I was a socialist, a moral puritan. I thought drinking and partying was decadent and bourgeois.'

As a young immigrant, Lee supported himself by washing dishes in a run-down restaurant in Baker Street, before enrolling at drama school. It was here that he met a more bohemian crowd who introduced him to a new world – the world of Soho.

'The first time I went to Wardour Street I was taken to some dive bar, and suddenly there was a knife fight between these butch lesbians and a local pimp. I fell in love with it all right there,' Lee recalls with a wide grin. 'I had read all the books from America by William Burroughs and Jack Kerouac, and I was attracted to the low life. I was young and curious, and this was dangerous and fun. There were all the musicians, actors, artists and clubs – but there were also a thousand prostitutes between Park Lane and Shepherd Market. I'd never seen anything like this – the pimps and the gangsters, and the male prostitute dilly boys hanging around Piccadilly Circus. I was fascinated by that whole world, and became a sort of journalist and explorer, trying to document it.'

Britain in this era was only just emerging from the drab, grey monotony of the post-war years. Rationing had only ended in 1954. The 1956 Suez Crisis exposed a country that 'had lost an empire and had yet to find a role'. For all that people may now romanticise the Teddy Boys, the years between the euphoria of VE Day and the free love explosion of the later 1960s were culturally sullen, parochial and inward-looking.

The exception was Soho. This was the era of the Colony Room on Dean Street, where artists, actors and writers like Lucian Freud, Peter O'Toole, Francis Bacon and Dylan Thomas would drink, flirt and argue. Racially mixed jazz bands played swing in basement clubs, and homosexuals could live relatively openly. Soho was a sliver of Technicolor in a country still living in black and white. It also set the scene for the first convulsion of what would come to be known as 'youth culture'.

The Mods were the first great cultural expression of the baby boom generation. Born just after the war, by the early 1960s they were just hitting their late teens – and they wanted to dance. Mods wore sharp suits, fought pitched battles with their rival tribe, the Rockers, and held all-night soul music parties in legendary Soho dives like the Scene, the Flamingo and the Marquee. It was into this netherworld that Lee Harris was drawn.

'I became very close friends with Lionel Blake, who managed the Scene Club. The parties there were incredible. The young Mods were amazing dancers, the girls all had their hair cut short and everyone looked very slick. I saw Chuck Berry and early line-ups of the Who playing, and would hang out with Brian Jones from the Rolling Stones.

'The kids would go dancing all night – then, at 5am everyone would spill out onto the street. You would walk down Wardour Street and there would be hundreds of these teenagers – 15-16-17-year-olds, all staggering around in the morning light.'

But, nobody dances all night without some extra fuel. And the fuel these kids ran on was French Blues, Black Bombers and Purple Hearts.

Amphetamines were first developed in the 1880s. They had been given to soldiers by both sides as performance enhancers during the Second World War, and throughout the 1950s were widely prescribed as diet pills and as a pick-me-up for tired housewives. Anthony Eden himself was prescribed Purple Hearts throughout the Suez Crisis.[1]

They were also absolutely central to the Mod scene of the early 1960s. Soho was awash with pills. Teenagers would get tattoos reading 'SK & F', standing for Smith, Kline & French, the pharmaceutical company that manufactured Purple Hearts. The clubs rang with drug rhymes like 'feeling down, try red and brown' and 'have no fears with green and clears'.[2] Kids would forge prescriptions and rob pharmacies to keep the scene supplied. Lee Harris looked on at all this with growing unease.

'There's no better drug to keep you dancing all night than amphetamines,' he explains, 'but the reason for all those so-called riots in seaside towns that the papers wrote about was that the kids would come out of the clubs at 5am, but still be completely high on the pep pills. So, they'd all drive out to Margate or Clacton just to have something to do because they couldn't sleep. And that's when the violence would erupt. I was there in Brighton when they were smashing all the shop windows – like the famous scene in the film *Quadrophenia*. They were all blocked on pep pills – that's the word they used for being high, "blocked".'

The Mod 'riots' of the mid-1960s were heavily reported in the press. Articles were loaded with images of leather jackets and motorbikes, using the symbolism of American films to whip up the fears of an older generation. In reality, these 'riots' were extremely rare, with relatively few arrests. Headlines like DAY OF TERROR BY SCOOTER GROUPS, from the *Daily Telegraph*, and WILD ONES INVADE SEASIDE in the *Daily Mirror*, now seem fairly ridiculous.

In fact, it was exactly the reporting of these disturbances that led the criminologist Steve Cohen to coin the phrase 'moral panic'. This is an essential term. It refers to when 'a condition, episode, person or group of persons emerges to become a threat to societal values and interests; its nature is presented in a stylised and stereotypical fashion by the mass media.' The dynamic of cynically constructed, media-driven moral panics is one that recurs over and over throughout this story.

But, for Lee Harris, a far greater concern than media-hyped street brawls were the horrors.

'Kids would take 80 or 90 of these pills over a weekend,' he continues. 'It was sixpence for a Purple Heart – they did far too many and would get amphetamine psychosis. They called it *getting the horrors*. I would find these kids shivering and jabbering, totally terrified. It could take days for them to come down, so I would try and take care of them.

'My family had fled to South Africa as refugees from Lithuania, but my father died and I was brought up in a Jewish orphanage. I think because of that I couldn't see young people in pain and not try and help. I became a sort of guardian figure for some of these kids. If I found someone in a bad way I would bring them back to my flat and make them a cup of tea. I had a typewriter and a tape recorder, and sometimes I would let them talk about what they were experiencing – it seemed to help. Later, I used some of those recordings to write my play *Buzz Buzz*, based around the pep pills scene.'

It was this role as a protector of young amphetamine users that was to change the course of Lee Harris's life – and ultimately, the entire direction of UK drug policy.

'Early in 1964, I was on my way home and I stumbled on this kid on Wardour Street, in a really bad condition. He'd taken maybe 90 Purple Hearts and was having terrible horrors. His heart was racing, he was seeing bugs climbing the walls. So, I helped get him back to his family's flat in Maida Vale.

'It turned out that this kid had a history with pills. His father knew nothing about drugs and was desperate – he didn't know what to do. So he called his local MP, who came down to the house personally to see if he could help. That's how I met Ben Parkin.'

Ben Parkin was the Labour MP for Paddington. He had recently made a name for himself by exposing the corrupt property baron Peter Rachman, and was now looking for a new socially progressive crusade to increase his profile. In Lee Harris, he saw an opportunity.

'We got the kid to bed,' Lee continues, 'then Parkin took me aside. He said he was worried about these pep pills and wanted to raise questions in Parliament. Only, he didn't really know anything about them – but I did, so he asked if he could give my phone number to a journalist he knew. I was worried about how the pills were affecting the kids as well. But I didn't know quite what I was getting into.

'I went home and got some sleep, but that very afternoon my phone rang. "Hello, it's Anne Sharpley from the *Evening Standard* – Ben Parkin said I should get in touch."'

Anne Sharpley is a minor legend of British journalism. A trailblazing woman in a chauvinist era, she had made her name by sailing on the *Windrush* as it carried the first West Indian immigrants to Britain in 1948. Later, when covering Winston Churchill's state funeral, she filed her copy from the nearest phone box, then cut the telephone cord to make sure no rival reporters got the scoop. Sharpley had been Parkin's go-to journalist during his Rachman campaign, and now she was looking for a pills story.

'I took Anne on the most glorious tour of Soho,' says Lee, beaming. 'I showed her all the dives, took her to all-night dances at the Scene and showed her how the kids were using pills. We became very good friends and stayed in touch for years afterward. I helped her with lots of other stories.'

The result was the headline I SEE SOHO'S PEP PILL CRAZE splashed across the front cover of the *Evening Standard* on 3 February 1964, followed by THE NON-STOP WORLD OF PILLS PARADISE the next day.

The two stories are a fascinating mix of genuinely interesting observation and exactly the kind of lurid sensationalism that would set the template for so much drugs reporting for decades to come.

Sharpley acutely notes that:

[The teenagers] are looking for, and getting, stimulation not intoxication. They want greater awareness, not escape. And the confidence and articulacy that the drugs of the amphetamine group give them is quite different from the drunken rowdiness of previous generations on a night out.

But she also peppers her copy with references to 'tireless, sleep-free talkative super-teenagers … drifting from club to café, moment to moment, day to day with a strange, sterile energy that their new craze gives them.'[3] The piece ends with a call for legal controls on Purple Hearts, and notes that Ben Parkin MP will be raising the issue in Parliament.

Parkin did indeed speak in Parliament that very Monday. The points he raised were so similar to Sharpley's articles as to make the collusion obvious.

This media play had its intended effect. On 7 February, the Home Affairs Committee authorised the preparation of a bill for the control of amphetamines. In fact, the original bill was supposed to include barbiturates – believed by the medical community to be far more dangerous. But the burst of publicity around pep pills led the committee to focus solely on speed.[4]

While the deliberations on the bill were taking place, the *Evening Standard* realised it had found a winning formula and launched a Purple Hearts crusade. That month saw headlines including: PURPLE MENACE; THE PURPLE HEART PLOT; COME ON, TEENAGERS, STAMP OUT THE PILL-PUSHERS; PURPLE HEARTS ACTION; PURPLE HEARTS IN WEST END; and NOW YARD CAN STEP-UP WAR ON PURPLE HEARTS. The tabloids were figuring out that drug scares sell papers.

In late March the Stimulant Drugs Bill weaved amphetamines into the Drugs (Prevention of Misuse) Act of 1964. *The Times* noted the rushed nature of the debate, calling the result 'hastily constructed legislation', while *The Economist* was blunter, labelling it 'a singularly ill-conceived bill'.[5]

For Lee Harris, though, the outcome was very different. 'After that first Anne Sharpley piece came out, my phone started ringing off the hook. I suddenly became the stringer for anyone wanting to film or write about the drug scene. I had everyone through, from the *Sunday Times* to Granada Television, week after week. They'd call up and say, "We need a room with junkies fixing, and they have to be willing to go on camera." So I'd have to round up all these junkies, and keep them all night to be ready for filming in the morning. Keeping junkies in one place overnight is bloody hard work you know.

'And it's funny, when Ben Parkin did his speech in Parliament, he talked about how the *Evening Standard* had spent thousands of pounds on this intense investigation. Well, I certainly never got more than fifty quid.'

It's impossible to set an exact start date for the British War on Drugs. The most obvious candidate would be the Misuse of Drugs Act of 1971. But the roots go deeper. And something in Lee Harris's story – the triangulation between an ambitious MP, an ambitious journalist and a self-appointed moral crusader – seems to lay a template for everything that was to come after.

The first casualty of any war is the truth, and the War on Drugs is no exception. If you wish to understand the modern concept of 'fake news', you need only look at how drugs have been reported for at least the last 60 years. Drug reporting has consistently focused not on accurately reflecting events, but on how it makes the reader *feel*. Every war ever fought has had a propaganda front. The tabloid press have, more often than not, served as the propaganda arm of the War on Drugs.

There had been drug scares before – the furore surrounding the death of the actress Billie Carleton in 1918, or the racist demonisation of the Chinese opium seller Billy Chang in 1922, to take just two examples. But, the dynamic that developed in the 1960s represented something new. The War on Drugs developed as an explicitly generational conflict. Across the UK, mothers and fathers who had lived through the Depression and the war watched their children pursuing trends they didn't understand, and thus feared. They clamped down to maintain control.

Unfortunately, their efforts often ended up actually putting their children at greater risk. There was another dynamic set in motion in 1964 that was to repeat itself again and again as the War on Drugs developed – the law of unintended consequences.

The Stimulant Drugs Bill utterly failed to stop kids taking amphetamines. The *Pharmaceutical Journal* reported in 1965 that:

> Even the severe penalties imposed by the Drugs (Prevention of Misuse) Act seem not to have deterred to any obvious extent those who misappropriate and misuse drugs – notoriously those of the amphetamine mixture type.

Even as the Mod culture of London gave way to hippy flower power over the coming years, amphetamine use exploded across the country as the Northern Soul movement took over with all-night parties at clubs like Wigan Casino and Manchester's Twisted Wheel.

But, while the architects of the 1964 Act didn't manage to stop kids taking speed, what they did manage to do was get them into heroin.

In the early 1960s, the tiny drug subcultures that existed in Britain stayed strictly separate – the Mods didn't hang around with cannabis-smoking jazz fans, who wouldn't be seen dead with the heroin users and junkies.[6] In the wake of the 1964 Act, these divisions began to break down. It began with the pharmacy robberies.

One of the main supply routes for pep pills had been employee theft – people working for pharmacies would simply walk out with a box of pills and sell them on. Now that possession of Purple Hearts had been criminalised, employees became less willing to take the risk. The gap was quickly filled by robberies and hijackings.

In 1966, 16 of Salford's 47 pharmacies were broken into. At a single pharmacy burglary in Kings Norton, 50,000 tablets were stolen. The rash of pharmacy robberies spread right across the country. What is crucial about these burglaries is that it was *only* the amphetamines that were stolen. They didn't break in, sweep everything they could into a sack and sort it out later – they knew exactly what they were looking for, and took only the speed. The *Pharmaceutical Journal* noted:

> The offences carry identical characteristics. No excessive damage is caused and the stock remains intact except a small range of specified drugs. The offender can recognise these tablets and capsules at sight.

To combat this explosion of 'drugstore cowboy' robberies, the Home Office brought in new rules dictating that all pharmacies must keep *all* controlled drugs in a secure, locked cabinet. This meant pharmacy burglars just had to work a bit harder and move a bit faster. One burglar interviewed by the sociologist Andrew Wilson recalled:

> The first time we came across the new DDAs gerrin' it open were a right job ... we didn't have two screwdrivers, you needed two good screwdrivers ... but it was often noisy so you had to sweep everything into a bag and get out as quick as you could.

The burglars now didn't have time to hand-pick the amphetamines – they just swept everything into their sacks. But the

Purple Hearts were now being stored along with heroin, barbiturates and other drugs and the burglars were accidentally ending up with swag bags full of opiates they didn't know what to do with. So, they did what any entrepreneurial villain would do – they found people to sell them to. Suddenly, amphetamine users and heroin users began mixing in a way they never had before. For the first time speed users were introduced to the use of needles.

Traditionally, Mods were 'pill-heads' – it was central to their sharp, cool self-image. Now, mixing with heroin users, the taboo around needles broke down. Once people had learned to inject speed, it was a much easier step to injecting heroin – shooting one drug was much like shooting another. Another of Wilson's interviewees recalls that this is:

> what led to cranking and consequently to junk … a lot of people on t'nighters turning to junkies … They cranked the speed. People who cranked speed tended to keep the company of others, they were a clique inside a clique.

Heroin use rocketed among the Mod community. The legal attempts to control Purple Hearts had inadvertently broken down the distinct drug culture that Anne Sharpley had originally described, creating Britain's first significant population of poly-drug users.

The story of the War on Drugs is a story of the law of unintended consequences. At their height, the Soho Mods of the early 1960s were maybe a few thousand people. But, in the story of how the government tried to control Purple Hearts, one can see, in its tiniest, most embryonic form, exactly the dynamic that would be replayed over and over, with ever-increasing ramifications, for the next six decades. And it all started with a conversation between Lee Harris and Ben Parkin in a Maida Vale flat in 1964.

For Lee himself, though, there were intensely conflicted feelings around the part that he played.

'First off, the clubs were all raided,' he explains. 'I was there – I watched the police storm in and all the Mods just throw their pills on the floor. My great friend Lionel Blake got busted and got 15 months for running a "disorderly house". I put together an affidavit that he was a good person, and went to visit him in prison.

'I definitely had a moral conflict. I never wanted to destroy the scene. But I couldn't see kids that young in trouble with pills like that. I tried those amphetamines and couldn't stand them. But, I always felt ashamed of my role in prohibition. I've spent the rest of my life trying to make up for that mistake.'

When everything really changed for Lee, though, was when he tried another controversial drug just gaining popularity in the mid-1960s – cannabis.

'We'd heard rumours and stories of this strange stuff called marijuana or Indian hemp – mainly in the West Indian community. Then one night, I was walking down Oxford Street with this Irish guy, and he said, "Here, try a bit of this." Well, my conversion came right there!

'I think I saw how so many people were being treated, and I realised, "Oh hell! I've come all the way from South Africa because I hated the state banning everything – and yet here I am, being instrumentalised in another system like that." That's what drove all my future activist work.'

Lee reorientated his entire outlook and became a lifelong activist in favour of legalising cannabis. He mixed with the musicians, artists and psychedelic explorers of the hippy era, becoming a central figure in the legalisation movement. In the 1970s, Lee opened Britain's longest-running head shop, Alchemy, on London's Portobello Road, and published *Homegrown*, the country's first 'weed magazine'.

Over time Lee Harris has become a minor cult legend of the British bohemian scene. In 2016, at 79 years old, he stood in the election for Mayor of London, representing the Cannabis Is Safer Than Alcohol party – and picked up over 20,000 votes. But, the dynamic he unwittingly helped establish back in 1964, tying together the tabloid press and grandstanding politicians, represented the beginnings of a process that was about to reshape fundamental aspects of British life and culture.

2

Killing the British System

A Lost History

We live in a drug-saturated culture. Anyone reading this has experienced a world of rave music, *Trainspotting*, Bob Marley, American presidents who claim they didn't inhale – and British prime ministers who admit that they did.

It is almost impossible for us to reimagine ourselves back to a Britain in which drugs were virtually unknown. But by far the most striking feature of the drugs scene of the mid-1960s is just how tiny it was. In 1945 there had been four convictions for cannabis in the whole of the UK. In 1964 there were 342 registered British heroin addicts. Drugs were something the vast majority of people simply didn't know about.

With a few exceptions of some, largely West Indian, cannabis use in Notting Hill and a few port cities like Liverpool and Cardiff, the entire mid-1960s British drugs scene was pretty much contained in the web of Soho streets between Charing Cross Road and Green Park. This book is about how certain decisions were taken that transformed this tiny, insular community into the millions of users that we see today.

Prior to the nineteenth century, drugs now illegal were widely used across Britain. In a country without universal healthcare, 'poppyhead tea' was commonly brewed as a painkiller and folk remedy. Later, opium was imported and sold everywhere from high-street pharmacies to rural grocery stores.

This was all completely legal. Most people used opium or laudanum (a tincture of morphine and codeine) purely as a medicine. A few, such as the writers Samuel Taylor Coleridge and Thomas De Quincey, took opiates seeking pleasure and mind expansion. Queen Victoria herself was fond of both opium and cannabis, before being introduced to cocaine later in life.

As technology and trade progressed over the nineteenth century, new professions emerged. Old-fashioned folk healers and apothecaries gave way to a new class of professional pharmacists, who gradually took control of drug supply. In 1868, the Pharmacy Act placed opium under pharmaceutical control with minimal regulation.

This was the birth of what came to be known as 'the British System'.

Within the tiny group of academics who study drug policy, the British System of treating heroin addiction is widely and fiercely debated. Outside this narrow clique, it is virtually unknown – an idea lost to history.

The story of the British System – of what happened to it and what it tells us about Britain as a country – is crucial. This is not only a story that every British person should know, but one from which people around the world can learn profound lessons as well.

The British System is a slippery concept. Some experts argue it isn't a system at all, but an overlapping 'system of systems', or a 'system of not having a system'. But all these interpretations boil down to one essential idea – that drug addiction is not a moral category, but a medical issue that should be treated by doctors, not law enforcement. This springs from age-old liberal traditions in British political life – traditions that favour custom over writ, personal liberty over state power and pragmatism over blind obedience to rules.

Crucially, the British System stands in absolute opposition to the American model, in which illegal drugs are seen as a moral evil in themselves, and prohibition by law enforcement the only approach to deal with them.

Throughout the First World War, cocaine was widely used as a dental anaesthetic and medicinal pick-me-up. Harrods offered small packages of cocaine and morphine as 'A Useful Present for Friends at the Front', which became a common train-station gift for girls to give their boyfriends as they left for the trenches.

Then came the foreign troops. By 1915, a quarter of a million Canadian troops were stationed in Britain. Rumours began to spread that these Canadians were using cocaine for pleasure, rather than root canal surgery. Soon *The Times* was thundering that cocaine was 'more deadly than bullets', and in July 1916, cocaine, morphine and several other drugs were brought under the Defence of the Realm Act – the same Act that had first introduced pub-licensing hours in 1914.

In fact, the rumours of rampant cocaine use had been absurdly exaggerated, if not completely invented. The entire furore turned out to be based on a single Canadian major stationed in Folkestone, who had arranged one sting operation to buy a packet of black-market cocaine from a West End prostitute. The select committee appointed to examine the problem reported back that 'there is no evidence of any kind to show that there is any serious, or, perhaps, even noticeable prevalence of the cocaine habit amongst the civilian or military population of Great Britain.' But of course, by then newspapers had been sold, laws passed and, in the midst of the Great War, the country had other pressing concerns.

Britain emerged from the war a nation transformed. The relationship between the individual and the state was being fundamentally renegotiated. Women got the vote, and the first governmental Ministry of Health was founded in 1919. Debate immediately began on whether the medical profession or the Home Office should take the lead in the regulation of drug use.

The United States, the rising power on the world stage, had banned all drugs with the Harrison Narcotics Tax Act of 1914, and was strongly pushing their moralising, prohibitionist approach across the world. Sir Malcolm Delevingne, the relevant official at the Home Office, had some sympathy with the American outlook. He received furious opposition from the medical community. W.E. Dixon, reader in pharmacology at Cambridge, wrote to *The Times* in 1923:

> We do not seem to have learnt anything from the experience of our American brethren ... cannot our legislators understand that our only hope of stamping out the drug addict is through the doctors, that legislation above the doctors' heads is likely to prove our undoing and that we can no more stamp out addiction by prohibition than we can stamp out insanity?[7]

Looking at the numbers, he had a point. In this era the heroin addict population of the US numbered in the hundreds of thousands, Britain's in the hundreds. Eventually a committee was formed to consider these questions, under the leadership of Sir Humphry Rolleston, President of the Royal College of Physicians.

The Rolleston Committee, formed in 1924, deliberated over a series of 23 meetings and called over 30 expert witnesses. The result was the British System as it came to be known among international policymakers. Doctors could use their own discretion in prescribing heroin to treat addiction, with loose overall control remaining with the Home Office. For the next four decades, this pragmatic system was to save Britain from developing any hint of a US-style heroin black market run by gangsters.

It's important to note that none of these decisions were taken out of some altruistic concern for drug addicts. This was about protecting the right of doctors not to have the Home Office telling them what to do. With only a few hundred drug addicts in Britain at the time, this was considered a very minor issue, essentially boiling down to a turf war between two newly modernising professional classes – the medical community and the Home Office bureaucracy.

What is striking about the discussions and reports of the Rolleston Committee, though, is their consistent sobriety. There is not a hint of the moralising hysteria that characterised similar discussions in America. Drug addiction is always spoken about as an 'unfortunate condition' – but never as 'evil', never as a moral failure.

And, for roughly four decades, the Rolleston System more or less seemed to work. Between 1936 and 1953 the number of known drug addicts in Britain fell from 616 to 290, before rising again to 454 by 1960.

Compare this to countries that adopted a prohibition model – Canada had roughly 150,000 addicts and the US 350,000. It is no wonder that the British fought tooth and nail to preserve their system against the encroachment of the American model, which was being aggressively pushed on them.

The American approach to drug policy has been defined by two key historical features – moralising fervour and racial prejudice. It began on the railroads.

Thousands of Chinese workers came to America during the mid-1800s to build the Central Pacific Railroad. Once the railroad was complete, however, they were immediately regarded as a threat to white workers. In 1882 Congress passed the Chinese Exclusion Act, the only US law to ever ban immigration solely on the basis of race.

One method of stirring up anti-Chinese hatred was to attack the practice of opium smoking. No matter that morphine and laudanum were popular medicines throughout the US; Chinese opium was seen as a threat to American Christian morality, and particularly to American Christian women.

By 1881, as the Exclusion Act was being debated in Congress, reports began flooding out of San Francisco of opium dens where 'white women and Chinamen sit side by side under the effects of this drug – a humiliating sight to anyone with anything left of manhood'. Newspaper editorials thundered that the Chinese opium menace must by wiped out lest it 'decimate our youth, emasculate the coming generation, if not completely destroy the population of our coast,' and that for white Americans, smoking opium was 'not at all consistent with their duties as Capitalists or Christians.'[8]

Then, in 1898, America became an imperial power, conquering the Philippines in the Spanish–American War. Charles H. Brent, the openly racist Episcopal bishop of the Philippines, despised opium users, and appealed to President Roosevelt to ban this 'evil and immoral' habit. By 1905 Brent had succeeded in installing the first American prohibition regime – not in the US itself, but in its new Pacific colony.[9]

Unfortunately, the ban completely failed to actually curb opium use in the Philippines. Bishop Brent decided this must be the fault of the booming trade in China, and wrote again to President Roosevelt, urging that the United States had a duty to 'promote some movement that would gather in its embrace representatives from all countries where the traffic and use of opium is a matter of moment.'[10]

In the American debate, drug addiction had long been framed as an infection or contamination of white America by foreign influences. Now that vision was internationalised. To protect white American moral purity, the supply of drugs from overseas had to be curtailed at their source. As the campaigner Richard P. Hobson had it, 'like the invasions and plagues of history, the scourge of narcotic drug addiction came out of Asia'.[11] The idea of international control of the drug trade was born.

In 1909, America succeeded in convening the first International Commission on Opium in Shanghai. Representing the US were Bishop Brent and the doctor Hamilton Wright, who was to become a major force in the American prohibitionist movement. The Americans had originally wanted to convene a formal conference, rather than just a commission, but had been blocked by another international power – Great Britain.

After lengthy discussions, the commission adopted a number of non-binding resolutions, crucially the principle that 'the use of opium for non-medical purposes is held by *almost* any participating country to be a matter for prohibition or for careful regulation.'[12] Once again, the bloc that insisted on the inclusion of the word 'almost' was led by the British delegation. This was the beginning of a pattern repeated throughout the next 50 years. Great Britain consistently took a leading role in resisting the international prohibitionist approach aggressively pushed by the US.

This resistance was down to a number of factors. Britain still operated a monopoly on the opium trade and certainly wished to protect her business interests. In turn, the Americans thought that by opposing opium they could curry favour with Chinese authorities, to undermine Britain and advance their own commercial interests in the country.

But, alongside this, there was also simply a different view of what drug addiction meant.

The British resented America's 'overtones of high-minded-ness and superior virtue'. These issues were a source of serious friction with the US. Occasionally it got personal. One frustrated Foreign Office official reported back that Hamilton Wright's wife, Elizabeth, was 'incompetent, prejudiced, ignorant, and so constituted temperamentally as to afford a ready means of mischief-making.'

But it was difficult for the US to push the prohibition of drugs on the rest of the world while not enforcing it itself. Wright began spearheading a fresh campaign for full drug prohibition within the US – once again built almost entirely on racial prejudice.

But this time, a new drug had emerged to capture America's fevered imagination, with another racial minority to persecute. The drug was cocaine, and the minority, African-Americans. In 1910, Wright submitted a report to the Senate stating that 'this new vice, the cocaine vice ... has been a potent incentive in driving the humbler negroes all over the country to abnormal crimes.'[13]

There was an explosion of headlines linking black people to cocaine use and criminality. The *New York Times* ran a typical story under the headline NEGRO COCAINE FIENDS – NEW SOUTHERN MENACE. The story tells of 'a hitherto inoffensive negro', who had reportedly taken cocaine and been sent into a frenzy. The local police chief was forced to shoot him several times to bring him down. Cocaine, it was implied, was turning black men into superhuman brutes. As the medical officer quoted in the article bluntly put it, 'the cocaine nigger sure is hard to kill'.[14]

This hysteria resulted in the Harrison Narcotics Tax Act of 1914, instituting the prohibition of drugs across the United States. Over the next 50 years America would aggressively seek to internationalise this prohibition across the world.

In 1925, just as the Rolleston Committee was completing its work in London, a new international opium conference convened in Geneva. The British were central in spearheading opposition to the international controls demanded by the US, causing the American delegation to walk out of the conference. When the US urged the complete international prohibition of cannabis, all but three member states voted in favour – the rebels were Great Britain, the Netherlands and India.

Bishop Brent's response to the setback in Geneva was that: 'Christ and his religion are brought under reproach and open shame.' The gulf between this religious condemnation and the sober, medical language of the Rolleston Committee could not be more striking. Time and time again, Great Britain was the country that stood opposed to this moralising American language – and was one of the last developed nations forced to adopt the American system.

Harry J. Anslinger was appointed head of the US Federal Bureau of Narcotics in 1930. Alcohol prohibition was about to be repealed, and this tiny department must have seemed like a dead-end posting. But Anslinger embarked on a campaign of political and media manipulation that was to build drug prohibition into a key plank of US domestic and foreign policy. He was to remain head of the FBN for 32 years, serving under five presidents and holding his office longer than any other senior civil servant save Herbert Hoover.

Anslinger was in many ways the architect of the modern War on Drugs – and the archetype of the moralising drug warrior. To him, drugs were a moral evil in themselves. Users were 'criminals first, addicts afterwards', and the only way to rid the world of this evil was a punitive, law enforcement approach. Anslinger was ruthless in his crusade, often stooping to methods that were unethical and, at times, actually illegal – particularly in the monitoring and persecution of artists, scientists and intellectuals he saw as a threat.[15]

He was also a race baiter. In order to whip up hysteria in the press, Anslinger incessantly played on racial fear and prejudice, linking cannabis to Hispanic people, cocaine to African-Americans and heroin to the Chinese.

Chinese men, he warned, had 'a liking for the charms of Caucasian girls', using opium to force them into 'unspeakable sexual depravity'. The increase in drug addiction, he insisted, was 'practically 100 per cent among Negro people', who would party with white women, 'getting their sympathy with stories of racial persecution. Result: pregnancy.'

Anslinger was not content to simply wage his crusade within the US. Throughout the 1930s he lobbied the US government to pressure the rest of the world to adopt a prohibitionist approach.

Then came the Second World War. Every country in the world emerged from the war significantly poorer, save one – the United States. Anslinger and his underlings lost no time in leveraging America's newfound hegemony to force the other nations of the UN towards a prohibition model. They ensured that versions of the Harrison Act were written into the laws of the occupied Axis powers, and Anslinger had himself appointed as the US representative to the Commission on Narcotic Drugs of the newly formed United Nations.

Every aspect of international relations, from military protection to trade deals to aid programmes, became a carrot or a stick to coerce other states to adopt the American way. Charles Siragusa, a high-ranking FBN agent, laid out these bullying tactics explicitly, 'most of the time ... I found that a casual mention of the possibility of shutting off our foreign aid programmes, dropped to the proper quarters, brought grudging permission for our operations almost immediately.'[16]

The British resented Anslinger's heavy-handedness, and did their best to undermine his efforts, fighting to preserve the British System. The British delegate to the CND complained that, had it not been *for the white drug problem in the USA*,[17] other nations might have been left alone to pursue their own drug policies. Another UK representative expressed his frustration that at the CND, 'the Chairman Anslinger ... continually confused his position as Chairman and as US representative.'

In 1953, Anslinger pushed through the United Nations Opium Protocol, leading to a furious backlash in Britain. *The Times* published an editorial titled THE CASE FOR HEROIN, forcefully arguing the wisdom of the British System of prescribing to addicts over moralising American-style prohibition.

From there, it took over a decade of US bullying, but eventually Bishop Brent's dream of a blanket international ban on illicit drugs was realised. The 1961 UN Single Convention on Narcotic Drugs was passed, intended to bring the confusing tangle of all previous drug treaties and conventions into line.

This was an American policy, serving American interests. It was the result of a US-drafted, and US-sponsored, resolution – and the hallmarks of crusading American prohibitionism are threaded through its core.

The 1961 Convention is the only convention in the history of the UN to use the word 'evil'. 'Addiction to narcotic drugs constitutes a serious evil for the individual and is fraught with social and economic danger to mankind.'

Torture, apartheid and nuclear war are not described in these terms. Genocide is referred to in UN documents as an 'odious scourge' or 'barbarous acts', but never as actually 'evil'. That the UN, founded in the ashes of world war and the Holocaust, finds drug addiction the only phenomenon worthy of this word is a testament to just how heavily American moralising pressure was brought to bear.[18]

The Single Convention laid out the international standard of placing drugs in different 'Schedules' to determine their levels of danger, the punishments for trading them and their potential benefits to medicine and science. This Convention forms the basis for almost every individual country's drug legislation, including that of the United Kingdom.

The Single Convention was to have a profound effect on life on the streets of Britain. As soon as the UK became a signatory, it was inevitable that the British System would come under attack. Even so, the British still fought a valiant decade-long rearguard action to preserve their way of 'doing drug policy'.

To understand how this played out, we have to go back to Soho.

In 1959 there were 62 known heroin addicts in the UK. By 1964 this had risen to 342. This was a tiny, insular community, almost entirely contained in London's West End. Under the British System, addicts were registered with the Home Office, received prescriptions for heroin from their GP and picked up their drugs at high-street pharmacies.

One former user, writing anonymously under the pen-name 'Barbateboy', has written a memoir that creates a striking picture of this era:

> I first used Heroin in 1963, I was 18 years old … I had read Cocteau, De Quincey, Kerouac and Burroughs and was ready to try new experiences. I met a junkie called Gaoler, and after much persuasion he agreed to share his 'scrip'.
>
> My first hit was a mixture of heroin and cocaine. I injected it mainline. It was amazing – I had the strongest high ever. I was not hooked, but from then on until I was 21 I regularly fixed mixtures of heroin and cocaine. I spent an entire weekend holed up in a bedsit off Westbourne Grove shooting up heroin and a large amount of cocaine.

All of the drugs I used were obtained legally on doctor's prescription from a clutch of chemists around London. There was Boots at Piccadilly, Blisses in Kilburn, John Bell & Croyden in Wigmore St.

Very few chemists stocked these drugs and so over time I ran into most junkies who were 'scripping'. It was a small world. There were the medical personnel for whom proximity and ready supply overcame scruples. Ex-military and sailors who started raiding field kits or who had smoked opium on tours. Fools like myself on a false pilgrimage for self-exploration, or simply to indulge personal hedonism. Also, a few 'tourists' from countries with harsher drug regimes. There seemed to be very few routes into this closed scene, which was almost entirely separate from the growing hippy cannabis and acid scene. A camaraderie existed and we would gossip and discuss which Doctors were cool and which were severe.

The drugs were of course pure, British Pharmaceutical or BP. The heroin came by the grain (which is about one sixteenth of a gram), consisting of six tiny tablets called jacks, which perhaps gave rise to the expression 'To jack up'. On private prescription it cost one and tuppence a grain, the cheapest hit in town. Half a jack was as much as a non-user could stomach. The cocaine was a shining white powder a bit like crushed mothballs. Fresh syringes and needles came with every 'scrip'. There was very little reuse. I met many people from taxi drivers to set designers who held responsible jobs and lived otherwise normal lives.[19]

The British heroin scene was so small in this era that we know the precise addresses of the pharmacies where addicts picked up their gear. Almost every account of this era stresses the importance of Boots at Piccadilly Circus and John Bell & Croyden in Wigmore St. These two chemists controlled most of the British heroin supply. Reflect on that for a moment – there was a time in living memory when the two biggest heroin dealers in Britain both had W1 post-codes, didn't engage in gang wars and paid their taxes every year.

The Home Office official in charge of overseeing all this was Henry 'Bing' Spear, a somewhat legendary figure in international drug policy circles.

Bing Spear was a unique character. He did not just take care of administering a system – he took care of the addicts themselves. The eulogy at his funeral in 1985 spoke of how

> he knew virtually all the addicts … he knew their birthdays, where they came from, everything. They'd go and see him in his office in Whitehall, just drop in for a cup of tea … When addicts had no scripts he would phone round to find doctors who would write out more. He took special care of the new addicts, determined to keep them away from criminal suppliers.

> Another user recalled the story of a merchant seaman who had become addicted to heroin while aboard ship, wrote to Spear and found him waiting quayside, prescription in hand, as his ship docked back in England.[20]

The idea of a senior Whitehall official taking such personal care of the people they serve seems extraordinary today. The image of a drug addict – a group on whom such stigma has now been loaded – dropping in for tea at the Home Office to discuss their problems sounds absurd. But it was not always so. Under the British System, drug addicts were not stigmatised or seen as moral failures. They often lived otherwise 'normal' lives, with jobs and families, and were simply helped to manage their condition in the least harmful way possible.

Under the shadow of increasing American pressure on the international scene, a new committee was formed in 1958 under Sir Russell Brain to consider issues relating to drug addiction in Britain.

The first Brain Report was published in 1961. It found that 'after careful examination of all the data put before us, we are of the opinion that in Great Britain the incidence of addiction to dangerous drugs … is still very small'. The committee argued that the apparent increase in addict numbers was not down to more people actually using drugs, but was simply because people already using them were only now becoming known to the system.

The report was simply wrong. The number of addicts was rising, even if by numbers that seem minuscule today. The world was changing, and a new generation of drug users was emerging. The addicts of the 1930s and 1940s had been largely middle-aged – often doctors who had got too curious about their own medicine cabinets. The new generation was primarily young, middle-class men – males outnumbered females three to one – who had read some De Quincey and William Burroughs, and were trying to experiment and rebel.

This is significant. Drug use in Britain began in the middle classes, and then spread to the working class. This is the exact opposite to the pattern in the US, where drug use slotted into Social Darwinist theories as a vice of the poor.

The first Brain Report is generally considered a failure – if not an outright whitewash. Bing Spear, among others, condemned it for ignoring issues in the British System that, had they been confronted head-on, might have saved the system as a whole. But perhaps there is another reason that the Brain Committee reported as it did?

In the mid-1950s the net was closing in. Harry Anslinger and the American establishment despised the British System, speaking against it openly in their propaganda. The British knew that pressure was mounting for an international treaty, which would inevitably be drawn on American terms.

In 1955, the British representative at the UN's Commission on Narcotic Drugs, Johnnie Walker, wrote to the Home Office warning that pressure was mounting for an international convention, and that the Americans would look for any excuse to force Britain to the table.

Walker's correspondence shows that both he and the Home Office were aware of the 'first real sign of a significant increase in heroin addiction for very many years.' So, why did the Brain Committee report there was no rise in addiction, when it was clearly acknowledged elsewhere?

In the closing line of one of his memos, Walker neatly sums up the philosophy of the British System.

There is a limit to what the State should attempt, and the deprivation of personal liberty for medical reasons is far too serious a matter to contemplate unless there is overwhelming evidence of the need for it because of some widespread and particularly virulent social problem. This need does not exist in the United Kingdom.[21]

This last sentence is key. Some have argued that in order to defend the British System from American attack, the government needed to produce a report showing that there was no significant increase in British heroin addiction.

We shall likely never know whether the Brain Committee was deliberately set up as a whitewash. What is certain, though, is that its failure to address the fairly minor problems that were appearing in the British System laid the foundations for the chaos that was to follow.

For a history of the War on Drugs, there seems to have been quite an important element missing so far – the police. Where was law enforcement in all this?

The answer is that they were barely present. For the police of the 1960s, drugs were considered deeply uninteresting. Chasing drugs simply wasn't seen as 'real police work'. Being a proper copper meant going out and catching burglars and robbers. Under the British System, policing drugs generally meant inspecting pharmacists' records to make sure supplies weren't going missing, and the occasional cannabis bust on a West Indian café. It was seen as boring, unglamorous and certainly no way to get ahead in your career. To really advance, any ambitious young detective wanted to be working on armed robberies and murders.

Where the police did take an interest in drugs, it was generally down to the personal interest of an individual officer. Lee Harris, still deeply involved in the Soho drug scene, remembers exactly how drugs policing of the era worked.

'In Soho there was one cop, Sergeant Patrick, who would harass all the junkies,' he explains. 'He'd follow them after they'd picked up their supply at Boots, then hassle them and kick them about. He was awful, everyone knew him – it was personal with him, he just hated drug addicts. He had no understanding of their situations.

'At this point I was living in this big flat in Earl's Court, which became known as the Hang Out Club. All the junkies would come there, and I did my best to take care of them. They used to call me the High Priest. I never touched heroin myself, but sometimes there would be 14 junkies at my place. Some were hippies, some just strays that had come down from Scotland or

Ireland. They would fix, or go through withdrawal, and I'd try to take care of them. Some of these people had terrible personal problems. They were very vulnerable; half the girls were on the game. There were no real charities for drug people in that time, and they had no one to help them.

'So, one evening I'm heading home to Earl's Court, and I see Sergeant Patrick at Earl's Court station. He'd followed me from Soho. Then, a few days later, I get a knock on my door – and there he is. He had no warrant, and I wasn't doing anything illegal. But he came in and gave me a warning not to have junkies in my house.

'I didn't know what to do, so I phoned my friend Steve Abrams, who arranged a meeting for me with Bing Spear at the Home Office. I went there just to ask him to get Sergeant Patrick off my back, but ended up staying for about two hours. He was very interested in what I had to say – so I explained to him how the scene worked. In those days you could just call a top civil servant and arrange a meeting like that. And I think they did make a call and tell Sergeant Patrick to lay off me.'

Once again, we are looking at a different world. The drugs scene was so tiny in this era that drugs policing meant one copper following someone home – then that person appealing straight to the cop's boss at the Home Office.

One of the primary reasons the police were so uninterested in drugs was that, unlike today, there was not seen to be any connection between drug-taking and other crime. Under the British System, drug addicts simply didn't need to steal to feed their habit.

In the late 1960s the Ford Foundation, the giant American charitable institution, sent the journalist and future congressman Edgar May to Britain, to examine how the British System compared to American prohibition. His report is absolutely fascinating, especially concerning the role of the police and their utter dismissal of the idea that using drugs somehow magically 'causes' criminal behaviour.

May writes:

Unlike the United States, Britain has no national police agency for drugs. London police colleagues sharply differ with their American counterparts over one vital aspect of the drug problem: the connection between crime and addiction.

No one in England – from the toughest London detective to the most liberal-prescribing clinic physician – suggested to me that narcotics addiction increases criminal behaviour. This does not mean, of course, that drug addicts are crime-free. On the contrary, a significant number of addicts engage in criminal behaviour, and some criminals are addicts. But in England there is no cause-and-effect relationship.[22]

The idea that drugs necessarily cause criminal behaviour is an American concept, springing directly from the American mode of prohibitionist policing. The British System, while it lasted, protected the UK from this sort of criminality. It was only after that system was dismantled under American pressure that the stereotype of the 'junkie criminal' began to take hold.

The British System was known throughout the world – and not just by policymakers. Word spreads fast on the addict grapevine. In the 1960s many American and Canadian heroin addicts emigrated to the UK, purely in order to sign up with a GP who would write them a prescription with no hassle from the police.

Particularly well known was one group of around 91 Canadian addicts who arrived in the mid-1960s. Most of them actually returned to Canada fairly quickly, but a group of 25 stayed, and ended up taking part in a detailed study of the differences between their lives in Canada and in Britain. This is extraordinarily significant because it is perhaps the only data available anywhere regarding a single group of people who have lived both under the British System and under prohibition.

At home, the Canadians spent 25 per cent of their addicted years, a combined total of 141 years and 2 months, in jail; in England, less than 2 per cent, a combined total of two years and five months. At home, they compiled 182 offences; in England, 27. At home, in the high addict-crime category of theft, which included robbery and burglary, they committed 88; in England, 8.

Not only did they commit far fewer crimes, but, while in England, many of them were crime-free. In Canada, 16 of the 25 had committed five or more crimes, with one of them recording more than 20 separate offences. In Britain, none committed more than four offences and nearly half were never charged with any unlawful behaviour.

Despite the fact that the Canadians consumed far more daily heroin than the London average, many of them became jobholders and led fairly normal lives while in England. Their living accommodations were far more stable.

The employment record showed the most dramatic difference between the two countries. In Canada, only one addict claimed to have worked steadily while addicted. In England, the majority (13) worked full-time, and four worked part-time. Six had held the same job for at least three years ... 'For once we could work and live like humans,' the addicts said, 'There is less trouble from the

police ... we don't constantly have to be paranoid ... there
is less pressure ... there is no need to steal.'[23]

This is a completely unique and extraordinary set of data, and
explains why the police in this era were so uninterested in drugs
– they simply didn't cause very much crime.

Another key aspect of policing the British System was
that there were almost no drug dealers to pursue. Addicts got
their gear from Boots – there was no black market. Bing Spear
recalled the head of the Metropolitan Police Drug Squad telling
a meeting of the Forensic Science Society in 1962 that 'we have
never found – or received reliable evidence – of heroin being traf-
ficked in London in any other form than a tablet.'[24] Since tablets
were how addicts received their gear from pharmacies, this indicates that there simply was no black market in operation.

One widespread rumour of the criminal underworld was
that in 1963 representatives of several New York mafia crime
families came to London, and met at the Hilton Hotel to discuss
whether they should develop a drugs syndicate there. They
ended up deciding there was no point. Why bother when doctors
were already supplying?[25]

Most of the product that supplied the New York heroin
crisis of the 1960s and 1970s was supplied through Corsican
organised crime groups – the famous 'French Connection'. They
processed the raw opium from Turkey, and imported it into the
US in collaboration with Sicilian Mafiosi and their American
relatives.

This network dominated the American heroin business for
nearly two decades. Yet, somehow, they never thought to set
up shop in the UK – just over the English Channel. Whatever
else one may say about the British System, it seems to have
prevented the formation of the black market, and the sort of
organised crime drug syndicates, that sprang up across America.

So, what happened? How did the British System fall into crisis? How did we get from a Britain with no drug dealers to the Britain we know today?

To answer these questions, we have to look at the 'junkies' doctors'.

By 1964, the number of heroin addicts known to the Home Office had risen to 342.[26] As quaint as this may seem today, in the mid-1960s it was a cause for concern, and in July the Brain Committee was recalled to take a fresh look at the situation.

The committee reported in 1965. Their analysis was that the rise in addict numbers was down to 'the activity of a very few doctors … not more than six … who have prescribed excessively to addicts.'

This was half true. There was indeed a loose group of doctors who took care of addicts – usually around ten operating in London at any one time. The rise in addict numbers, however, was not down to six of them – it was down to just one. As Russell Brain himself exclaimed to the committee at one meeting, 'Well gentlemen, I think your problem can be summed up in two words: Lady Frankau.'[27]

Lady Isabella Frankau is a fascinating character. Trained in psychiatry, she operated an independent practice before another doctor, Dr P.M. Stanwell, invited her to assist him in treating addicts in 1957. Gradually, however, Stanwell became concerned with the liberalism with which she handed out prescriptions. The two fell out, and Frankau struck out on her own.

By her own estimate, she prescribed to over 500 addicts between 1958 and 1964. She prescribed without question. Any addict could come to her, claim that they had lost their tablets, or that their usual NHS doctor was on holiday, and she would scribble out a new scrip. As one addict recalled, 'I just asked for what I wanted and she took my word. If you spun her enough story she would believe you.'[28]

Word went round the addict networks like wildfire, and Frankau became a magnet for heroin users, including celebrities like Marianne Faithfull. When the great American jazz trumpeter Chet Baker came to London, she was his first stop. 'She simply asked my name, my address and how much cocaine and heroin I wanted per day,' he later recalled.

But, Lady Frankau was no drug dealer. She may have been described by other doctors as a 'well-meaning fool', but no one has ever suggested she wrote prescriptions for money. In fact she often waived her consultation fee for poorer patients and reports came back that 'it was by no means uncommon at West End pharmacies to find prescriptions endorsed "charge to my account"'.[29]

Unfortunately, her patients had no such scruples. Some addicts realised they could pick up extra supplies from Frankau, then sell them on. The writer Alexander Trocchi became notorious for this on the underground scene. This was the first emergence of a 'grey market' in Britain – drugs acquired legally, but sold illicitly.

But the real problems began in 1967 when Lady Frankau died. Or as one contemporary wrote: 'when she died, not having warned the Ministry of Health of her intention.' Suddenly, the hundreds of addicts who had relied on her were cast adrift. Into this gap in the market stepped Dr John Petro.

Petro is a strange and somewhat shadowy figure. Born John Piotrkowski, he came to the UK from Poland at 11 years old, studied medicine at Cambridge and became one of the first doctors to administer penicillin with Alexander Fleming. Then in 1966, he was knocked over in a road accident. Unable to practise, by 1967 Petro was facing bankruptcy.

Unlike Frankau, Petro wrote prescriptions to survive. He didn't even have an office, but would hold court at all-night coffee bars in Soho, or the café at Baker Street Station, scribbling out prescriptions on napkins and cigarette packs.

Then someone tipped off the papers. The *Sun* and the *Daily Mail* both led with front-page stories: DOCTOR HOLDS DRUG CLINIC IN A CAFÉ and DRUGS CLINIC IN STATION BUFFET. Over the next few months, Petro's chaotic practice became an incessant tabloid circus. Finally, in January 1968, Petro was invited onto David Frost's TV programme to explain himself. Immediately after the broadcast, he was arrested. The arresting officer was none other than Sergeant Patrick, Soho's one-man drug squad.

Though his actual prescribing was not illegal, Petro's record-keeping didn't pass muster, and he was eventually fined and struck off the medical register. However, while he was in the process of appealing against this decision, he switched to prescribing methedrine, injectable speed, further accelerating the crossover between the heroin and amphetamine scenes. The tabloids continued to stalk Petro mercilessly, until finally his appeal was rejected and he faded into poverty and obscurity.

Since this era, there has been much knee-jerk criticism of the so-called 'junkies' doctors'. Much of this criticism has come from the United States, and most of it is, as Bing Spear wrote, 'grossly unfair'. There were a few corrupt figures like Frankau and Petro, but the vast majority of doctors who got involved in this world are acknowledged to have done so out of genuine concern.

When the *Sunday Times* ran a feature on the junkies' doctors in 1969, they observed:

all of these doctors have some unusual quality about them – some direct element of the 'outsider' in their make-up; strong political opinions; the status of exile; or perhaps an unusual degree of professional compassion. And it is

possible as a result of this that they succeed in acting as
a link between the outcast addicts and normal society.[30]

Most important to recognise, though, is that all these doctors
were acting to fill a vacuum of the government's own making.
The Second Brain Committee had made certain promises, and
those promises had been broken.

The Second Report of the Brain Committee had made two central
changes to the British System. The first was that only doctors
licensed by the Home Secretary would be allowed to prescribe
to addicts. The second was that specialised treatment centres
would be created to treat addicts, and wean them off drugs.

The creation of treatment centres was significant in that
it meant responsibility for drug issues within the medical
community was switched from GPs to psychiatrists. This
'psychiatrisation' of addiction was another step in the American
direction. Psychiatrists had long dominated the medical discussion of drugs in the US, pushing the idea that addiction was a
disease that they alone could 'cure'. As Caroline Fazey writes,
'[the] psychiatrists who took over treatment decided that the
U.S.A. knew best, and addicts could be cured of their addiction.
Abstinence became the universal goal.'[31]

The growth of this American-style, abstinence-based approach
obviously spelt trouble for the British System. But the most
pressing problem of the proposed treatment centres was simply
that they never got built.

One of the most famous of the doctors who prescribed to
addicts was Dr A.J. Hawes. Known as a kindly, if eccentric, character, he ran an old-fashioned practice near Tottenham Court
Road. On 31 May 1966 he wrote to the Minister of Health,
Kenneth Robinson, enquiring where some of these treatment
centres were to be found in London.

On 22 June, the Ministry replied, listing nine hospitals with 'already established outpatient facilities'. Hawes promptly wrote to each of these hospitals. The response was extraordinary. Every single one denied having any specialist provision for addicts, and claimed the Ministry must have made a mistake in naming them.

Kenneth Robinson had promised doctors that, 'we shall not bring in the regulations prohibiting prescription by general practitioners for addicts until we are satisfied that the hospital facilities are adequate'. This commitment was simply not honoured, and the consequences were devastating. The licences for GPs to prescribe were withdrawn, and addicts were simply cut adrift with nowhere else to turn.

The *Sunday Times* picked up on the story, running a feature headlined THE STRANGE CASE OF THE MISSING TREATMENT CENTRES, and followed it up with a series of hard-hitting reports on the issue. Eventually several centres were put together, but by then the damage had been done. The needless delay between withdrawing supply and providing care had opened up a gap in the heroin supply. It was into that gap that the British black market was born.

In September 1965, Dr Hawes wrote to the *Observer*, warning of the effects of hastily withdrawing the doctor's power to prescribe.

To cut off supply by prescription would be easy; it has already been done in the United States where doctors are not allowed to prescribe for addicts, with the result that the provision of drugs has become a flourishing industry and addiction there increases yearly.[32]

In November he followed this up with a letter to *The Times*, sounding the alarm at what he was seeing on the street.

The most threatening portent is that addicts are telling me there is plenty of the stuff to be had on the black market, even though the source from overprescribing doctors is drying up. It looks as if big business which has been waiting in the wings for so long has now taken over the stage and is playing the lead. So we may look for an explosion in the teenage addict population as the months go by.

Unfortunately, this is exactly what happened. Addicts could no longer get prescriptions, so illegal heroin began trickling into the country to satisfy demand. As it happened, this did not initially come from Italian-American mafia organisations, but from Chinese Triads working out of Hong Kong. Little red packets of South-east Asian heroin, stamped with an elephant design, began littering the gutters of Gerrard Street in London's Chinatown.

We can pick up this story in the memoir of the anonymous addict, Barbateboy, that we followed earlier:

> The tabloid press had got all-judgemental about the practice of prescribing drugs. Wilson's government, impotent in other respects, needed to be seen as effective ... almost overnight all junkies were cut off from their supplies.
>
> The contraband trade in Chinese heroin mushroomed. Nothing pure about it. A wrap of brown, white and black (unrefined opium) powder which had to be ground and then boiled in a spoon and sucked into the syringe through a wadge [sic] of cotton wool. There was no way to assess the strength of the dose. Over the next year I lost about six friends to overdose, all experienced junkies. The whole junkie scene exploded. It became a 'pushed' drug, and the number of users grew as they got younger.

Measured by effect heroin will always be one of the cheapest drugs, and being addictive, one of the most sustainable and profitable markets for gangsters.[33]

The pivotal phrase here is that heroin became a 'pushed drug'. Under the British System, with heroin prescribed by doctors, there was simply no financial incentive for gangsters to import the drug, or for one user to introduce it to another. As prohibition creeps in, everything changes.

As soon as heroin is outlawed, the potential profits of a black market become almost limitless. Dealers have a huge incentive to actively get more people addicted, and the easiest way for any user to finance their own habit is to sell a bit themselves. It is a pyramid structure in which every link in the chain is incentivised to introduce more people to the habit.

This is how the street-level heroin market works everywhere that prohibition has been attempted. It was in this era that it was first unleashed on Britain.

On 26 March 1969 *The Times* reported the first seizures of illicit heroin in the UK. Curiously, the journalist who wrote the report was Norman Fowler, who went on to become Health Secretary during the heroin crises of the 1980s.

Dr Hawes wrote yet another letter to *The Times*, referring back to his previous warnings.

I hear from my heroin addicts that the drug is now appearing on the black market in powder form, which has never been available before ... It looks as if my dismal prophecy of large-scale heroin merchants waiting their opportunity of a shortage in the black market ... has come to pass ... The Ministry of Health does not seem to understand the implications of what they are doing. Nevertheless, they soon will.[34]

No one involved in making these decisions can claim they weren't warned. The undermining of the British System in this era, under international pressure from the United States and internal pressure from the tabloid press, would eventually lead to horrors almost unimaginable at the time.

For our anonymous heroin addict, Barbateboy, however, this is exactly the point where the story takes a more positive turn.

About this time I took LSD for the first time and realised there was more to life and consciousness, so I started to make a determined effort to wean myself off heroin ... I took the hippy trail overland to India and the 'Hashish Cure'.

I spent about a year there. I cleaned up. I could see the junkies and speed freaks before they recognised me and I stayed away from them. I did smoke a huge amount of high-grade hashish, and eventually hitched home from Kathmandu with a pregnant girlfriend. We were broke but we picked hops, then apples and started a new life as a family. I went into business as a builder and she trained as a teacher, and neither of us touched white drugs again.

I think getting clean depends on various factors. First one has to hit bottom and realise a change is necessary. Then one has to be able to change one's social geography, someone cleaning up is a challenge to junkies and they can be a bit like vampires coming round all the time trying to seduce you back to smack. They only need to get lucky once, and then they don't have to think of their own weakness. Then, most important of all, one has to fill the void with a new mission, a passion, a raison d'etre [sic]. I think after getting clean one remains a non-using junkie for at least five years and unless there are new horizons, objectives; whatever, in ones [*sic*] life the sheer meaning-less [*sic*] makes it very difficult to stay clean.[35]

It is also exactly at this point that acid, hashish and the hippy trail all make their appearance in the national story. In 1967, just as the failure to deal with a few rogue doctors was under-mining the entire British System, the Summer of Love exploded across the country. A new generation found their voice in the Beatles, Stones and Jimi Hendrix. And that, in turn, began the reaction that would lead straight to the Misuse of Drugs Act of 1971.

3

How to Sell a Newspaper

The Road to 1971

'They're selling hippy wigs in Woolworth's, man,' laments Danny, the perpetually spaced drug dealer in the cult film *Withnail and I*, 'the greatest decade in the history of mankind is over.'

The 1960s that Danny is talking about are not the ten years as they appear on the calendar. The 'sixties' have become an idea, a symbol, a projected self-image for the baby boom generation. Amid all the hippies, acid, free love and other familiar clichés, it's now almost impossible to separate truth from self-mythology.

Even at the height of the hippy movement, its defining drugs – cannabis and LSD – were largely the preserve of a very particular crowd. The image of an entire nation of 'flower children', all smoking dope and tripping out, is largely a creation of later culture looking back. *Withnail and I* actually came out in 1987.

Cannabis and LSD did, however, take up a huge space in the national imagination. Stories about pot and acid sold papers, so stories about pot and acid got printed. It didn't hurt, either, that the crowd that used them happened to include a lot of pop stars, actors and celebrities.

The 1960s were an era of profound generational change. For the vast majority, the most revolutionary new drug of the era was the contraceptive pill. But, rock stars don't get busted for carrying the pill – so the nation, and the press in particular, turned their hunger for outrage on marijuana and LSD. It started with Donovan.

Donovan was a singer-songwriter in the mid-1960s, Bob Dylan-ish mould. He was right at the centre of London's bohemian, hippy crowd, with lyrics explicitly referencing hash-smoking in 1965, before the Beatles had even released *Rubber Soul*.

In January 1966, the BBC ran the TV documentary *A Boy Called Donovan* which featured a friend of the singer smoking a joint at a party. This brought Donovan to the attention of Nobby Pilcher.

DS Norman Pilcher had been transferred from the Flying Squad to Scotland Yard's new drug squad in 1966. At the time, this was a very clear backwards move in the career of any detective. The Flying Squad was an elite force, and drug squads were still seen as barely a step above traffic wardens. But Pilcher soon realised he could make a name for himself by busting singers and celebrities.

He developed an extremely dubious relationship with the press, exchanging tip-offs for photo opportunities. Pilcher was soon the scourge of the London music scene. When the Beatles sang about 'Semolina Pilchard, climbing up the Eiffel Tower' in 'I Am the Walrus', it's Pilcher they were sending up.

In June 1966, Donovan was asleep with his girlfriend at his flat in Maida Vale; his friend Gypsy Dave was in another room with his own girlfriend. Pilcher and his drug squad burst in at 1.30am, tearing Donovan and his girlfriend from their bed and finding a little bit of hash.

Donovan ended up getting a £250 fine, quite stiff for the era, and a criminal record that damaged his touring career. Press coverage of the bust focused on the fact that both Donovan and his girlfriend were naked, with the heavy implication of some sort of 'drug-fuelled orgy' – despite the fact they had been asleep at the time. Featuring at least one naked girl became de rigueur for press coverage of celebrity pot busts for the rest of the 1960s.

The tabloids had worked out that celebrities and drugs shifted papers, and in early 1967, the *News of the World* ran a lurid three-part series of features under the title POP STARS AND DRUGS: FACTS THAT WILL SHOCK YOU. As part of this 'investigation', the paper had infiltrated the Rolling Stones' inner circle and managed to get a slightly addled Brian Jones to speak openly about his drug use. The only problem was that the paper couldn't tell one long-haired musician from another, and reported the dope confession as coming from Mick Jagger. Jagger promptly sued for libel – and the paper went to war.

In a creepy foreshadowing of the scandals that would eventually bring the paper down, the *News of the World* illegally tapped both Keith Richards's and Mick Jagger's phones, and gave the police underhanded tip-offs for raids. Trevor Kempson, one of the journalists put in charge of sabotaging the libel case, recalled in a 1998 interview, 'There was no doubt that it was a pride and personal thing ... The paper was embarrassed at not recognising Jagger from Jones ... They wanted to get the Stones badly, and the best way to get them was to get someone on the inside, which was easy'.[36]

On 12 February, Keith Richards's home in Sussex was raided, and Jagger and Richards were both arrested.

The reporting of this raid was particularly bottom-of-the-barrel. Marianne Faithfull had just taken a bath and was wrapped in a blanket, so of course the papers focused on the naked woman. Rumours spread that the police had caught Jagger and Faithfull in an outlandish sex act involving a Mars Bar. The bust probably just added to the Rolling Stones' bad boy image, but women are rarely afforded that luxury. The prurient sniggering was to dog Marianne Faithfull throughout her career.

On 29 June, Mick Jagger was sentenced to three months for possession of four amphetamine tablets that he had bought perfectly legally in Italy. Keith Richards got a year for allowing cannabis to be smoked in his home.

The response was immediate and explosive. The editor of *The Times*, William Rees-Mogg, surprised many by taking Jagger's side in his famous leader, WHO BREAKS A BUTTERFLY ON A WHEEL?, publicly labelling the arrest the political stunt that it plainly was.

The kids on the street took their protests straight to the source, Fleet Street. Mick Farren, an author and musician central to the 1960s scene, recalls the night in his book *Watch Out Kids*:

The general opinion was that a protest should be made the same evening at the News of the World building. Everyone split to spread the word, and agreed to meet at midnight for the demonstration … At about a quarter to twelve we arrived at the News of the World to find that about fifty freaks had shown up. It was disappointing, but it didn't last. From then on hippies began to show up in droves, until by twelve-thirty the narrow streets around the newspaper building were thronged with a weird assortment of people. Hippies came with drums and flutes, political heavies in leather jackets. Superstars drove around the building in limousines. A rock band equipment manager blocked the street with his truck.

The police were totally unprepared. Accustomed to protests that were planned and publicised for weeks in advance, they had no rules for dealing with these dial-a-mob tactics. It took them at least an hour to raise a force capable of dealing with the 1,500 freaks paralysing the newspaper building. So unprepared were the police that most of the people they did arrest had to be released because the arresting officers could not be found in the confusion.

The protests continued for two more days. The second day (Friday) the audience at UFO, the weekly rock/multi-media concert, left the club and marched to Piccadilly, where they found the police, equipped with dogs, waiting for them. After an hour of scuffles and abuse the crowd returned to the club, where a number of people were treated for cuts, bruises and dog bites.

On the Saturday things got a little heavy. Late in the evening between two and three thousand kids showed up in Fleet Street again, with the intention of blocking the street so the Sunday newspaper could not be shipped out. The police, this time, really had their shit together. In addition to uniformed pigs operating in force, hurling people back on the sidewalk and attempting to split the crowd into small groups, detectives and plainclothes men mingled with the demonstrators with orders to 'pick out the ring leaders.' As I was pushed across the road by the uniformed squad four of these infiltrators grabbed me, dragged me into a door way and worked me over with their fists and boots.[37]

The record producer Joe Boyd called these protests the 'peak of the sixties'. It's interesting that the sixties should have hit their peak not with a protest outside Parliament, but a tabloid news-paper. As far as we're aware, this is the only time the press have been directly and publicly held accountable for their consistent inaccuracy and shady practice around drugs reporting.

In the end, Richards's conviction was overturned, and Jagger's sentence was reduced to a conditional discharge. But the merry dance between the tabloids and the police continued. It was Trevor Kempson of the *News of the World* who made the Rolling Stones tip-off, and 'was clearly working closely with police in return for scoops when raids and/or arrests were made'.[38]

When Nobby Pilcher went after John Lennon in 1968, the press were there before the police – having been sent in advance by Pilcher to ensure a good photo of him slapping the handcuffs on a Beatle. In the end, Pilcher failed to find any dope on the raid, because Lennon had in turn been tipped off by Don Short of the *Daily Mirror*. Journalists were obviously playing both pop stars and police.

The role of the press in creating national hysteria around pop stars and drugs cannot be overestimated. If the American war on drugs was at least in part manufactured to satisfy racial prejudice, then its British franchise was at least in part manufactured to sell papers.

But what about the cannabis users who didn't happen to be pop stars?

Up until the mid-1960s, cannabis use in Britain had been the preserve of a small number of jazz musicians, West Indian immigrants and the occasional bohemian cultural explorer.

In 1955, 235 people were convicted of cannabis possession in the UK. By 1965, this had risen to 626. Then the number doubled to 1,119 in 1965, and then rose again, to 2,393 in 1967. Once again, these figures are almost comically low by today's standards – but they become much more interesting when you break them down.

In 1963, 296 offenders were officially recorded as 'white', and 367 as 'coloured'. By 1967 the numbers were 1,737 'white', and 656 'coloured'. The first year that white Britons outnumbered black in cannabis convictions was 1964. Curiously enough, that's about when the British establishment began to pay attention.

On 1 February 1967 the academic and campaigner Steve Abrams published an article titled 'The Oxford Scene and the Law'. This was a fairly well-balanced run-down of contradictions in existing UK drug laws, but it contained an assertion that as many as 500 Oxford students, and several dozen dons, used cannabis. The tabloid media picked up on this, and the article was republished in the *People* without Abrams's permission.

This set off a minor storm at Oxford, with the university denying the allegations – and hundreds of students enthusiastically backing them up. As the dust settled, the vice-chancellor of the university wrote to the Home Secretary, Roy Jenkins, to request an urgent enquiry into British recreational drug-taking. The result was the formation of the Wootton Committee.

This committee, chaired by Barbara Wootton, Baroness Wootton of Abinger, was officially named the Sub-Committee on Hallucinogens, and was part of the newly formed Advisory Council on Drug Dependence, a group of specialists set up to advise the government on drug policy.

The committee was tasked with looking into the rising popularity of LSD and cannabis, beginning its work amid the charged atmosphere of spring 1967. Then Hoppy went to trial.

John 'Hoppy' Hopkins was a Cambridge physicist turned photographer and activist – and one of the key figures of underground London bohemia. In early 1967 he was arrested for possession of a small amount of cannabis. Instead of pleading guilty, which would probably have resulted in a fine, Hoppy chose to make a political stand by going to trial. He lectured the judge about his views that cannabis should be legalised, and that the laws against it were an affront to personal liberty. The judge responded by calling him a 'pest to society', and sentencing him to nine months.

The sentence caused huge anger throughout the London scene. On 5 June, Steve Abrams, who had by now formed the drugs research group SOMA, met with the author Barry Miles at Paul McCartney's house. They decided to take out a full-page advertisement in *The Times* calling for the decriminalisation of cannabis possession. The Beatles agreed to pay £18,000 for the advertisement, which eventually ran on 24 July.

The headline called the law against cannabis 'immoral in principle and unworkable in practice', and was signed by the Nobel laureate Francis Crick, the novelist Graham Greene and all four members of the Beatles, as well as a number of doctors, MPs and other high-profile figures. The ad caused enough of a stir to alter the course of the Wootton Committee's enquiry, causing them to focus exclusively on cannabis, rather than on hallucinogenic drugs as a whole.

While the Wootton Report certainly did not recommend legalising cannabis, it presented a sober assessment of its growing popularity among young people, and a general affirmation of the liberal principles that underpinned the British System.

> Cannabis is less dangerous than the opiates, amphetamines and barbiturates, and also less dangerous than alcohol … An increasing number of people, mainly young, in all classes of society are experimenting with this drug, and substantial numbers use it regularly for social pleasure. There is no evidence that this activity is causing violent crime, or is producing in otherwise normal people conditions of dependence or psychosis requiring medical treatment.

Significantly, Wootton also included the recommendation that 'possession of a small amount of cannabis should not normally be regarded as a serious crime to be punished by imprisonment'.[39]

The tabloid press immediately exploded with stories that the report was 'soft on drugs'.[40] James Callaghan, the Home

Secretary, was furious. He publicly accused Baroness Wootton of being 'over influenced' by a 'lobby' seeking to legalise cannabis. Wootton shot back in a letter to *The Times*, defending the integrity of her committee and calling Callaghan's accusations offensive.

But for Callaghan, and for sections of the press, the argument was never simply about the legal status of one particular drug. Cannabis use had become symbolic of something else – a new generation with its own rules, which was asserting itself and casting aside the boundaries of the past. If they couldn't stop young people listening to rock 'n' roll or having sex, they could crack down on pot. In Parliament, Callaghan railed that cannabis use was 'another aspect of the so-called permissive society'.

But Callaghan was eventually forced to compromise. In 1970 he put forward a Misuse of Drugs Bill, which, though it ignored most of the suggestions of the Wootton Committee, did actually reduce the penalties for simple cannabis possession. Callaghan's bill was intended to bring together the contradictory hotchpotch of existing British drug laws, and bring the UK into line with the UN Single Convention of 1961. But Callaghan never got to pass it.

The general election of 1970 saw Labour ousted, and the Conservatives take hold of government. In a highly unusual move, however, the new Home Secretary, Reginald Maudling, reintroduced Callaghan's exact bill without addition or modification.

The two Commons debates on the Misuse of Drugs Act are long, occasionally fascinating – and often very much the opposite. Perhaps most interesting is that, despite being only a few months apart, the tone of the two debates is profoundly different.

The first reading took place in March 1970, with Callaghan still Home Secretary. The overriding impression is of a group of people who know very little about the subject they are talking about, but at least have the common sense to recognise their own ignorance, and demand more research.

Dr Michael Winstanley MP summed up the post-Wootton controversy, saying:

> much of the difficulty was created not by the nature of the report itself, but by what the Press had to say about it ... we know nothing like enough about cannabis. It is not right, therefore ... to pontificate one way or another on this question. I entirely agree that we need study, and we must reserve our opinion until we have the result.[41]

Michael Foot restated the traditional, British System position on drugs.

> The approach of ignorant horror to these matters is not the way in which to deal with them adequately, particularly if approaching the matter in that spirit means that innocent people, including innocent young people, shall find themselves in prison.[42]

There were also several clear warnings about following the American prohibition model, including this from William Deedes:

> America has had Draconian penalties for the misuse of dangerous drugs – heroin, marijuana, the lot – and she has tried hard to enforce them, yet abuse in America has spread like an oil fire in a timber shed ... We need credibility as well as severity.[43]

By the time the 1970 election had come and gone, and the bill came forward for a second reading under a new government, the change in tone was dramatic. In his own opening remarks, Reginald Maudling sows the seeds of moral panic, insisting, 'we are dealing with a symptom of a deeply troubled society ... trading in drugs merits the severest punishment, but, nevertheless, possession itself will remain a serious criminal offence'.[44]

In this second reading one begins to pick up far more of the moralising American approach. Drug addicts are referred to as 'the lowest of the low', with 'deficient personalities', and the word 'evil' makes its first appearance with Percy Grieve's speech:

> I cannot accept ... that this evil has come to stay and cannot be rooted out. If we can get at the suppliers and the sources of supply, and deal with them with the severity which their offences demand, we shall have gone a long way to rooting out this new evil in our midst.[45]

The Misuse of Drugs Act was given Royal Assent on 17 May 1971. Almost exactly one month later, Richard Nixon gave his famous War on Drugs press conference in Washington, DC.

The British War on Drugs had been officially declared, but what did the Act actually entail? It's a complex piece of legislation, but one can pick out a few threads that, over the next few decades, would have profound consequences, played out on the streets of Britain.

The most headline-grabbing clause of the MDA was that it brought the UK into line with the UN Single Convention of 1961 by separating various illicit drugs into different classes. Heroin, cocaine and LSD were designated Class A, while cannabis and amphetamines were considered Class B.

While this cleared up some the derangement of earlier laws whereby someone caught with cannabis could be sent to prison, while someone caught with heroin could be sent to the doctor, in fact the Wootton Report had called for treating cannabis entirely separately from other illicit drugs.

> We believe that the association of cannabis in legislation with heroin and the other opiates is entirely inappro-

priate and that new and quite separate legislation to deal specially and separately with cannabis and its synthetic derivatives should be introduced.[46]

The idea that cannabis, heroin, amphetamines, etc. are completely different chemicals, and might require completely different laws, is one of the great what-might-have-beens of the War on Drugs. Lumping them all together was itself an encroachment of American-style drug policy.

The MDA refocused attention away from possession of drugs, and towards prosecuting dealers and traffickers. The maximum penalty for possession of cannabis was reduced from ten years to five, while the penalty for supply of heroin was increased from ten years to life.[47]

This simply brought drug policy into line with most other aspects of law, whereby if you seek to profit from a crime you will be judged more harshly. If you punch someone in a pub fight and they fall over and die, you will likely receive a lesser sentence than a professional hit man who murders for money in cold blood.

However, this rationalising move was undercut by the introduction of an entirely new concept in drugs policing – possession with intent to supply. This is where if someone is caught with, say, five grams instead of one, the police and the courts could assume they intended to supply drugs to others, and charge them as a dealer.

This was to have profound consequences on the streets. Over the next few years, as the police worked out how to use these new powers, the application of possession with intent to supply was to fundamentally transform how the policing of drugs worked.

The parameters of what constituted intent to supply quickly expanded. Suddenly, a cop who found a roll of clingfilm in someone's flat could declare them a dealer. Drug dealers often use one- and twopence pieces to weigh their product, and before long cases started appearing of police officers declaring intent to supply because someone had pennies stored in 'suspicious places' in their homes.

Most significantly, if you're a cop or a drug squad detective, it's far easier to get a search warrant for possession with intent than simple possession. So, the creation of this new category led to far more people getting their doors kicked in.

The Act also gave the police wide-ranging new powers to stop and search. Under Section 23, police could detain someone – without formally arresting them – remove them from their location and strip-search them.

Interestingly, though, the very first section of MDA actually had nothing to do with law enforcement, but mandated the formation of the Advisory Council on the Misuse of Drugs (ACMD) – a supposedly non-political panel of experts – to advise the government. This was an incredibly important move towards maintaining the British tradition of sober, scientific analysis. In the United States, this role is undertaken by the Drug Enforcement Agency itself, which is much like letting Goldman Sachs write the laws governing financial regulation.

However, over the coming years, the role of the ACMD was to become bitterly politicised. It has made hugely important contributions, but has also been sidelined when politically convenient. It may say something about the current government that, at the time of writing, the relevant paragraphs about the central role of the ACMD are mysteriously missing from the text of the Misuse of Drugs Act on the Home Office website.[48]

The global War on Drugs was born with the advent of international American imperialism in the late 1900s. The path of its development has directly mirrored the path of that imperialism ever since. Prohibition was born in the occupied Philippines

– then re-imported back into the US with the passing of the Harrison Act in 1914.

After the Second World War, the War on Drugs was exported across the world. It came to Britain along with Elvis Presley, rock 'n' roll, colour TV and the United States Seventh Army stationed in Europe during the Cold War.

This was a moralising movement, rooted in racial and religious prejudice. It sprang from a specifically American vision of society, whereby the interaction between the citizen and the state is dominated by law enforcement – the sheriff with a badge and a six-shooter.

Britain had historically maintained an utterly different approach to drugs.

In British legal tradition crimes are separated into two essential categories. There are crimes that are *mala in se* – wrong in themselves (murder, robbery, sexual assault, etc.), and there are those that are *mala prohibita* – wrong only because they are prohibited. Drug law fits entirely into the second category. Despite the generational moral panic of the 1960s, there has never been a legal sense in this country that drugs are a moral wrong *in and of themselves*.

When writing up any crime, there is a space on the form where the arresting officer is required to record a victim. For crimes like murders and robbery, this is obvious enough. But one can only imagine the awkward moment when the first arrest was made under the MDA, and the copper turned to his sergeant, saying, 'Sarge, who am I meant to write down as the victim?' To this day, when drug arrests are made in the United Kingdom, the victim is, absurdly, recorded as 'the Crown'.

The British fought a long rearguard action to preserve their system. In the end, it could not bear the weight of what can only be called American cultural imperialism. Like almost every other country in the world, Britain succumbed and became a signatory of the UN Single Convention, a projection of US power and influence.

But, in fact, the British System wasn't killed completely. Even under the terms of the Misuse of Drugs Act, it is actually still technically legal for a doctor to prescribe heroin to patients in the UK. Instead of banning prescribing outright, the Home Office simply made doctors apply for a special licence – then stopped issuing them. Doctors who do display an interest in the area are often discouraged, and even quietly let know that it might harm their careers. As Bing Spear wrote in the 1980s, 'the British System is not dead, it has just been under psychiatric care.'[49]

There's also an ironic coda to this story. In September 1973 – just two years after the Misuse of Drugs Act – Nobby Pilcher was convicted of perverting the course of justice. He had been extorting money from people he had fitted up on false drug charges. The speed at which the corruption set in is shocking. As we shall see, over the coming years and decades this corruption, unique to drugs policing, would spread right throughout British law enforcement.

Now that it had been declared, the War on Drugs was to fundamentally transform the nature of British criminal justice and, indeed, society at large. To begin tracing how this story was to play out, we need to go to the badlands south of the river. We need to go to Brixton.

4

Riots

Peele's Principles on the Streets of Brixton

Saturday, 11 April 1981 was an exciting morning for Alex Wheadle. He leapt out of bed, and raced straight across Brixton to the Soferno B record shop. There he found a crowd of other young black men, all wired with a similar state of feverish, tight-wound tension. Today was the day they were going to hit back at the police.

'That Saturday morning all the record shops were completely packed,' Alex explains. 'Even party guys and dealers, guys who were usually night people, were all there at nine in the morning. See, in Brixton the record stores were really the local hang out. You could listen to music, but also check the flyers for where the good sound systems were going to be on Saturday night. And Soferno B was one of the main ones – Soferno was a local dude, with his own sound system and everything.

'But that Saturday morning, it was tense. There were like 50 people there, it was buzzing, but also nervous. We were looking out the window at the police – and they were looking back at us. They knew something was happening too. Usually they patrolled in twos and threes, but today it was much bigger groups. We stared them down, they stared right back. It was like a Sergio Leone film.

'Then, in a flash – Soferno B's just empties! Everyone rushes out. There was a cab driver, down at Atlantic Car Hire, who was stopped on a cannabis search. But the police that morning were really upping their intimidation – so they didn't just arrest him, they really roughed him up.

'Then this guy, Johnny Brixton, who was a bit older than the rest of us, he did something none of us kids ever saw – he protested. He got up in this policeman's face about how the cab driver was being treated. So, the policeman got right back in his face. Then – BLAM – Johnny Brixton just stepped up and sparked the copper out.

'That was the moment. Everyone just surged forward. I came in just as the police started fleeing – they ran for their lives. I think for every young, black kid there, that sight of the police running away – after everything we'd been through – that was one of the most exhilarating moments of our lives.'

The Brixton riots had begun.

In the early twentieth century, Brixton had been designed as a pleasant suburb for the newly emerging middle class. It had handsome Edwardian townhouses, good transport links to central London and a smart modern department store on the high street.

By the 1970s, however, Brixton had become one of the most deprived areas in Britain, its very name synonymous in the press with poverty, violence and criminality. It was also home to Britain's largest Afro-Caribbean community, now well into its second generation. Britain had brought immigrants from the West Indies to help rebuild the country after the Second World War, but was now struggling to integrate their British-born children. This pattern was repeated across British inner cities, particularly Toxteth in Liverpool, where riots also broke out in 1981, and pockets of Manchester and Birmingham,

By the time Alex Wheadle was hitting his teenage years in the late 1970s, relations between this community and the police had reached an all-time low. Brixton was in crisis, with a street robbery rate double that of the next worst borough in London.

In April 1981, Brixton Police decided to clamp down, and launched Operation Swamp 81, flooding the area with plain-clothes officers and making close to a thousand stop and searches over six days, predominantly of young black men. The operation only served to further enrage the local community and destroy what trust they had left in the police.

Then, on the afternoon of Friday, 10 April, a young man named Michael Bailey was playing Space Invaders in a café on Railton Road. He got involved in an altercation with some other youths, and was stabbed in the abdomen. He ran out of the café and down the street, past two uniformed officers who were busy searching another kid.

The cops spotted Bailey's wound, stopped him and called for an ambulance. However, trust in the police had been so corroded that word went out around Brixton that the police were actually arresting Michael, even as he bled out. Many believed that the police had injured him themselves. The first small skirmishes began.

Alex Wheadle remembers exactly where he was when he first heard the news.

'I was in a pub on Brixton Hill. This young lad comes running in shouting, "Dem police kill a yout'!" That rumour went around from estate to estate. From that moment we knew something was going to kick off. The feeling was just like, "No, they can't just kill us – this has gone too far. Now we have to stand up." We never questioned the idea that the police would kill a lad – why would we? It totally lined up with our experience. Everyone had this nervous excitement because we knew that finally there would be a confrontation.'

How had an entire community got to the point where they would find it completely believable that the police would murder one of their own? How had this absolute breakdown between police and community come about? Alex Wheadle finds it very easy to explain: 'The first time I got beaten up by the police, my friends all laughed and said, "Oh, now you've been christened." Because this, or something like it, happened to almost everyone I knew.

'It was when I was 16, on a stop and search for weed. I had seen them coming, and had dropped my little bag – so they didn't find anything on me. But they still took me in under suspicion. They wanted us to fear them – and I did feel fear, pure fear.

'I wasn't taken to a charge officer. I was just pushed straight to the cell. A few cells down, someone was getting the crap beaten out of them. I could hear every scream. That was worse than the actual beating. I knew that was going to be me in about ten minutes.

'Then they burst in like, "What you been doin', you fucking nigger? Who you dealin' for, nigger?" Then just bang, bang, bang. I tried to cover myself, but there's only so much you can do. Eventually they got tired of kicking me, and just started laughing and walked out.

'I think they then checked my age and found out I was only 16. So, they dragged me into a police van, drove me up Brixton Hill towards where I lived, and chucked me out while the van was moving at about 15 or 20 miles an hour. I remember just feeling pure, pure hatred.

'The next time, I was picked up outside a club called Bali Hai in Streatham. This was a nice club – not like some rough party, but a nice one where you'd dress up nice and bring your girl. So, I was in the line with my 1970s safari jacket and all that on – then the police grab me.

'What they did back then was throw you down on your belly on the floor of the police van. Then all their heavy boots come down on top of you. It was humiliating. That's the word. I think every young black kid felt that humiliation.'

When Brixton Police launched Operation Swamp 81, it was ostensibly targeted at cutting street robbery. But Alex is very clear about where the roots of the conflict between the youth of Brixton and the police really lay:

'Nine times out of ten it was about cannabis – that's what got you stopped, it was always, "We're searching you for possession of cannabis." Maybe one time out of ten it might be, "You fit the description of a mugger."

'Now – I wouldn't have loved the police no matter what, but if they had been searching for blades or weapons or something, I think we at least would have understood that. There were knife fights back then – there were muggings. But the targeting around cannabis was different, that didn't just piss off the professional drug-dealer guys – it pissed off everyone in the area. That's how me and my friends saw it.

'Everyone knew what happened to you if you ended up in Brixton police station. Back then there were no taped interviews or anything. You'd hear about a friend of yours who got picked up by the police, and now he can't come out for six weeks because his eye's out of shape. And you'd just think, "Are you serious? For a £2 draw?" You'd have six policemen coming up to you – for a £2 bit of weed. It's not a knife, I'm not mugging anyone – all we wanted was to be normal teenagers and have a bit of a dance on the weekend.'

When the Brixton riots kicked off in 1981, facing off against Alex and his friends was a young police officer named Peter Bleksley.

Peter was new on the force, and his experiences in the riots were to fundamentally affect his development, both as a cop and as a person.

'That Friday afternoon I was in a Divisional Support Unit,' Peter begins. 'There were about a dozen of us patrolling in a people carrier, going to trouble hotspots to reinforce those areas. Peckham was just down the road from Brixton, and we also had a lot of deprived estates where we spent most of our time.

'Most of us had been working long hours, and Friday is "Poet's Day" – "Piss Off Early, Tomorrow's Saturday". So, a lot of people had gone off already. We were about to go back to the nick ourselves, when the shout went up for urgent assistance on Railton Road.

'There were three of us left in the van, and we thought, "Yeah, we'll have a bit of that." So, I got on the radio – the bloke on the other end heard we were a DSU and assumed there would be a dozen of us. He didn't know most of us had fucked off early because it was Friday.

'So, we turn up at Railton Road and it was just beginning to kick off. There were two or three Brixton units there, and it was like a Mexican stand-off.

'We had a few shields in the van so we got those out. Then the bricks started to fly. As bad luck would have it, there was building work down the road, so no one that weekend was short of ammunition. More and more units started racing up, but at this point it was still just skirmishes. But this clearly had the potential to escalate quickly. You could just feel it.

'After the Swamp Operation, the police were just as on edge as the public. It was a tinderbox. I could absolutely see how those rumours about the young lad who got stabbed would be believed. If you were a young Brixton kid, sure you'd believe that.

'There were massive crowds on the street – people came out in force. This was very obviously not the kind of thing that could be put down in the usual way – crack a few skulls and trust people would soon bugger off. On the Friday it stayed as just skirmishes, but because of the numbers on their side, there wasn't going to be any reduction on our side – so we just kept calling in more units.'

This was perhaps the critical moment of the entire weekend – the last chance to de-escalate the situation and avoid a full-scale riot. The police didn't take it. Peter continues his story:

'Eventually, late Friday there was a big powwow at Brixton police station. Our sergeant came out of the briefing and said, "Right, what we're going to do is patrol in a never-ending circle up Railton Road and Tulse Hill, then back round. But under no circumstances do you get out of your van. No matter what you see – no matter who provokes you." So, we started this convoy – a line of vans going end-to-end around Brixton, till the early hours.'

Peter pauses, takes a sip of his coffee and takes a moment to choose his next words carefully.

'That was frankly the stupidest fucking decision I have ever come across in my life. It was just waving a massive red rag at a bull. All it served to do was raise the tension. You could feel it getting cranked up and cranked up.

'So, the whole night it was us in our vans, driving round and round, with the crowds lined up just shouting abuse. At one point, the landlady of this pub came out – because she'd seen us going around for hours. She flagged our van down, and slung in a crate of light ales. She was a white lady, perhaps she related to the police in a more old-fashioned way. So, we all got a few light ales while we were driving this mad circuit around Brixton.

'Of course there was no mobiles in those days, and we all had to phone home to let them know we wouldn't be back that night.

I asked another lady if we could use her phone. We did a whip-round for some coins and I was last on, so I just hid the coins under the phone – so she'd find it when she next dusts the room or what have you. Well, when we came back around on our next circuit, this same lady came running up to us and threw that money straight in through the window, saying, "Don't you dare insult me."

'But, we basically carried on in this ridiculous endless loop, just winding everybody up until the early hours. It wasn't until the next morning when that built-up tension really exploded.'

This image of one community screaming abuse at the police, while another – just on the other side of the road – clings to a vision of law enforcement from a previous era, taps into a very deep theme of what the story of the British War on Drugs means.

The War on Drugs in Britain has often been vicious, brutal and terrifying. But, even at its worst, this country has never approached the violence of the US, or the murderous chaos of much of Latin America. However, there are a few ways in which Britain is central to this global story.

The first is the lost history of the British System. The second has to do with a set of fundamental questions about the very nature of law enforcement. Who are the police, and what are they for?

The world's first modern, professionalised police force was established in Britain by Sir Robert Peel, in 1829. Through many changes and evolutions, this is the essential model on which almost every advanced nation has founded and developed their own law enforcement services to this day.

Peel laid out nine foundational principles of modern policing, designed to separate the new professional force from the arbitrary, haphazard policing of the past. The Peelian Principles are what all modern law enforcement, however imperfectly, is built on.

The key phrase comes from Principle 7: 'The police are the public and the public are the police.' The idea that all policing must be done with the consent of those policed is the foundation of all modern law enforcement. It is what separates free countries from police states – and it is one of the greatest British contributions to world civilisation.

Now, go back to that image of the Brixton riots – one community giving police officers light ales, another hurling bricks and abuse. This one image is a perfect illustration of how Peel's Principles are supposed to work, and of just how ugly it gets when they go wrong.

The Brixton riots, as well as those that broke out at the same time in Toxteth, Liverpool, traumatised Britain. In a panic, the government appointed Lord Scarman to undertake a full-scale enquiry into the riots and their causes.

The Scarman Report is one of the key moments of modern British history – attempting a fundamental overhaul of the relationship between the police and ethnic minorities. It did not succeed.

The failure of the Scarman Report was down to several key blind spots in its research. The report details how poor housing, high unemployment and social exclusion sowed the seeds of fury in the Afro-Caribbean community across the country. But, while poverty and poor housing may have formed the background to the riots, they were not the trigger.

These were anti-police riots. Their target was very specific. Something had happened to policing in Brixton to make the area explode. Something had torn the police apart from the community.

Where Lord Scarman does deal with policing, he rightly draws attention to the Suspicious Persons Act, or 'SUS' laws. Derived from the Vagrancy Act of 1824, these laws essentially gave any police officer the right to nick anyone they didn't like the look of. All they had to say was that the person seemed to be acting with the 'intent to commit an arrestable offence'. These laws were routinely abused, and were despised in Brixton for obvious reasons – they were repealed soon after the riots in 1981. But, even where Scarman does touch on policing, there is still a massive, crippling blind spot.

The Scarman Report is 255 pages long. The word 'cannabis' appears exactly zero times. The word 'drugs' appears once. The line that Scarman, and those who came after him, failed to draw runs straight from the Misuse of Drugs Act in 1971 to the riots in Brixton almost exactly a decade later. A fundamental thread in the breakdown of trust between the police and the community in 1970s Brixton was the early stages of the British War on Drugs.

Drugs policing is qualitatively different from other forms of modern police work. Aggressively policing actions that aren't wrong in themselves, but only wrong because they are prohibited, places very particular strains on the Peelian bond between the police and the community.

The polite parliamentary discussions we looked at in the lead-up to the MDA of 1971 led directly to smashed windows in Brixton in 1981. To trace how, we need to look again at the stories of Alex Wheadle and Peter Bleksley.

At the time of the riots there were only a few years between them: Alex was 18 and Peter 22. Both had tough upbringings, not that far away from each other – Alex grew up in care in south London; Peter came from a working-class single-parent family in Bexleyheath. But, somehow these two young men ended up on opposing battle lines as Brixton burned.

'If you're trying to understand drugs in Brixton culture, you have to go back to my father's generation,' Alex begins.

'My dad arrived in the mid-1950s from Jamaica, and cannabis really wasn't around that much. Back then if a guy wanted to score, they'd go up to the Flamingo Club and places like that in Notting Hill where black American jazz dudes hung around.

'A lot of the time they weren't even allowed into the white clubs, so they started putting on their own dances and parties – bringing over that sound system culture from the Caribbean. Obviously a few of the more entrepreneurial types realised people wanted some weed, and started flying it in from Jamaica.

'By the time I was a teenager, there was also the whole Rasta influence. I can't emphasise enough how important Bob Marley was. We saw the artists coming over from Jamaica – Dennis Brown, Sugar Minott, Gregory Isaacs. When you're young you want someone to look up to – and those guys were it.

'So, basically, if you were living in Brixton from the mid-seventies onwards, smoking a spliff was like drinking a cup of tea. It was everywhere – blues dances, parties – everywhere black people congregated.

'A lot of the blues dances and squats were centred around Railton Road – which we used to call the Frontline. There were a lot of run-down properties – God knows who actually owned them – but people would set up little businesses selling booze from the basement, little shebeens. And that's mainly where you'd go to buy your weed. You might recognise a dealer, and get either a £2 draw, a £5 draw or a £10 draw.

'Most of us were unemployed, so we'd just get a £2 draw before a party or a dance. Early evening was rush hour on the Frontline – everyone would get their £2 draw, get their Special Brew and hope by the end of the night they'd have a girl as well. That was just the culture. We were just trying to have a good time – until the police would come and beat you up.

'I started going out to these parties at 14 or 15, like any other kid. It was just part of our lives. I remember going to see *Saturday Night Fever* – and on their Saturday night in that bit of New York, that's what they did. On our Saturday night, this is what we did.'

Alex has described the culture surrounding drugs that he grew up with. But those drugs had to be supplied by someone – they were part of a growing market. We press Alex for more detail on the exact structure of the Brixton cannabis trade.

'For dealers, the Frontline was the prime spot – it was the best territory,' he begins enthusiastically.

'If anyone tried to move in on that, it could lead to occasional violence. I saw people chased off with ratchets and axes – there were no guns, but you'd see the odd big knife here and there.

'We called the main guys Line Mans. They'd stand there and sell weed with one hand, while flicking their ratchet with the other. It would make that distinctive noise – so you'd know they were armed, and not to mess with them. In those days it was more often just the threat of violence, rather than violence itself.

'Then you had the stick-up boys, who would wait for you to score – then creep round the corner and mug it off you. That happened to me once or twice. When you're faced with a blade you just go "I like my smoke, but I like my face more."

'It was all weed – I hardly ever saw anything like cocaine or heroin. If people were using that I would have seen it. There was a little bit of speed going around, just for the all-night parties, but really it was all weed, straight from Jamaica – not like the greenhouse stuff they're smoking today.

'And it was all individuals. There were no gangs. Those individuals could be pretty intimidating – but in comparison to what happened later in the 1990s, it was really pretty gentle.'

As our conversation progresses, Alex gets more and more insistent that we understand that Railton Road represented much more to the Brixton community than just a place to buy weed. This was the beating heart of an entire community.

'The Frontline was almost like a safe space for us,' Alex insists.

'There was drinking and there was gambling – but that's where the record shops were where we would all hang out. It wasn't just a drug-dealing place – it was a sort of home. It was where we could breathe easy and feel a bit free for once.

'That's where the best blues dances were. The difference between a party and a blues dance was that at a blues dance, a sound system would take control of an entire house. It could be a squat or something, and they'd bring in a generator and run the entire place. They'd take money on the door and run the bar.

'And if you really wanted to be cool, you partied on the Front-line. That's where you would first learn to dance with a girl. Then you could say "I'm a man now."

'And the weed thing was an important part of that. It was a little local industry. People would take their money from selling a bit of weed, and set up their own sound systems to do parties – or set up loads of other businesses. You'd have thought Margaret Thatcher would have been proud – they were real entrepreneurs. The weed trade was an economy in itself. It was a way of surviving for many people, and it was part of the community.

'That's why we resented the police so much for coming down on it so violently.

'The pressure ramped up over the late 1970s. The way we saw it, we weren't mugging people, we were just having a little smoke at a party. But they came down so hard on us. That's why we began to really hate the police. It got especially bad when they brought in the SPG.'

The Special Patrol Group, or SPG, was an elite unit of the Met, established in the 1960s to target high-crime areas and respond to terrorist threats. If detectives generally aspired to join the Flying Squad, uniformed cops could aim for the SPG. By the 1970s, though, the unit had gained a nasty reputation for brutality and heavy-handedness. In 1979 they were engulfed in controversy over the killing of the teacher Blair Peach at an anti-racism rally, and were eventually disbanded in 1986.

It's significant that even as a teenager, Alex was aware of exactly which police squads were particularly nasty. But he goes further, highlighting the specific tactics that were most responsible for driving the police and the community apart.

'Funnily enough with cannabis – you wouldn't smoke it at home,' he explains. 'Everywhere else was fine, but not with your mum and dad upstairs.

'But then the police started raiding people's houses for weed. And those raids were savage. They'd smash in the door; tear up the floorboards. This was the 1970s, so everyone wanted those nice sideboard cabinets in their hallway – and the police would smash them up.

'They weren't looking for weapons or stolen goods – it was just weed. That smashing up of people's parents' houses led to deep, deep resentment. They were attacking our families. Suddenly, these first-generation immigrant parents who wanted to be respectable, who went to church and had worked to finally get their own home, were having their houses smashed up. That created problems between the generations, and I can't even tell you how much it made us hate the police.'

What Alex is describing is a form of policing unique to the War on Drugs – a form all too familiar to those with a police background, like Neil Woods.

As a rookie cop Neil was assigned to a team raiding a flat for stolen property – TVs, VHS players and the like. Neil geared himself up for a 'proper raid', like he'd seen on American cop shows as a kid. So he was quite surprised when his sergeant, an experienced veteran on the force, simply walked up and knocked on the door. The door swung open to reveal a very sheepish-looking thief, who knew he'd been caught and simply turned and led them into his living room, where the stolen TVs were piled up.

It was only when Neil started working with the Derbyshire Drug Squad that he first experienced the archetypal image we now have of a police raid – the battering ram taking down the door; a dozen hard coppers bashing their way in, shouting at the top of their lungs; the occupants brought down on their bellies as fast as possible with maximum force; the cops tearing through the flat, upending every stick of furniture in the place.

There is a very simple reason for these different styles of policing. TVs can't be swallowed. Laptops can't be flushed down the toilet.

Doing a drugs raid, the object is to get in as fast as possible, causing the absolute maximum panic, fear and confusion. You need to prevent anyone trying to swallow or flush their stash. Obviously, you don't want to lose your evidence, or have them injure themselves by ingesting a big pile of drugs – but also, if you smash in someone's door, and *don't* find any drugs, then the police force has to pay for the damage.

So, drug squad DIs are massively incentivised by their budget requirements to make absolutely sure that at least some drugs are always found. This means always going in as hard and fast as possible. It is a recipe for planted evidence and corruption.

When Alex talks about how police tactics destroyed the black community's trust in law enforcement, he is talking specifically about the War on Drugs. This is reinforced when we speak to another former police officer who took part in the Brixton riots. Brian Paddick was a young constable when he was rushed down from Holloway to reinforce the police lines on Railton Road. Soon after, he was posted to Brixton full-time, and went on to rise to the position of Commander of Brixton Police. After leaving the police he was made a baron, and we interviewed him at his offices at the House of Lords.

'I did my bit at the riots,' he begins, 'then January of the following year I was posted to one of the Railton Road patrols as a sergeant.'

'It was myself and six constables, patrolling Railton Road and the surrounding area. Always with a vanload of riot cops parked round the corner, in case we got into trouble – which we never actually did.

'So, we're out on patrol, and someone has their handbag snatched. We chase the guy we think is responsible – and he ducks into an illegal gambling den on Railton Road. We knock on the door, and this older guy opens it. We say we were chasing someone and we think he came in here. The guy asks what we want him for – and we say a handbag snatch. The guy goes back in, and a couple of minutes later he comes back, pushing the guy we're after out in front of him by the scruff of the neck.

'Then, a few weeks later, a similar thing happens. This time we're chasing a suspect we think has cannabis on him. And this guy also runs into the same building – I suppose it might have been some sort of safe house. We knock on the door again, the same older guy answers. Again, he asks what we're chasing the person for – and I say it's because we think he's got cannabis on him. He slammed the door in my face. He didn't say a word – just slammed the door. That stayed with me for a long time.'

This is the starkest possible illustration of how drugs policing is fundamentally different from other forms of law enforcement – and of just how seriously it can divide the police and the community. To explore how this plays out at street level, we need to pick up Peter Bleksley's story, and discover how he ended up policing the Brixton riots in the first place.

'To go back a bit, I grew up in Bexleyheath,' he explains. 'I left school at 16 and got involved in quite a lot of petty crime – shoplifting, gambling, criminal damage, drinking and stuff like that. I was young and directionless – it was only finding the police that changed that. As soon as I walked into the training school in Hendon, my life completely transformed. I came top of my class, and at 18 I was posted as a constable to Peckham. And that's when I got a very rude awakening. I quickly realised that I knew fuck all about the world and had a lot to learn.

'Coming from where I did, in that time, I had no knowledge of other cultures. I simply didn't know any black people growing up. There were a couple of Asian kids at my school, but no one with Afro-Caribbean heritage. Then, suddenly I land in Peckham – still as a teenager – and I'm expected to police a huge Afro-Caribbean community. I've said before that I wasn't racist when I joined the police – I didn't know anyone to be racist against – but I became racist through being in the police.

'The other thing I didn't know anything about was drugs. Even as a tearaway teenager, we simply didn't have any. I knew all about alcohol. I knew all about throwing up into a carrier bag, then hiding it so my mum didn't find it – but I'd just never seen drugs. But now, in Peckham, I had to learn about drugs very fast – right from the start.

'Usually you weren't actually allowed out on patrol until after your 19th birthday. But I made such a nuisance of myself that they finally allocated me to a very senior PC to come along for a search of a blues dance – and told me to stick by this senior officer at all times.

'We crashed in and it was pandemonium. The music screeched off and people were getting thrown against the walls. Of course, there were drugs all over the floor – because as soon as they heard the police smashing through the door, they all dropped their dope.

'But, what I learned that night was that drugs could fly. Because somehow they flew off the ground, into people's pockets – and by the time we got back to the station there was a prisoner for all those drugs.

'And that senior officer I was with went straight up to the speakers, and stuck them with a knitting needle, which totally ruins them, without leaving any visible damage. Then he went through the entire record collection, stamping on each record. That's just how it was in 1978 – I believe that raid would have been on a drugs warrant.'

This is classic War on Drugs policing. It is what destroys the trust between police and community. And Peter is absolutely clear that this was not an isolated incident.

He goes on with a sigh: 'I was just 18, but I very quickly learned that to nick a West Indian lad for a small amount of cannabis for personal use would always be regarded as a good arrest, and you might get a good report from your supervisor.

'I can't over-intellectualise the connection between drugs policing and general police racism. There was no space between them. It was just, "that culture had drugs." If they were black, they had drugs – that was it.

'I can't speak about high-up policy. Back then I was a foot soldier – I was in the day-to-day fight. I'm sure I must have nicked some white people for drugs, but I struggle to remember one. Overwhelmingly, it was indivisible in our minds – the black population and cannabis; one meant the other.

'There was a well-known phrase: "black and white, stop on sight" – if you ever saw a black person and a white person together, you automatically stop them – because what would a white person and a black person ever want to be doing together?

The police had converted me into a vile, racist thug. I would genuinely describe myself then in that way.

'The chief superintendent and his superiors wanted figures. They wanted people on the charge sheet. They kept track of each of us with little cards pinned to the office wall, like a tournament. So, if you're an 18-year-old kid walking the streets of Peckham near the end of the month, heaven help you. Because some copper might be on 96, but if they hit 100, the detective sergeant will get the drinks in, and they'll have a piss-up in the office. And, in that office, pinned to the noticeboard, were Rastafarian dreadlocks that had been ripped off a prisoner's head.'

It was only as Peter became more experienced, and advanced through the ranks, however, that he began to realise that this was not just an issue of the brutalising day-to-day battles of street-level policing. Drug policy and police racism were deeply intertwined all the way up through the criminal justice system, often in very subtle ways.

'I discovered that I actually had a talent for police work. I just had a nose for it. I could look at someone and just know they're up to something. So, I became a renowned thief-taker among my peers.

'There were some at Peckham who were complete fit-up merchants. Policing back then was far less sophisticated – there was really nobody to hold us to account. We weren't aware of words like "accountability" and "justification". We just went out and did what we did – and if you were a young, black man you could easily get fitted up.

'With the SUS laws, all a copper needed was to say he saw two "overt acts". He could just say that a suspect was seen trying two car doors, or looking at two houses, and nick them – that's it. So, if someone had the misfortune to fail the "attitude test", as it was called, they would get nicked and fitted up.

'But if you fail the attitude test, you're fair game for a kicking. In the back of the van on the way to the police station there's no one watching, and you might just get a straightener. Welcome to Peckham in the late 1970s.

'But when it comes to court, if you say you're innocent and have been fitted up – suddenly you're questioning a police officer's evidence. And at that point any previous convictions – and they were usually cannabis convictions – become fair game for the prosecution to reveal to the court.

'So, you end up with a lot of barristers advising their clients to plead guilty – to take the fit-up, rather than actually fight their case. I can't tell you how prevalent that was. The corruption and racism wasn't just at the point of arrest, it was all the way through the system.

'This was pre-PACE, and pre-Scarman. In those days the only evidence required was the police officer's word – what he happened to write down in his pocketbook. Everyone else was powerless.'

For a young black man in 1970s south London, getting caught with a bit of cannabis didn't just mean a conviction and possibly a beating. It meant not being able to defend oneself against false allegations from then on. How could this sabotaging of the safeguards that are meant to underpin criminal justice not drive the police and the community apart? Even at this early stage, the drug war was already beginning to corrupt the system.

Probably the most significant result of the Scarman Report was the Police and Criminal Evidence Act of 1984, or PACE. The idea was accountability and oversight. Whenever you watch a TV cop show and see them flip on a tape recorder in an interview room, that's PACE at work. Previously all that was required was an individual cop's word about what they happened to remember.

In the old days, the first thing a cop would do was try to extract a confession from a suspect – to 'verbal' them. After PACE, policing became about using the evidence to build a picture of what actually may have happened.

PACE was a very necessary revolution in British policing. 'Verballing' was a blueprint for abuse and corruption, made clear by landmark cases like that of the Birmingham Six, in which false confessions regarding an IRA bomb attack were extracted through torture. But, as unbelievable as it sounds now, there was a time when a police officer's word might have been considered to merit the benefit of the doubt. In a situation in which the Peelian Principles are working, in which 'the police are the public and the public are the police', it's not inconceivable that the community might place more trust in a copper's word.

What we see in the 1970s is that trust breaking down. The entire idea of what a police officer represented in British society was being radically transformed. Of course, this was a complex picture, to do with deep changes in society as a whole. But there is no doubt that the passing of the Misuse of Drugs Act in 1971 was a key landmark on this road – a landmark that was utterly missed by Lord Scarman and those who came after him.

The Scarman Report shied away from declaring the police institutionally racist – that would come 18 years later with the Macpherson Report, following the murder of Stephen Lawrence. The media reaction to Scarman was equally ambiguous, shot through with images of disease, sickness and poison. The *Sun* raged about THE HATRED THAT IS POISONING BRITAIN, while the *Telegraph* warned, SCARMAN TELLS OF 'DISEASE THREATENING OUR SOCIETY'.[50] As in so much reporting of this ilk, it is often murky as to whether these papers are trying to convince their readers that the 'disease' in question is racial prejudice, or multicultural society itself.

What both Scarman and the surrounding media missed was the critical role that the development of drugs policing played in causing the riots. But perhaps there's a good reason they missed this – the very people who might have alerted them didn't trust the system enough to even talk to the enquiry. Alex Wheadle certainly didn't. 'A lot of people from my generation didn't want to give evidence to Scarman,' he explains. 'We thought it was a trick. We didn't trust the police at all. Even if our house got broken into we probably wouldn't call the police.'

When the relationship between police and community breaks down, even the investigation into the causes of a problem gets sabotaged. Decades later, we are still feeling the effects of failing to address these issues.

For both Alex Wheadle and Peter Bleksley the Brixton Riots were life-changing events – though in very different ways. Alex has an almost resigned nonchalance as he tells about the fallout that weekend in 1981 had for him.

'Immediately after the riot, parties sprang up everywhere. I honestly didn't even know about the looting – for me it was about confronting the police – but suddenly people had this booze they'd nicked, and we all partied. You had to be careful going between the estates because the SPG patrols were still everywhere, but there was an amazing vibe in the air.

'I was living in a Lambeth Council Social Services hostel, and even four weeks after there was still plenty of stuff floating around that had been lifted during the riot.

'So, the police battered down the door – bang, bang, bang – and took me and about five others down to Brixton nick. It was the same procedure as before – they put you in a cell for a long time to make you stew without knowing what's going to happen. Then they come in and beat you. After the kicking they left me overnight – then charged me with causing an affray, resisting arrest and assaulting a police officer.'

Alex was sent to prison, where a Rastafarian cellmate intro-duced him to the books of Chester Himes, Richard Wright and John Steinbeck. After his release, Alex became a successful novelist, often writing about Brixton life. In 2008 he was awarded an MBE for his services to literature.

Peter Bleksley has none of Alex's calm acceptance. When he talks about how the riots affected him as a person, you can feel the anger is still there.

'My unit had done the Friday and Saturday, so we got stood down on the Sunday,' he begins.

'I still remember driving home and thinking over and over about how close I'd come to not driving home. And a voice inside me just went, "Fuck that – I'm not going to wear that uniform any more."

'I knew that in Peckham and places like that the police were never going to win a popularity contest. But that weekend, there were people there who actually wanted to kill me. Only, they didn't want to kill me, they wanted to kill the cloth I wore and what it represented. That had a deeply, deeply profound effect on me.

'I almost started to convince myself that if they went out for a drink with me and got to know me, then it would be all right. But then I realised, No it wouldn't, because look what I've become. So, I thought about jacking the cops in period – but somewhere deep down I knew I was good at catching thieves, villains, robbers. CID had already tapped me up once, but I'd turned them down to stay on the street.

'Then I came into Peckham station on the Monday. Over the weekend a shoe shop had been looted. One of the sergeants was boasting about how he'd fitted up a six-foot-two-inch black man with the theft of a size seven ladies' shoe. That was the last straw. I really said, "Sod that – I am never wearing that uniform again."

'After that moment everything changed. I never uttered another racist word or committed a racist act. I saw the world in a completely different light. That's really how I started on the path of becoming a detective, and eventually making it onto the crime squad.'

Peter went on to become one of the Met's most celebrated under-cover agents, bringing down very high-level drug dealers and international organised groups. He was one of the original founders of SO10, Scotland Yard's dedicated covert policing unit, and since retiring has become a successful author, television consultant and media commentator on policing matters.

Reflecting on his long and highly distinguished career, he says with a sigh, 'I look back now and think: well, are there less drugs and guns on the streets because of what my colleagues and I did? And of course the answer is an emphatic no. The whole drugs thing is a joke. I could wallpaper my bedroom with commendation certificates – they sit in the loft gathering dust. What a waste of time.'

5

Phoney War

Utopian Hippies and Media Hype in 1977

You can see how Smiles got his name. He flashes a craggy, mischievous grin, which combines with a mane of Gandalf-white hair to create an instantly engaging, roguish sort of charisma. Yet, for all his friendliness and piratical charm, when Smiles hears one of us is an ex-undercover cop he refuses to have us into his home. We do our interview by Skype.

This is understandable. Smiles has experience with undercover coppers. He was a key suspect in one of the most famous – and perhaps most overhyped – police operations in modern British history. The Operation Julie LSD busts of the mid-1970s have become the stuff of legend, generating massive headlines at the time and book deals for the detectives involved ever since. But none of the principal players in the greatest acid ring in history has ever really spoken out – until now.[51]

We also spoke to Stephen Bentley, the undercover detective who was sent to infiltrate Smiles's LSD distribution network. To hear the same events recounted by both a major drug dealer and the undercover who investigated him turns out to be a very interesting dynamic.

The story of how Smiles's and Stephen Bentley's lives inter-
sected also opens a fascinating window into how the War on
Drugs did – and did not – operate in the 1970s. It begins at
Glastonbury.[52]

Today, the Glastonbury Festival is a corporate behemoth –
the music industry's biggest 'heritage' acts playing to massive
crowds, who have forked out serious money for the privilege. But
it started off in 1970 as little more than 1,500 people gathered
around one stage.

The following year, the festival was taken over by the hippy
icon Andrew Kerr – partly funded by Winston Churchill's granddaughter, Arabella. The iconic Pyramid Stage went up for the
first time, and tripping out along the West Country ley lines
became a key rite of passage for those on the blossoming 1970s
psychedelic scene.

But Glastonbury was only one of many festivals to spring
up in this era. Beginning with Phun City in 1970, and building
through key events at Windsor, Watchfield, Stonehenge and
many more, the free festivals grew from a series of random
parties into a fully fledged movement. The squatting communes
that had sprung up throughout British cities in the late 1960s
were being evicted one by one. Their residents took to the road,
and the free festivals continued many of their radical experi-
ments in communal living and consensus politics – as well as
their anarchic, hedonistic spirit.

Most of these festivals had no entry charge at all. Food was
free or very cheap – as were the plentiful supplies of the movement's drug of choice: LSD. In the sixties, acid may have been the
preserve of a select clique of mystics and pop stars, but now it had
become the favoured drug of a movement seeking mind expansion
and new modes of living. In 1969 there had been 159 criminal
convictions for LSD in the UK; by 1972 there were 1,457.[53] These

were still relatively tiny numbers, but the movement had high visibility, and attracted outsize attention from the press.

Mick Farren, who organised the Phun City Festival, laid out his aims as 'attempting to provide a three-day environment designed to the needs and desires of the Freak, not just a situation set up to relieve him of his money.' One of the attendees recalls, 'A genuine Californian hippy in long white robes holding a plastic bag with thousands of hits of pure acid came along trying to give us some tabs, but all the people around the fire was [*sic*] already surfing on clean high-quality acid and everyone had more than enough anyways.'

The author William Bloom recalled an early Glastonbury experience: 'nearly everyone was tripping at one stage or another. Sometimes it was being given away ... The festivals would not have been what they were without hallucinogens.'[54] This is not a picture of the drug war as we have come to know it, with ruthless gangsters peddling drugs for profit. These were hippies, often giving their product away in the belief that it would create a new consciousness and a better world. Their utopianism may have been naïve – perhaps even ridiculous – but they were not violent murderers.

The authorities didn't quite know how to handle this growing movement. The response seemed to shift from ignoring the issue in the hope it would go away to serious violence – as at the 1974 Windsor Festival, where hundreds of police brutally battered unarmed festival-goers, including women and children.

But some elements within the police did eventually begin to act with a touch more intelligence. Undercover detectives began infiltrating the festivals disguised as hippies and brought back samples of the LSD available. These samples were then tested by scientists at the Central Research Establishment at Aldermaston – and eventually landed on the desk of a detective inspector with the Thames Valley force named Dick Lee.

Lee began piecing together evidence of a new type of ultra-high-strength LSD that was becoming increasingly common throughout the festival circuit. This new acid also came in a brand new form, different to the sugar cube and liquid LSD the police had been used to since the 1960s. These were tiny triturated, moulded tablets, known to the hippies as microdots. They changed everything.

The birth of the microdot can be traced back to one day in 1967, when the American writer David Solomon met a brilliant young English biochemist named Richard Kemp in Cambridge. Solomon was an 'acid intellectual' who wrote extensively about LSD, and was a friend of the psychedelic guru Timothy Leary. He turned Kemp on to acid's mind-expanding potential.

Kemp then moved to Paris to work with the enigmatic American drug trafficker Ronald Stark. While there, he stumbled on a revolutionary new method of producing LSD without chromatography, and was able to create perhaps the purest acid ever made. He eventually moved back to England and began turning out this new super-strength acid in earnest, distributing it via a dealer named Henry Todd.

However, Kemp then discovered that Todd was halving the dose in each trip to double their profits. To Kemp, this was a gross insult to his product. He'd never got into the acid game for the money – he genuinely wanted to 'turn people on' and change the world. He split from Todd, and moved to the small Welsh village of Tregaron to restart his production line with David Solomon, away from the London rat race.

Todd, in turn, promptly hired another hippy chemist, and friend of Kemp's, named Andy Munro, and set up a new lab in Hampton Wick on the outskirts of London. These two operations remained completely separate – Kemp and Todd didn't see each other again until they wound up at the same police station after the Operation Julie busts. But, with two labs now both pumping out ultra-high-strength acid, the microdots began flooding the psychedelic scene. In 1971, they had made up 5 per cent of all LSD seized by police; by 1975 they hit 80 per cent.[55]

This was the acid that Dick Lee began finding on his under-cover festival operations. And it wasn't just being sold in Britain. Kemp and Munro's microdots were showing up all over the US, Europe and Australia. By the mid-1970s, 50 per cent of world supply was thought to originate in the UK.[56] Something needed to be done.

So, on 17 February 1976, Dick Lee was given permission to form a special squad to investigate this new wave of LSD. A hand-picked team of 25 officers was put together, drawn from 11 separate police forces. The name Operation Julie was taken up in honour of sergeant Julie Taylor, one of the few women on the squad.

Stephen Bentley clearly remembers getting the call to join the operation. 'I was immediately excited because it was a way to get off the drug squad I was working on. I hated that squad to be honest, chasing potheads meant nothing to me.

'When I started CID in my early twenties, I was doing real police work in tough areas like Kirby – investigating murders and serious crimes. Then I got moved to this drug squad in Hampshire. That was really looked down on – it was seen as a poor relation. We had had two detective constables and one DS to cover the whole of the north of the county. It wasn't seen as a big priority at all. The whole organised crime dimension hadn't developed yet, and we were just going after really small dealers.

'So, when Dick Lee called me, it was a chance to get off that squad. I'd also heard about LSD in the media. The papers were full of the false stories about kids wanting to fly off skyscrapers. At the time I believed all that, so I signed right up for the squad.'

* * *

After surveillance confirmed that Richard Kemp was indeed running an acid lab in Tregaron, Dick Lee approached Bentley about undertaking an undercover operation in another tiny Welsh village nearby called Llanddewi Brefi. The target was a major player in the acid distribution network, known only as 'Smiles'. Bentley was partnered with another detective, Eric Wright. Together they worked on developing a cover story – and began growing their hair out to blend in with the hippies.

But who was Smiles, the mysterious acid dealer at the centre of this supposed conspiracy? And how had the biggest drug ring in Britain ended up in an out-of-the-way village like Llanddewi Brefi in the first place?

'I joined the army at 15 on an apprenticeship – to get away from an abusive stepfather at home,' Smiles begins.

'I came out after a few years, and basically lived on the road for a while. It was the late sixties, and I was very swept up in the whole hippy movement that was kicking off. I ended up in Birmingham, but had made friends all over the country.

'Originally I was just into drinking and smoking a bit of hash in the shebeens around Birmingham, but then more psychedelic drugs started coming in and I knew some Americans who were into that scene in London. Acid was so easy to carry that when Americans were coming to Europe to travel it became a bit of easy money for them. It was sort of an underground currency, really.

'Then this guy John Preece approaches me in a pub in Birmingham and asks if I can get some acid. He gives me £35, and I zip down to London and get it for £25. So, I've made a tenner and have done my first drug deal. But when I bring those trips back, John says I can come and live in his house. So I do that – and we set up a nice little dealing business, running up and down to London for hash and LSD.

'I have to say, acid changed my life – it was a real force for good for me, and we absolutely thought we were doing something good for the world. I wanted everybody to understand that everything is absolutely and inextricably connected. I wanted people to understand that everything we do has an impact, so that if we change what we do, we can make the world a better place. That was absolutely the main drive.

'I remember we were up in Cannon Hill Park in Birmingham, and I had a thousand trips of very powerful Clear Light acid from America. I split the bag with my teeth and all these trips fell into my beard, so I just started picking them out and eating them – then we wandered around the park giving them away to people. It was an amazing moment. What we were doing back then had nothing to do with any modern sort of "drugs business".

'Eventually, I moved down to London – and actually got a line on what I later realised was Kemp and Todd's LSD. But, then a friend in Amsterdam let me down on an acid deal, which put me out of that game – and shortly after, I got busted with a tiny amount of hash and got a fine. That's when my wife and I decided to get out of the city, and moved up to Llanddewi Brefi.

'We were part of the back-to-nature hippy movement, and it was completely idyllic. I was making a bit of money importing hash to Canada – buying it for a hundred quid in London and getting a thousand Canadian dollars for it over there. There was a particular brand of suitcase called a Spartanite, which had this plastic shell with an aluminium frame – it was basically custom-made for drugs smuggling. You'd go on a plane or a boat, and there'd always be loads of hippies walking around with these really smart suitcases, it was funny really.

'Then I ran into Russ Spenceley, who I knew from the old days, and asked if there was a way back into the acid scene. And I ended up actually slotting in higher up the chain than I'd been before. We were moving the stuff that Andy Munro was making down in London. Russ or Leaf Fielding would bring it to me – and I had the connections to get it out to the world. These were just connections I'd made over the years – so I suppose I became the key link on the distribution side of things.

'And there was huge demand! We were shifting between 80,000 and 100,000 trips a week. It really took off, and turned into a regular sort of trade. And it was all done completely on trust. I'd get 100,000 laid on – then, having sold some, I'd send a bit of money back up the line. Then, if I had another order coming in, I could still get another 100,000. It was all trust, and as far as I know, no one ever broke that trust.

'But really we were just living a simple life up in Wales – and taking as much of this great new acid as possible. My friend Buzz and I would go out to the pub, then drop a handful and go tramping around the hills. You come back off one of those trips and it's like you're pouring your essence back into your body. You bring back a bit of everything and everyone you've experienced. You really form extraordinary connections and friendships.

'And I got on with everyone in the town as well. I was a working-class lad and suddenly I had loads of money. I didn't know what to do with the bloody stuff, so I spent it, gave it away and went on the piss. Nobody in Llanddewi had any money – so I was buying everyone's drinks all night, which is also a good way to make friends in a Welsh village. I got on with everyone there. They were all my friends.

'But, the mad thing was, I had no idea that Richard Kemp was based just down the road in Tregaron. The two operations were completely separate. It was just blind, ridiculous coincidence that these two high-strength-acid operations happened to be based in these two little villages in Wales. Andy Munro is a good friend of mine to this day, and his acid was absolutely superb, really top of the line – but I do have to be honest and say that Kemp's was a tiny bit better.'

* * *

These were not 'drug dealers' in any modern sense of the term. Gangsters as we know them today aren't known for wandering around parks giving their product away for free to expand universal consciousness. And they certainly aren't known for running major distribution networks solely on trust.

This was the scene that Stephen Bentley was sent to infiltrate. He arrived in Llanddewi Brefi looking for a drug dealer – what he found was Smiles propping up the bar at the local pub. In his memoir, Bentley records that from their first meeting Smiles was immediately open and friendly, even offering to introduce Bentley and his partner to the local faces.

Smiles tells a very different story.

'Buzz and I were minding the pub in Llanddewi Brefi, and these two Herberts come in. The first thing I said was, "What will it be then, officers, two halves – we are on duty aren't we?" I knew immediately by their reaction they were coppers. They didn't look comfortable in their skin, they were just wrong – I knew it from the off. It's instinctive – if you're living outside the law, you look for it all the time.'

There might well be a touch of after-the-fact bravado in this. If Smiles was so sure that Bentley and his partner were cops, why did he proceed to hang out and smoke dope with them for the next eight months or so?

'It was a case of keep your enemies closer,' he insists. 'There was also a story fed into the local community that there was an IRA safe house up in the hills – and that's what they were looking into. I kind of wanted to believe that, I suppose. I was rationalising things away – also helped by the booze I think.

'But to be honest, those two were very peripheral. They were just sort of there, hanging around – but they were never a big part of my world. I never did any actual business in front of them. I smoked a lot of dope with them, sure – but that was sort of normal where I'm from. And, to be fair, Bentley was fun to have a drink with. I didn't like Wright, though – I didn't like his manner or his vibe at all.

'The only time I ever doubted my intuition was one incident where there was a drunken confrontation between Bentley and the local Welsh PC. That made me stop and think. But then they'd do things like claiming they had a load of high-grade Moroccan hash – but then showing me this crap from Karachi that they'd obviously dug out of some police evidence locker. They just didn't know what they were talking about – and in the end, I don't even think those two actually produced any of the serious evidence against me.'

In his book, Stephen Bentley also relates the story of the drunken confrontation with the Welsh PC. That part of his legend-building, at least, seems to have worked.

In all, Bentley and his partner spent around eight months under cover on Operation Julie. One must never discount the psychological pressure of having to live as someone else, but speaking to Bentley, it becomes clear that most of the 'work' involved here consisted of getting drunk and smoking hash with Smiles and his hippy friends. In our interview, he sums it up succinctly, 'Most of the time it was a hoot. It was great!'

The summer of 1976 was one of the hottest on record. Bentley and Wright lived out of an old 'hippy van' in the Welsh mountains, with carte blanche to operate as they saw fit. In his book, Bentley outlines their usual working rhythm: 'Our routine became one of using our mountain retreat to bathe and breakfast. Refreshed, we would drive up the mountain road to explore the beautiful landscape ... We never failed to use our rock pool for some nude swimming to escape the heat of the midday sun. Then, it was time to work. The pubs were open.'[57]

Once in the pub, their job was to gain Smiles's trust. This was made much easier by being able to buy rounds at the bar on their police expenses. As Bentley recalls, 'The average wage in Britain in 1976 was £72 per week. My expense claims alone were in the region of £40 to £50 per week … Our pay was for a 40-hour, five-day week … we would claim for eight hours over-time every day we spent in Llanddewi Brefi.'[58]

Perhaps it's small wonder Bentley considered this part of the operation a 'hoot'. Though he and Wright were undoubtedly conscientious and dedicated to the job at hand, it would quickly become clear to them that they had nothing to fear from Smiles. As Smiles himself says of his crew, 'We never threatened anyone, or did any violence. It was a loose affiliation of people who did business on trust. We hadn't even imagined the sort of violence and intimidation that came after.'

In fact, what's most striking – and almost touching – about the way Stephen Bentley talks is just how close he felt to Smiles himself. This is not some form of Stockholm Syndrome. There is a very real acknowledgement that Smiles broadened his horizons, and opened his eyes to an entire range of experiences he otherwise would never have dreamed of.

'He introduced me to Joan Armatrading and Steely Dan,' Bentley writes. 'I will always be grateful to him for that. He also introduced me to Buddhist meditation. He had a whole room that looked like it was a shrine dedicated to Shiva. It was de rigueur to sit cross-legged in meditation with him and chant "Om". The sound repeated and uttered in a slow melody. This was irrefutable evidence that I had adopted a new persona! The meditation was often preceded by inhaling marijuana. Unlike a former President of the United States, I did inhale! Big time! … I came so close to warning Smiles. I wanted to do that. It was a fight to subdue a strong urge to tell him all. The vast majority of this lot were decent people. Smiles was a great guy, I loved his company and got very close to him. I loved his wife and kid ... I don't think any of the people I was investigating were a threat to anybody.'[59]

There was, however, one moment during his deployment when Stephen Bentley did genuinely believe he was in danger. It had nothing to do with Smiles.

Another hippy drifter, going by the name of Blue, turned up in Llanddewi Brefi and quickly befriended Bentley and Wright. Then, Blue introduced a Canadian friend named Bill, who claimed to have serious connections with the South American cocaine cartels and was looking for a way into the UK market.

This was obviously an entirely different proposition from Smiles and his idealistic hippy friends – but far too intriguing not to pursue. Bentley and Wright strung Bill along for a bit, seeing if they could eke out any more information about his supposed operation. They ended up on a rowdy, drunken night out in Liverpool – then, in the midst of the party, Bill asked them straight out, 'Are you guys cops?'

Bentley writes:

The words rolled around inside my head ... He raised one hand next to my head ... his joined forefinger and middle finger ... imitating a gun. The fingers touched my skin. He silently mouthed the silenced spitting sound as two imaginary shells splattered my brains out of the gaping exit wounds at the far side of my head. Pop! Pop![60]

Bill's threats never went further than that, and no cocaine was ever actually produced. The prospective deal soon petered out, and Bentley and Wright went back to partying and Buddhist meditation with Smiles. To this day, however, Stephen Bentley harbours the suspicion that Bill was himself actually an under-cover agent working for the American DEA.

For Smiles, though, it goes much further. He is convinced that not just Bill, but also Blue himself, was working under cover.

'Just before Blue turned up, Buzz and I had gone to London,' he begins. "We stayed at a flat that belonged to a guy called Johnny – who was heavily into the cocaine business. Now, none of us lot ever dealt with coke at all – we might take a bit if it floated across our path, but we never sought it out. But then, when it came time to drive back to Wales, the car wasn't running properly. So we stopped at a garage, and someone had very obviously tampered with the wheels. I later learned that customs had been watching the flat the whole time – I suppose they messed with the car to slow us down and put a tail on us.

'Johnny was busted not long after that – and then this guy Blue turns up in town, talking all this nonsense about cocaine. He told all kinds of tales about how he could get it in for £7,000 a kilo and all that. I wanted nothing to do with him – but Wright and Bentley got close to him. They started spending more time with Blue than they did with me. To this day, I'm absolutely convinced that Blue was an agent provocateur for the customs.'

When the Operation Julie busts eventually went down, Blue was nowhere to be found. He had disappeared and, to our knowledge, has never turned up on any police record since.

Over 25 and 26 March 1977, 800 police officers undertook synchronised raids across 87 properties across the UK; 120 suspects were arrested. Eventually 1.1 million tabs of acid were discovered and destroyed, along with 1.3kg of pure LSD, which the police claimed was enough to make 6.5 million more.

Smiles remembers the busts well. 'I'd been out drinking with Buzz and my sister-in-law till about 1.30am,' he begins. 'Then at

5am – BANG – the door goes. Before I can even react they're up the stairs, and there's a gun to my head.

'My wife and sister-in-law are taken away. The kids, who were two and nine, go over to the people next door, and I'm hand-cuffed to this copper as they spend hours searching the house. I mostly just stayed silent – there was nothing to be gained by saying anything.

'It was all going swimmingly at first. I never kept any acid in the house, so they weren't really finding anything. Then they got a call from one of the busts in London where they'd found a load of money in a packet of dog food. So, they drag me into the kitchen, pick up this box of Alpen, and ask if there are any drugs inside it. I say, "No, of course not." So, they take their tweezers and open it up – and 14,000 quid falls all over the floor.

'At that point I got a few slaps and a tune-up. The cop I was cuffed to dragged me out of the room and this other fella really gave me a few. There must have been at least six of them, all plainclothes, all getting frustrated because they weren't really finding anything.

'Eventually we all ended up at Swindon nick. I was taken into this long room in the basement, and there were all these other people – everyone looking at each other and just thinking, "What's going on?" That was the first time I met guys like Richard Kemp. Out of the whole operation, I only really knew Russ Spenceley. I had no idea how big a thing it was that I was involved in. The first time I had any inkling was in that room. I had never thought of what we did as a criminal conspiracy – I knew it was against the law, but not *really*.

'They had to clear the whole top landing of a remand wing, and stuck us all together on it. Then they started putting various people in cells with each other, to create tensions and see who would talk. Some people did, some didn't. None of these guys were real professional criminals.

'One of my distributors, Doug Flannagan, managed to get himself down to a two-year sentence because of what he knew about Princess Margaret and Roddy Llewellyn taking acid. Those rumours are absolutely true. He used to visit the commune where they were conducting their affair, and supply hashish, cocaine and LSD.[61] The only thing I ever said to the cops was that some of the hash that Buzz was caught with was actually mine. So he ended up just getting 12 months for simple possession.'

The Operation Julie busts sparked a media frenzy. Every major paper covered both the busts and the trial that followed. The BBC extended its usual 30-minute news bulletin into an hour-long special for the first time, and Stephen Bentley recalls 'several of the squad members making phone calls to every news desk in the country.'[62]

Much of the coverage quickly slipped into the usual lurid sensationalism of drugs reporting – to the point of ludicrous tales of a plot to put LSD in the water supply.[63] As in the later trial of Howard Marks, another 'nice guy drug dealer', the media seemed to fixate on the fact that many of the defendants were university-educated professionals – an aspect even noted by the judge at sentencing: 'I regret very much ... that severe sentences are to be passed on people with excellent characters, excellent professional qualifications, and others in possession of very considerable scientific skill.'[64]

In all, 15 defendants went to trial over one month at Bristol Crown Court. They received a total of 124 years in prison. Richard Kemp and Henry Todd both got 13 years, Smiles got 8.

'Your knees go a bit when you hear eight years,' he says, sighing. 'But that first night when we got back to our landing at the prison, the guy came round with our tea, and we all got a little piece of dope with it as well. One of our number had smuggled it in, and sent a piece to all of us on our first night after the conviction.

'I remember that night was the first episode of *The Hitchhiker's Guide to the Galaxy* on the radio. So I got stoned and listened to that – which helped lessen the sting. There was always a way to get stuff smuggled into prison. I remember taking acid inside and listening to the BBC Proms on the radio. I did my time, but it never changed any of my ideals. My life after prison was still dedicated to expanding consciousness and changing the world. And I think a lot of people haven't had half the fun I have.'

Here, Smiles breaks into a roar of laughter, and once again flashes his pirate's grin. But for Stephen Bentley – and indeed, the police at large – the long-term results of Operation Julie's success were far more ambiguous.

'What should have happened,' Stephen Bentley insists, 'is that our 25-man unit, drawn from 11 different forces, should have formed the basis for a national drug squad – with Dick Lee in the vanguard. *The Times* even did a leader supporting that idea. But, because of parochial politics and petty jealousies in the police, that never happened. Back then they didn't go in for aggrandising and elitism – there was a distrust of specialist squads.

'I don't think the bosses had any idea what was about to happen with the drugs trade. I remember interviewing Doug Flannagan, and he said straight out, "You guys have done a great job, I take my hat off to you. But you know, things are going to get a hundred times worse now. The heroin scene is about to explode in the country – you guys have no idea what's about to happen."

'And I remember thinking, "What the hell is he on about?" But he was right. These guys were tuned in. We should have listened to them.'

In the end, 6 of the 25 Operation Julie officers left the force shortly after – including both Dick Lee and Stephen Bentley, for whom the pressure of returning to the mundanity of 'regular' police work after his rock-star deployment proved too much to bear.

Smiles is more specific about exactly how Operation Julie – and the general crackdown on the hippy psychedelic scene that began in the late 1960s – shaped the future of the country: 'Loads of people were getting busted for doing pot and acid scams in the sixties and seventies. So, they go to jail and start mixing with bank robbers and all manner of people. And that's when that type suddenly realise the profits that can be made – with abso-lute minimal risks. So, suddenly they all rushed into drugs. The quality declined, the price went up and the real violence kicked off. And now you see the situation we're in today.'

Since the 1970s, Operation Julie has achieved an almost cult-like aura, spawning a mini-industry of insider memoirs, TV dramas and the Clash song, 'Julie's Been Working for the Drug Squad'. One can see the appeal. There's something almost charmingly quaint about this story of Welsh villages, tripped-out hippies and bumbling cops who have to make it up as they go along with plucky British derring-do.

But one thing it wasn't – in any meaningful sense – is the War on Drugs. Smiles and his crew made a bit of money off the LSD trade, but they were simply not a drugs gang in the way we understand the term today. Stephen Bentley lived under the psychological pressure of a double identity, but the most dangerous thing he actually experienced was someone – who may well have been a cop himself – pointing a finger pistol at him.

Perhaps most surprising is just how much Stephen Bentley himself agrees with this assessment. 'The BBC said Operation Julie was the start of the War on Drugs,' he says with a smirk. 'I've even used that as a handle now and again, because it makes people sit up. But I don't really believe it's accurate. I don't think anything we did was really a "drug war" – or that a war even really existed back then.

'I even ask myself did Operation Julie do society a disservice? If you look what happened after, what's on the market now and what young people have access to – they'd be far better off with Richard Kemp's acid. I know a lot of people will be horrified by me saying that, but I am saying it and I believe it's true. Let's have an open debate about this and not hide behind prejudices. I never tried Richard Kemp's acid – I have to be honest, I now wish I had.'

In his writing, Bentley's assessment is even harsher.

> In retrospect, Operation Julie was a waste of time. It led directly or indirectly to fine detectives lost to the police force. The efforts and skills were never utilised in the fight against real criminals. Julie was not the start of the 'War on Drugs'. It was just the wrong war.[65]

And this is, perhaps, the overriding impression one gets from speaking to these two men, decades after their lives intersected. Smiles seems absolutely at peace with the life he has led and the choices he has made; Stephen Bentley is still wrestling with the meaning his experiences carry.

For the most part, the War on Drugs in the 1970s was a phoney war. It was an interregnum between the dismantling of the British System, and the horrendous consequences that dismantling was about to wreak on the country. The violence was real enough for Alex Wheadle in Brixton, and for people of colour throughout the inner cities. But for the vast majority, the real drug war was still just a dark cloud on the horizon.

In the wake of the 1971 Misuse of Drugs Act, police forces across the country had been told to go off and form drug squads.

But it took a few years for them to actually figure out what those squads were meant to do, and how to use the new powers that the MDA had given them. In the meantime, they simply tended to follow the prejudices of the day – and lashed out at hippies and young black men. This formulation may seem crude, but every single police officer of the era who we have spoken to has fully agreed with it.

One of the great claims made about Operation Julie is that it forced up the price of LSD on British streets from £1.25 to £5. What people neglect to mention is that this information seems to come from a single interview, and the actual quote is, '*in the days following the Julie raids*, one acid tab now cost £5.'[66] New suppliers flooded in, and the market soon righted itself. By the time of Smiles's trial in early 1978, the price had gone down to £1.

When asked whether he thinks Operation Julie was part of the War on Drugs, Smiles himself gives a contemptuous snort. 'There is no War on Drugs, there's only a war on the people who take drugs.' As the 1970s drew to a close, the war that Smiles is talking about was set to begin in earnest. The phoney war was about to end. Britain was about to discover heroin.

6

Epidemics

The Heroin Crisis Breaks

Lisa chops the heroin into a small beige line, about three inches long. She lifts it to her face, and snorts it up with expert precision. Then she turns and smiles. 'Much better. Would you two like another cup of tea?'

We are in the front room of Lisa's flat. There's a widescreen TV set against the wall, matching three-piece furniture and an array of kitsch trinkets on the glass coffee table. This could be any suburban living room in any suburban flat in the south of England. The only difference is that Lisa has been a heroin addict for 45 years.

And the heroin we've just watched Lisa snort is no ordinary street smack. This is heroin supplied by the British state – prescribed to Lisa by her doctor, and provided by a pharmacist. It is completely pure, and to get it Lisa didn't need to encounter a single drug dealer, gangster or criminal.

Lisa is one of the last people in Britain to receive a heroin prescription. She knows of a handful more in her own region; there are maybe a few hundred others scattered across the United Kingdom. These are the last remnants of the British System. In this suburban living room we are sitting with a living fragment of a lost history – and, perhaps, with a vision of how we might shape our future.

The British System never died. When it came under came under attack in the late 1960s, heroin prescription was never officially banned – there was just a bureaucratic trick to make the licences very difficult to obtain.

Lisa first received her prescription in the mid-1980s, and has maintained it to this day. Lisa has a career. She owns the flat we are sitting in. She pays her taxes and talks lovingly of her daughter and granddaughter – neither of whom have ever touched drugs. Lisa credits this stability in her life to one thing and one thing only – the precious slip of paper she receives from her doctor each week.

Lisa comes back into the room, and hands us each our cups of tea. 'I've never been a thief,' she declares with some pride. 'People think, Oh you're a drug user, you must be thieving – but I wasn't brought up that way. You don't just start robbing and stealing – it's something you have to be taught.' She pauses, as if considering other paths her life might have taken. 'I've been incredibly lucky with my prescription. I can't even really describe it … it completely saved my life.'

Another interview in another suburban living room – this time in a small town in the Midlands. We get about 20 minutes into our conversation before Danny's mobile rings. He grabs it, giving us an apologetic look. 'Yeah, sorry mate, I'm a bit busy at the moment … I'll give you a ring back when I'm free, yeah?'

He puts the phone down and turns back to us. 'That was a dealer,' he sighs.

'I get pestered by dealers all the time. I don't even know how they get my number. A lot of them are Birmingham lads, looking to come here and set up. They call me and say, "We'll be up in a couple of days – you want anything?" It's constant – they come up, run the town for a few weeks, then move on before the police can get to know them. Then someone else just takes over. This is just a small town, but it must be a gold mine for them.'

Our interview with Danny lasts just over three hours. Over that time his phone rings eight times – an average of once every 22.5 minutes. Text messages ping in between the calls. Each time the phone goes, Danny gives us the same sheepish, apologetic look. Every one of these messages is a dealer looking to sell heroin and crack cocaine.

In this living room, the time-honoured laws of the drug world seem to have been reversed. In the old days, the first rule of scoring drugs was encapsulated in the Velvet Underground song 'I'm Waiting for the Man': 'He's never early, he's always late – first thing you learn is that you always got to wait'. Nowadays in small-town England, the market for Class A drugs is so huge that pushers cold-call potential users like any other salesman trying to close a deal.

Danny has been around long enough to remember how it used to work.

'It was nasty enough back in the day on Moss Side – people would try and rip you off if they could. But now, this little town is totally different. There's so many more guns about for starters. I've never seen anything like this place. It's amazing how easy it is to get it now. Almost every street I know has a dealer on it.'

Like Lisa, Danny been an addict for over 40 years. Unlike her, though, Danny is a daily contributor to Britain's vast criminal economy of drug pushers and gangsters. He buys his gear on the street, financing it through odd jobs and selling to other users. Even as he approaches official retirement age, he lives in a constant state of instability, anxiety and paranoia at the thought of another arrest leading to prison.

Despite both being long-term addicts of the same drug, Lisa and Danny's lives have taken extraordinarily different directions. The contrasts in how they manage their addiction could not be starker. However, there is one vital point of connection between them. The pivotal moment in each of their journeys occurred in a very particular time and place – a time and place absolutely crucial to understanding the story of the British War on Drugs. Both Lisa and Danny are products of the Merseyside heroin scene of the 1980s.

After the 'phoney war' of the 1970s, the eighties saw the real War on Drugs finally break on the people of Britain. And it broke hard.

This decade saw the entire structure of society profoundly transformed. These momentous changes created a drugs crisis in Britain unlike anything the country had ever faced. This new drug war wasn't confined to a few streets in Soho or Brixton, or to festival sites in the English countryside. It ripped right through the country, touching people at every level of society. This was the era of heroin.

Heroin is by far the most addictive and most dangerous of any of the major illicit drugs. If you're a gangster, you couldn't dream of a better customer base than a heroin-addict population. The American writer William S. Burroughs described heroin as 'the ideal product ... the ultimate merchandise. No sales talk necessary. The client will crawl through a sewer and beg to buy.'

More often than not, when prohibitionists talk about the horrifying effect of 'drugs', what they are actually describing is heroin. Many people talk glibly about cannabis being a 'gateway drug'. That concept is incredibly flawed, with little basis in evidence. But in the minds of those who say it, if cannabis is the gateway, heroin is the end of the line.

With other policies in place, Britain might well have been able to better weather these storms. But the gutting of the British System in the 1960s and 1970s stripped away the internal defences that had protected the country for so long. The authorities proved completely unprepared for the battles that were about to engulf them.

There were many reasons why heroin took hold of Britain in the 1980s. Some of them began half the world away. In 1979 Iran exploded in revolution. Hundreds of thousands of middle-class Iranians fled to the West. In many cases, heroin was the easiest way to transfer their capital out of the country. Rumours spread among intelligence circles that this was often accomplished with the collaboration of the SAVAK, the Iranian secret police. In Soho, crudely refined dark-brown Iranian heroin gradually began to displace the lighter Chinese and Thai.

At the end of 1979 another event took place that was to have a seismic impact on the global heroin trade – the Soviet invasion of Afghanistan. Over the coming years, the mujahidin who fought the Soviets realised they could finance their struggle through opium and heroin. Global production began an inexorable shift away from the Golden Triangle of Thailand, Laos and Myanmar towards the Golden Crescent between Afghanistan and Pakistan. Today, over 90 per cent of the world's illicit heroin supply originates in Afghanistan.

This shift was driven as much by technological advances as by wars and revolutions. Throughout the 1960s and 1970s, the Central Asian trade primarily worked by transporting raw opium to plants in Turkey, Sicily or southern France, where it would be refined into pure heroin. In the late 1970s refining plants began to be located near the poppy fields themselves in Afghanistan and Pakistan, which exponentially boosted the scale of production.

When Richard Nixon formally declared his War on Drugs in 1971, one of his first international targets was the 'French Connection' of Marseilles-based Corsican gangsters who supplied most of America's heroin. With American pressure and support, French authorities cracked down, imprisoning many of the Corsican bosses and disrupting their networks.

This neatly opened the door for the Sicilian mafia. By 1979 there were five well-known heroin-processing plants on the island, each with a capacity of around 50 kilos per week. With a wholesale price of $100,000 per kilo on delivery to the US, many economists estimate that these levels of profit, relative to company size, hadn't been seen in Europe since the seventeenth-century slave trade.

The major Sicilian crime families promptly started a war over this vastly profitable business. In the city of Palermo alone, 122 people were murdered in the heroin wars of 1981, 250 in 1982 and 123 in 1983.[67]

By sheer bad luck, these global upheavals happened to take place just as huge sections of Britain were undergoing a process of crippling forced deindustrialisation. Margaret Thatcher won power just after Britain's Winter of Discontent in 1979. Inflation peaked at 22 per cent in 1980, and the country fell into recession. In response, Thatcher embarked on a wholesale restructuring of the British economy.

This history has been argued through over and over again. But certain facts are inarguable – factories closed, mines shut down, communities were torn apart and young people found themselves without work. Unemployment hit 14 per cent. One could hardly have constructed a more virulent breeding ground for a heroin epidemic.

In 1971, when the Misuse of Drugs Act was passed, there were 1,049 known heroin addicts in the UK. The rate of new addicts held steady at about 700–800 for the next ten years, meaning that by 1979 the total could be estimated in the very low tens of thousands. By the mid-1980s this had exploded to an estimated 150,000.

When experts refer to the heroin crisis of the 1980s as an 'epidemic', they are not just reaching for a lazy metaphor. There may have been 150,000 heroin users by 1985, but these 150,000 were not distributed evenly throughout the country.

Instead, heroin addiction followed similar patterns to epidemics of other diseases – with users densely grouped in a few centralised 'ground zeros' of infection. London, consistently ahead of the curve in new drug problems, was one such centre. Another was Edinburgh, where the *'Trainspotting* generation' of heroin addicts utterly transformed the city. Perhaps worst hit, though, was Merseyside.

Liverpool and its surrounding areas have always occupied a special place in the drugs map of Britain. It comes from the docks.

By the time the MDA was passed in 1971, Liverpool already had a long criminal tradition of things 'disappearing' off incoming cargo ships. Liverpool gangsters were the first to realise the potential of the UK drug market. They simply added cannabis, heroin and cocaine to the shopping list of contraband they could bring in through their tightly controlled networks of dockworkers and paid-off officials.

This obviously generated huge profits, allowing them to consolidate their networks across Britain. By the time gangsters in the rest of the UK woke up, the Scouse firms were already so well established – and well armed – that few were able to really compete.

It's impossible to say for sure, but most of the people who contributed to this book – both criminals and cops – estimate that upwards of 60 per cent of the drugs coming into the UK still come in through Liverpool's organised crime networks. But the story of Merseyside in the 1980s has as much to do with drug users as it does with smugglers and gangsters. Because in Merseyside, the heroin epidemic was like almost nowhere else in Britain.

The Wirral peninsula follows the south bank of the Mersey, just over the river from Liverpool proper. This series of interconnected towns was once a world-renowned centre of shipbuilding. But in the 1980s the shipyards began to close. The vacuum they left was filled by heroin.

By 1988 the Wirral had a population of 340,000. Among them were 4,000 young adult regular heroin users. This is a staggering number – more than one in every 100 people.[68]

And these users were nothing like the old-fashioned addicts who had seen out the end of the British System in the 1960s. The old-fashioned 'Soho junkies' had largely been drawn from the middle classes. The 1980s saw the birth of Britain's drug *underclass*.

The regional unemployment rate in the Wirral was running at 20 per cent. Among heroin users it was an astounding 86 per cent. Over half of heroin users had no educational qualifications; few even finished their O levels.[69]

It was also only during the epidemics of the 1980s that heroin addiction became synonymous with crime. Under the British System there was simply no significant link between heroin addiction and criminality. No one needs to shoplift or mug people when they get heroin on prescription.

Evidently, there had been crime in northern industrial areas prior to the 1980s – largely focused around fighting and hooliganism. But the heroin black market changed everything.

In 1979 there were 2,824 domestic burglaries reported in the Wirral. In 1986 there were 10,238 – five times as many. The vast majority of these offenders were young adult heroin users specifically stealing to fund their habits.[70] Spikes of that scale, in such an invasive form of crime, are enough to destabilise entire communities. By and large people outside London still knew very little about drugs. Most people first learned about heroin only when they began to see groups of skeletally thin victims tracing their way listlessly down neighbourhood streets – or when their home got broken into.

In the poorer parts of Edinburgh and Merseyside it soon felt as though no family was left untouched. The authorities seemed powerless, and entire communities were traumatised. This was a terrifying new world for the people of Merseyside. It was into this world that Danny came of age.

'My family was very religious,' he begins.

'My dad was a church organist and choirmaster – we had to go every Sunday and sing in the choir. We had a nice house, an ex-vicarage in Runcorn. You could walk down the street and not get hassled. But our parents were very strict. The attitude was that children were seen and not heard. You know how some- times fathers will just put their arms round their children? That just didn't exist. There wasn't a lot of love in the house.

'And we were actually good kids. We didn't have a lot of options – this was back in the days of caning. So, we were well behaved, but because I felt unwanted I stayed away from home as much as possible. I still struggle with those feelings now.

'So, because of all that, the first thing I did when I left school was to get my own flat. I trained as a butcher and eventually got a job running a shop in Liscard on the Wirral.

'For the first time in my life I felt things were going my way. It was 1980, and I was 21 years old. I got married and had a daughter. I had a good job – a car and a house. I felt great really.

'Then I met this guy Graham, and became mates with him and his brother. We'd have a beer and a right old laugh – sort of lads about town. I was young and had a bit of money, and I was having a good time.

'So, this guy Graham kept saying to me, "Mate, try this stuff, have a bit of smack." I literally had no idea what he was on about. I had no idea it was heroin – because Graham just called it smack. I'd never tried any drug before, except alcohol. I'd never had a smoke of weed or anything. I'd heard of pot vaguely, but because of our upbringing I just didn't know what drugs were. I was actually completely shocked when I found out much later it was heroin.'

Once again, in our drug-saturated society, it is almost difficult to believe that a 21-year-old wouldn't know the street slang for heroin. But this story is repeated right across the country. Dr Roy Robertson, who was instrumental in treating heroin addicts in Edinburgh, recalls exactly the same dynamic at his clinic: 'I had teenagers who'd all left school together coming through the door, jaundiced and with needle wounds, asking for help. When I asked them what drug they were taking they said they were on "smack". I asked them if they meant heroin and they said, "No! smack".'[71]

One cannot overstate how much the heroin epidemic of the 1980s took Britain by surprise. People simply didn't know enough about drugs to be aware of their dangers. It was exactly this ignorance that was to prove Danny's downfall.

'Graham pestered and pestered me,' he continues.

'I'd say, "Let's go to the pub," and he'd always say, "Ah mate, just come round and have a smoke." When I look back now – knowing how things work – of course he had a plan to get me on the stuff. He knew I had plenty of money from my job.

'I wasn't really interested, but after months of this badgering from him, I was round at his flat one day, and he's sitting there on his bed with his piece of foil, smoking it – chasing the dragon. He got on at me again to try it, so just to shut him up I said, "Oh okay, go on then."

'He showed me how to do it – how to follow the little beetle of heroin tar around the foil. At first I kept missing all the smoke – it took me a few seconds to work it out. But then it knocked me for six. I felt sick and turned totally white, and my eyes were sort of fluttering like I couldn't control them. We were meant to go to the pub, but I just felt too sick and said I needed to go home. To be honest, I didn't really enjoy it at all.'

Unlike the South-east Asian heroin of the 1970s, the new high-grade Afghan was smokeable. Many people in the UK didn't realise what they were taking, because they assumed that heroin was something you injected. Story after story tells of people smoking heroin without knowing what it was, or assuming that because they were smoking instead of shooting, they couldn't get addicted. In the War on Drugs, the most dangerous weapon is often simply ignorance.

'A couple of months later,' Danny continues, 'we drove down to Graham's brother's caravan in Wales. He had some more of this smack on him, and we'd stop and do a bit on the drive down. But he also had a few bottles of Theakston's Old Peculiar – and what I noticed was a few swigs of the ale, plus a little line of the smack, gave a very nice feeling. I really remember that nice, warm comforting feeling.

'So, that whole weekend we were smoking it – Graham's brother and his missus were both on it regular. And it was a little while after we got back that I first bought some for myself. Graham was down visiting in my shop, and I said, "Yeah, get me a bit as well." It was about 30 quid's worth I think.

'I didn't know anyone else who did this stuff, and definitely not anyone who sold it. So, I just bought from Graham. I was financing his habit too.

'He was always "just popping in" to the shop while I was working, to see if I wanted some. I was probably using it a couple of times a week, and each bag would last me a couple of days. It was just a nice, natural feeling that blanked out all the problems. Looking back, Graham definitely had a plan to put it in front of me as much as possible.

'It wasn't until maybe six months later when I woke up one morning with real bad stomach cramps – real horrible shooting pains. Graham happened to be coming by my house and he goes, "Here have some this, that'll take it away." So I had a line or two again – and instantly it was gone. I felt instantly okay again. But even then I didn't put together that I felt bad because I didn't have the smack – I just thought smack was good for stomach cramps.

'I think that's the first time he mentioned it was actually heroin. I was shocked – I was like "Heroin?" I didn't know anything at all about drugs – I'd never even smoked hash. But this stuff just seemed to click with me. It filled a bit of a void and took away the negative feelings. I didn't even know smack was illegal. I sort of knew heroin was illegal, but not until then did I ever put the two together.

'I never ever forced it on my wife, but when she asked I let her try it, and she did take it up as well. I was properly addicted by then – taking it every day. It was wake up, reach for the foil. But, to be honest, I wasn't that bothered. Life was still pretty good, I was a manager of the business and I still had loads of money.

'Graham had made himself my only supplier. I just dished the money out to him, and of course every time I'd buy it, he'd take some. I just believed everything he said. We lasted over a year like that. I suppose I was very naïve, and I didn't protect myself.'

It is a symptom of just how naïve Danny really was that he thought a situation this precarious could ever last. He may not have been fully aware that heroin was illegal, but it very much was. And in a black market, it is the naïve ones – those least able to inflict violence – who inevitably get hit first.

'It was all going sort of all right until Graham was caught by the police,' Danny explains.

'He was selling it to a few others like me around town, he probably had around seven or so of us. Of course the police got interested in him, and he got caught with a couple of grams. So, in order to get his sentence reduced he told them I was selling it from my work.

'One morning he comes into the shop and sells me a gram, which was a decent amount at the time. Then about half an hour later he comes back and asks to buy half of it back off me – which was very strange. Usually Graham would always hang around and have a chat, but that day he was straight in and out.

'Next thing I know, this guy in a suit comes in and says, "We're police, we've got a warrant to search your shop for illegal drugs." It was a total shock. In my mind I wasn't a druggie – it was just this little bit of powder I liked. It was only then it started to dawn on me that this was actually a bit serious.

'They locked the door and told me to stand in the back while they searched the place. The whole time I'm staring at my cigarette packet lying on the table with my half-gram hidden in it.

'But what happened was, the other butcher down the road had seen all these big guys in suits come in, and he thought they were robbing us – so he phoned the police. So, suddenly all these normal bobbies surround the shop, with the drug squad lot inside.

'In all the confusion, I asked if I could have a cigarette, and they let me, so I managed to slip the half-gram out of the pack and swallow it. I thought I'd got away with it, but then they found the tube I used to smoke with, which had residue on it. When they sent it to forensics, it apparently had four micrograms on it.

'They took me to the police station, and the detective said straight out, "If you give us some names, then this will come back with nothing on it." He told me he could make this evidence go away. The problem was I just didn't know any names. The only person I knew was Graham, and I wasn't going to start dobbing people in. Though they'd only found that residue, the drug squad fella said, "We've had information that you've been selling it from the shop." I'd never sold any in my life at this point. There was only one person who could have said that about me.'

This is quintessential War on Drugs policing – inflating evidence to get a suspect to grass on higher-level dealers. The Misuse of Drugs Act is very clear that only a 'visible, tangible and measurable amount' of drugs can be used as evidence. There was one stated case, *R* v. *Boyeson* in 1982, that indicated that trace amounts of a drug could count, but it's very rarely used.

Danny had clearly been verballed. Had he simply 'no commented' the detective, there's every chance the case would have simply been thrown out. Danny was just unlucky he didn't have any evidence to trade – or the street smarts to invent some, as a proper hardened criminal probably would have.

Even more significant is that Graham was very likely made exactly the same offer – give us names or go to prison. At this point Graham would have faced a choice. He could give the names of the higher-level gangsters he bought his gear from – or he could name Danny. Danny wasn't likely to come after him with a shotgun; the gangsters very well might.

A mid-level guy who gets busted will always inform on his least harmful associates. This means that the only insurance policy real gangsters have is to be as brutal and terrifying as possible, to ensure that people are simply too scared to testify against them. The drug war is the survival of the most brutal.

Only the worst of the worst gangsters survive, and the police use their resources busting people like Danny.

This script is fundamental to how the War on Drugs works. And it's a script that was written during the heroin epidemic of the 1980s.

But for Danny, getting busted was only the start of his problems. This is the moment he was swept up as a tiny part of the vast epidemic ripping through the entire country. It's the moment he went from being an addict to being a criminal.

'I brought my wife and child to the head office, to try and soften the boss up,' he says with a sigh. 'But it did no good. I was allowed to leave instead of being formally sacked, but I'd still lost my job. My wife and I were both still using heroin, and I was now unemployed. The car went, the house went – I couldn't pay the mortgage and they repossessed it.

'It was devastating. I'd worked really hard to get that job. Of course, all that pressure just makes you use more. The first thing you notice when you try and stop is all these emotions come rushing back and you can't deal with them. The gear blacks all that out.

'I only saw Graham once after that. He came to see me and said he felt bad about me losing my job. But by this time there were other dealers. The heroin came into the area very fast – like, bang, it was everywhere.

'The council put us up in a high-rise estate over in Moreton, and there were two or three dealers just in my building. There were another few in the other block – God knows how many in the whole area.

'The explosion of heroin just kept growing, to the point where it seemed like everyone you met was on it. Suddenly there are these gaunt figures just walking around. When you're that addicted you don't even want to wash yourself. All you can think about from the moment you wake up is "Have I got enough? Where am I going to score?"

'That was me as well. I'd lost the plot. I was only interested in where the next hit was coming from. The guy upstairs at Moreton flats taught me how to inject. I think we shared the needle that day. I had no knowledge of not sharing needles – nobody did. I could tell you things that would make your hair curl.

'Then, of course, Tuinal came in – Tuinal, Nembutal, Diconal – all those barbiturates. I started injecting them too. There was a doctor in the neighbourhood who prescribed those, and all the junkies bullied him for scrips so badly the surgery had to get a bouncer just to keep us away.

'I wasn't a shoplifter – that just wasn't for me. I sold to other addicts though. Selling a bit of heroin was much easier. And it wasn't hard to forge Post Office books back then, you could usually just steam the stamp off another postal order.

'But the whole scene was getting violent now as well. At Moreton I went to score one time, and there were these five massive lads outside this dealer's door. I knew these guys – the Leary brothers – they worked for a serious gangster named Tommy. Basically if you were a dealer, and didn't get your gear from them, they'd do you in.

'So, I see them outside this door, and I think better of it and just walk on as fast as I can. Then I hear the crash of the door. He'd opened the letter box to see who was there – and they'd sprayed acid into his eyes and kicked in his door to smash him up with bats.

'Those flats in Moreton were awful. Every weekend I would go and see my sister, and every weekend I came back to find my flat had been broken into. It was all the other junkies knowing that I was away. It went on till there was really nothing left to steal.'

There is a grim inevitability to Danny's story. The pattern of addiction meaning a descent into poverty and crime was laid out in the 1980s. And Danny was once again about to encounter what the War on Drugs really means. His story was about to take its next inevitable step – prison.

'From that original smoking tube I'd received a six-month sentence, suspended for twelve months,' he continues. 'I don't think I'd ever knowingly broken a law before. I certainly had no previous convictions.

'But, at eleven months and two weeks into that suspension, I got busted walking up to another lad's house to buy some gear. The police were already in his flat busting him – and I knocked on the door and walked straight into it. That broke the suspended sentence. They got me on attempted possession, searched my house and found another smoking tube. So I went to prison and did four out of six months.

'I had to do my withdrawal in prison, but heroin was still pretty easy to get inside. You could get a little for a half-ounce of tobacco – enough to make you feel better.

'But then in prison I saw a whole other side of things, when I got a visit from the drug squad.

'In that bust that I'd walked right into, they'd found a big load of heroin thrown down the bin chute of the council flats. Well, Tommy and the Leary brothers had a bent solicitor in Liverpool, and he'd put together a few so-called "witnesses" to say that those drugs were mine. They were framing me up, and were getting paid half an ounce of gear each.

'So, I'm in prison sitting across from these drug squad guys asking me about this serious weight of heroin – more heroin than I'd ever seen. Of course I have no idea what they're on about.

'It didn't actually take long for these detectives to say, "Listen, we know it wasn't you. This solicitor has written out these state-ments for these five lads – we just had to question you about it." One of the lads had bottled it – he told the police he'd been forced to make the statement. So, the whole thing went away, but it was a stress I definitely didn't need in prison.'

Getting a corrupt solicitor to write up five separate false statements, for five separate witnesses, is no small achievement for any criminal gang. In earlier eras only people on the scale of the Krays or the Richardsons would have tried to pull a stunt like that.

Tommy and the Leary brothers were not particularly major gangsters. They were just another of the countless mid-level crews on Merseyside at the time.

There is one reason, and one reason alone, that a small-time gang like that could attempt a serious corruption of the criminal justice system – drug money.

The 1980s saw the emergence of the drug trade as the number one earner for gangsters. Turning heroin from a prescribed drug to a pushed drug had created a vast, unprecedented new market – and a new species of criminal emerged to fill it. These weren't solo entrepreneurs selling weed in Brixton, or utopian hippies trying to turn on the world. These were hardened gangsters recruiting networks of vulnerable addicts for profit. They made money and wielded power on a scale that previous generations of British criminals could only have dreamed of. And they were willing to engage in extreme violence to protect their territories. This – in its most embryonic form – was the emergence of the modern British drugs gang.

Perhaps the most terrifying aspect of the heroin crisis was how powerless the authorities seemed. The police simply had no experience of drugs on this scale. Busting a few hippies and young black kids smoking pot during the 1970s was no preparation for the violence of the new drug gangs – nor for the extremes to which a heroin addict will go to raise money for their score.

Throughout the late 1970s there had been a sustained attack on the remnants of the old British System. This was the era of Nancy Reagan and 'Just Say No'. The American model – based on enforced abstinence from all drugs – was being exported throughout the world, and the British treatment infrastructure was simply no longer there.

Prescribing licences had not been renewed; maintenance clinics had been shut down; access to clean needles had been restricted. The British System had been discarded in favour of the American, recovery-based, psychiatric approach. The sole aim was to force the addict off drugs as fast as possible – no matter their circumstances. The result was the national crisis that engulfed Danny and so many others across Britain.

But, sometimes it is exactly in the midst of crisis that innovation is born. Seeing that the official response to the epidemic was a shambles, a disparate group of Merseyside health workers and volunteers began working on a revolutionary new range of solutions. Eventually, these rebels would transform the whole of international drug treatment policy. But they began with a needle exchange on Maryland Street in Liverpool.

Throughout the 1970s the official line, imported from America, was that giving clean needles to addicts would *send the wrong message*. Much like religious charities that refuse to teach that condoms can prevent HIV infection, the thought was that if drug users wanted to preserve their health, they should simply not do drugs. This wasn't much help for people like Danny who didn't even know they were taking heroin until they were already addicted.

It was against this background that the health worker Alan Parry, and the Merseyside Regional Health Commissioner, Howard Seymour, took the enormously controversial step of setting up one of Britain's first needle exchange programmes.

It wasn't a grand affair – it started as a converted toilet in the Drug Training and Information Centre on Maryland Street. But, from that small acorn, an entire international social movement would eventually grow.

Based on the success of the needle exchange, Seymour, Parry and many others began developing a whole matrix of programmes and health schemes to protect drug users and the wider community. This was a disparate group, each addressing different aspects of the problem. But they were all working from a set of common principles, centred on reducing the harm that addiction causes, rather than 'curing' or judging addicts themselves. Eventually, these principles were given a name – Harm Reduction.

First defined by Dr Russell Newcombe of Liverpool John Moores University, Harm Reduction has since become an internationally recognised school of public health, encompassing everything from safe injection rooms in Canada to condom distribution in Africa. But the idea was born on Merseyside as a response to the 1980s heroin epidemic.

Newcombe laid out four key principles of Harm Reduction. The first was *pragmatism* – the drug worker had to recognise that not everybody was able to achieve absolute abstinence; the idea was to work with people where they were currently at, not where the worker wanted them to be.

The second was to remain *non-judgemental*. Drug users may behave poorly on occasion, but they are still somebody's son or daughter. Stigmatising attitudes – from drug services in particular – are a major reason why many drug users choose not to engage in treatment.

Next came requirements to be *user-friendly* and *relevant*. Harm Reduction workers were expected to make their services as easy to access as possible, and to give drug users what they actually needed, not what drug workers or society at large thought they should have.

In many ways these principles are drawn from the ideas that underpinned the old British System. In the face of the American 'Just Say No' model, it was revolutionary.

There are many names associated with the development of Harm Reduction on Merseyside, but by far the most famous – and the most controversial – is Dr John Marks.

In drug policy circles, Dr Marks is an almost legendary figure. The myth is usually of some sort of Robin Hood figure who just turned up in Liverpool and started giving out heroin to addicts. The truth is far more subtle. We tracked Dr Marks to Austria, where he now lives, and he agreed to tell us the real story.

'I was lecturing in psychiatry at the university,' he begins. 'Really, I was as straight as they come – wife, mortgage, three kids and a cat. Then this job came up as a consultant over in Widnes. We each had a town to cover for general psychiatry, but we also got allocated a speciality, and they basically said to me, "You're the new boy – you can have the junkies." I didn't seek this out, it just went along with the job.

'My predecessor there, Burt Brooker, handed the drug clinic over to me – and I was totally surprised, because he was prescribing them heroin! He ran an old Rolleston-era, British System clinic that had been going since the 1920s. There were still a few of them around the country that had never been shut down, and this one had just survived, plodding on completely legally, but simply ignored.

'People seem to think I started some sort of revolution, but the junkies were just something I inherited from Burt Brooker, I didn't invent this bloody thing.'

This turns the mythology on its head. Despite all the headlines he would eventually generate, Dr Marks didn't create anything new in Widnes – he was just continuing the old British System.

In fact, having been trained in psychiatry, he was initially hostile to the whole enterprise.

'To be honest, I found the addiction stuff just a bit of a nuisance,' he continues.

'I wanted to be busy with schizophrenia, mania and actual psychiatry. I thought giving out junk was crazy – I thought we were supposed to be getting them off the stuff and stopping them being addicts. Psychiatrists are very sensitive about being "proper doctors". That was the training – we're doctors, not bloody shopkeepers or pharmacists. But, Burt kept telling me, "It works John, It just works – just leave it alone."

'One of the addicts who came to the clinic was this lovely old docker named Sidney. He was a nice guy in his fifties – worked on the docks all his life, lovely wife, kids in school. And he was very philosophical about his heroin addiction; he said he'd been doing it all his life. I asked him if he wanted to come off and he just said, "No, I'm happy like this." So Sidney would come in once a week for his prescription, and basically he and his family got on all right.'

'To be honest, though, I put the whole thing to the back of my mind and got on with running the general psychiatry of Widnes. The junkies were just a bit of a chore every Thursday.

'But then there was a wave of stories in the press about drug abuse – junkies beating up old ladies, etc. So, Thatcher's govern-ment turned round and went, "Right – you're psychiatrists, you've got to do something about drug abuse." So, they put in a few million quid, and told everyone across the country to eval-uate what they were doing and see if it worked. I think this translated into about £20,000 for our region.

'My first thought was that this drug clinic was a load of rubbish – let's shut it down and save the money for a shiny new modern hospital. That's what I set out to evidence. So, I started working on this report with Russell Newcombe – we compared

Widnes with a town down the road called Bootle, which for historical reasons had just never had a clinic like ours. When we started I fully expected to find our problem would be worse in Widnes, because we were giving out bloody heroin.

'But, the results were actually the exact opposite to what we had expected – it was a complete lightbulb moment!

'By every measure we looked at, Widnes was doing much, much better than Bootle. We had a 93.6 per cent reduction in acquisitive crime, and a huge drop in morbidity – addicts in Bootle were dying, and those in Widnes weren't – and we had zero HIV infection.

'But, most importantly, we had a 92.4 per cent reduction in the incidence of addiction. This completely reversed everything I previously thought – the only way to measure how effective a certain system is, is to measure how many new cases of addiction arise. It's about the spread – the recruitment of new addicts.'

This is a crucial distinction. The 'incidence' of heroin addiction means the number of new cases of people becoming addicted – rather than the total number of heroin addicts in an area. Both Widnes and Bootle had a serious heroin problem, but a 92.4 per cent reduction in the incidence of new addiction is stunning. In Widnes people simply weren't getting hooked the way they were on the rest of Merseyside.[72]

This research is vital because the chance to analyse two similar areas with very different drug policies is extremely rare. It certainly forced Dr Marks himself to completely change his perspective.

'Having set out to convince them to shut down the clinic, I now realised that this was actually what was helping people, and I put much more effort into it.

'We were set up near the needle exchange, and would meet in groups of about 20, once a week. We also brought in a probation officer and a community nurse – and if anyone needed to talk to us about a problem, they could talk to us individually.

'The way I started to see peoples' lives change was amazing. I remember walking with one woman past a shop. She caught a glimpse of herself in the window and just said to me, "What am I doing, putting my kids through this?" But, as soon as she was on the script, she knew where her next fix was coming from – so she didn't have to spend all her money, time and energy on that. She got a job, went on a course and her kids were finally dressed properly.

'And of course, if anyone wanted to come off the heroin, we'd help them immediately. I always said, come in and we'll help you, but if you can't hack it, you won't suffer any consequences – you'll get your script back.

'In a lot of other programmes if you try and come off and fail, they won't let you back on the programme. But all that does is deter from people from trying. We could see amazing changes in people's lives happening all the time because we gave them stability.'

It was at this point that Dr Marks's path crossed that of Lisa, the addict we watched snort prescription heroin in her suburban living room. Her story illuminates the human reality of what John Marks's statistics describe.

'I was an adopted child,' Lisa begins.

'I don't think my mother ever really wanted to adopt, she had an alcoholic father herself. We weren't poor – but the house was very strict and very unloving. She never kissed me or hugged me from the day she adopted me to the day she died. I couldn't handle that cold, neglectful atmosphere, and ran away when I was a teenager.

'I went straight into the city and just stayed with random people who would let me sleep on their floor. For several weeks I lived in an abandoned car by the side of the road. This was still the sixties, so eventually some of the hippies took me in.

'I was introduced to heroin by this older girl I knew. She was a hooker – but very high-class. She had a lovely flat and all these fancy, gorgeous suits that she kept wrapped in cellophane. There were only a handful of addicts at the time, but she was one. She used to go to London once a week to get her stuff from a doctor. She let me stay because I looked after her cats while she was doing her trips there.

'But she didn't like getting stoned on her own, so she was always saying, "Go on, have a hit." And I was always like, "I'm not putting a needle in myself, you must be joking!" But eventually she convinced me and I let her inject into my hand. I was only 15 years old; she was 26.

'In all my life since – 45 years as a user – I have never, ever given it to someone for the first time. I think you just don't do that. But she gave it to me at 15.

'I didn't even like it that much at the beginning. You always throw up the first time, but after a while I learned to inject myself and that was it really. It changed the whole course of my life.'

Lisa is not exaggerating. From the age of 15, her life has been completely shaped by her relationship to this drug, and the different ways she has found to maintain her supply of it. She quickly found herself in a familiar spiral of poverty and petty crime.

'All I was concerned about was getting my gear,' she continues. 'And when it wasn't finding heroin, it was finding needles. I would go into hospitals and hide behind counters to try and rob a syringe or two. Back then you'd have five people queuing up for the syringe – then, six months later it would do the rounds, and you'd have a different five people all sharing that same syringe.

'The syringes would get so stiff you'd have to put Vaseline on the plunger to get it to move up and down. Sometimes the top of the needle would snap off – but you'd still have to force it into your vein. I can remember pushing it and pushing it, trying to get it in with the point broken – because you're going to get that needle in, no matter what.

'I met my first husband in that phase too. He was a user too, but he was always talking about how he wanted to stop. I just thought, "I like it. I don't drink; I don't smoke pot. Why shouldn't I do it? I'm not harming anybody."

'We moved abroad for a while and supported ourselves by selling gear. I stopped using for a year when I was pregnant, but started again afterwards. It's just something I need. We ended up moving back to Manchester, where my husband's mum was. But by then we were growing apart and he left.'

Lisa had arrived back in Britain just as the heroin epidemic was picking up gear. But by now, with a 15-year habit already behind her, she managed her addiction with almost professional precision – while still managing to get her daughter to school on time.

'By this time I really knew what I was doing,' she explains. 'I was never one for stealing, so I knew the only way to survive was to sell gear. I developed a group of about six hookers who were really good customers. I looked after them and they looked after me – it was a little sort of family. And it was on such a small scale that I didn't step on anyone else's toes. We went on for a few years like that. I was only selling to fund my own habit – I never went on the game myself.

'But, even though I was careful, I did eventually get busted. I was completely terrified of going to prison. I was terrified for my daughter.

'But there was this woman probation officer who was really nice. She was the one who told me about "this doctor in Warrington who has this novel approach". She made an arrangement with the judge to keep me out of jail if I went to see him. That's how I first met Dr Marks.

'I remember I walked in that first day, and he asked what I wanted to do with my drug use. I said what I thought he wanted to hear – that I wanted to stop. So, he immediately said, "Right, I'll have you a bed in the hospital this evening, and you can go and detox."

'Of course, I panicked. "Hang on a minute. I do want to stop, but not right yet."

'And he just laughed: "God make me good, but not today – is that it? Tell me the truth."

'So we talked through my situation and he tried me on methadone, but that had a terrible effect – I kept getting these jerky spasmodic movements and couldn't talk properly. So, eventually he put me on the heroin prescription.

'My entire life completely changed when I met John Marks. The whole chaos of the junkie life stops with the script. He wasn't soft or anything – he was very strict. They checked your urine and if you were scoring on the side you lost the script. But I would never buy it on the streets, or risk getting in trouble in any way, because that would jeopardise the script – and that script saved my life.'

Receiving her prescription allowed Lisa to regulate her lifestyle. But that meeting with John Marks was to determine the course of her life on a much more fundamental level. It gave her an entirely new purpose.

'Dr Marks came to me and said, "Listen, you know more about this than any of us. You've actually lived this life." So, I ended up working there – first as a volunteer, then as a paid member of staff.

'I did everything – scripts, key work, needle exchange, outreach work. I maintained my addiction with the script the whole time – I've never been off it. But, I ended up moving to Warrington, getting a mortgage and buying a house. It felt brilliant – it was an amazing feeling. That feeling of contributing is so important.

'I saw how the script transformed people's lives, just like mine. Suddenly they weren't getting arrested all the time. It wasn't that constant round of shoplifting and prison; fine after fine; probation and after probation; always living in the shadows.

'All of a sudden you get a script and all that's gone. Suddenly you can regulate your life. The main thing is stopping that crime. People would always say to me, "just not to have to wake up and have to go out on the streets and steal every day."

'I did outreach work – knocking on doors and saying, "I'm from the drug clinic." They thought I meant police, or I was going to grass them up. We really had to explain that we were there to help. People were in awful situations, with dirty needles on the floor and little babies crawling around them.

'But every single person I saw go into that programme was transformed. It was never just, "here's some heroin" – it was a whole support system, a team with a social worker, maybe a probation officer and a key worker. Not everyone got jobs and mortgages and stuff like that, but every single one left the street existence and transformed their lives.'

The War on Drugs is actually many different wars. There is the war between the police and the drug dealers. There is the war between different drug gangs. There is the war between the dealers and their own customers. And there's the war between the community and addicts driven to crime to pay for their fix.

Dr Marks's clinic effectively eliminated the latter strand of this conflict in Widnes. The 93.6 per cent drop in acquisitive crime between Widnes and Bootle that he and Russell Newcombe discovered is a staggering statistic that any police department would give their eye teeth to achieve. In fact, Marks & Spencer saved so much money through the reduction in shoplifting that they funded the first international Harm Reduction Conference, held in Liverpool in 1990.

But John Marks's clinic didn't just reduce shoplifting. About halfway through our interview, he touches on a little-explored, but crucial feature of how the entire drug world is structured.

'Let's say you're an addict with a one-gram habit,' he begins. 'It costs you about a hundred quid a day. Having to go out and steal the whole hundred pounds' worth is very risky and time-consuming.

'What's much more efficient is to find new users, and sell to them to finance your own habit. Any corporation would dream of having salesmen as motivated as a serious addict recruiting new users to get their own fix. It's the ultimate pyramid selling operation.

'All the social cost of mass addiction comes from that pyramid selling business. But the second there's a clinic where addicts can go to get their score on a prescription, the entire pyramid structure completely collapses.'

What John Marks is describing is the emergence of a key structural figure of the War on Drugs – the user-dealer.

In most movies and TV shows there are a few stock characters in the drug war – the ruthless gangster, the tough guy cop, the destitute addict, etc.

What's missing from that picture is that the key to expanding the pyramid scheme is the addict who sells in order to fund their own habit.

Think of how Danny was introduced to heroin by his 'friend', Graham. It is the archetypal story of an addict recruiting a new user to finance his own habit.

In turn, Danny went on to sell to support his own addiction. Though it is a point of pride that she never actively recruited new users, Lisa also sold heroin to maintain her own supply.

Most people with military experience will tell you the backbone of any army is its corps of non-commissioned officers. These are the corporals and sergeants who bridge the gap between the top brass and the frontline. The user-dealer is the NCO of the War on Drugs – creating the bridge between the world of the top-level gangsters and the chaotic poverty of the street addict.

A high-level player will usually surround themselves with a handful of user-dealers as both a conduit to the streets and a buffer from the police. If one of their user-dealers gets busted, they are easily replaceable with another addict desperate to maintain their own supply.

For their part, the police are quite happy to keep busting these user-dealers. As far as the cops are concerned, if you've sold drugs, you're a drug dealer. They can keep making easy arrests of small-time user-dealers to boost their statistics, while the real gangsters carry on their business, rarely ever seeing the street.

It was in the 1980s that the character of the user-dealer emerged as the main engine of the heroin pyramid scheme. If this era was an epidemic, these are the vectors by which the infection spread.

Perhaps surprisingly, the authorities were generally very supportive of these efforts. John Marks recalls his clinic's relationship with the police with a touch of gallows humour.

'We invited the drug squad down,' he says, with a wry giggle, 'and I remember one detective seeing one of our patients, and just blurting out, "I thought you were dead!" He'd been busting this guy for years, but then hadn't seen him on the streets for a while – and the usual reason an addict stops showing up before the courts is if they've died.

'So suddenly all these detectives are seeing all these addicts that they assumed had died, but they were all here attending the clinic and actually living their lives.

'The head of the Drugs Squad, Chief Superintendent Peter Dearie, actually said his officers had been monitoring our patients for months and hadn't found a single case of an addict in possession of drugs outside of their prescription. I'm sure a tiny amount may have leaked from our clinic onto the street, but even the police said it would have been a tiny, minuscule drop in the ocean.

'The idea of people selling prescribed heroin on is another myth. If you're a real junkie, you're going to take the stuff, not sell it. And no real junkie would jeopardise their script by even getting involved with that.'

We tracked down Chief Supt. Peter Dearie, today a Church of England reverend, to shed light on the police's role in the 1980s epidemic.

'I'm from Merseyside myself,' he begins.

'I was appointed DCI with the drug squad, just as the heroin explosion was starting. I had zero experience in drugs policing before this, I had been investigating murders and serious crime.

'So, I told the DI that I didn't really know anything about drugs, and he said, "Don't worry, there's a drug course starting next month."

'I said, "Oh that's good." And he replied, "Well, not really – you'll be running it."

'We started off with 12 officers on the squad, and within three years we'd gone to 42. I think other departments might have resented the resources we began to get, but it was absolutely necessary. It was a very serious situation.

'Most of my career was before the Misuse of Drugs Act – policing was much more civilised. With drugs raids you need different tactics because people fortify their doors, and the stuff gets shoved down the loo. We began smashing the pipe at the bottom of the house – grabbing the stuff coming down pipes, and just praying it was only drugs.

'In the early days I went on raids with my staff. And the sheer misery of the people we were dealing with really struck me. It reshaped my attitude towards drug abuse in general. There were an awful lot of people suffering, and the drugs were just making matters worse. So, when I learned about the needle exchange and so on, I was very supportive.

'The main issue was that if some young cop wanted to make a name for himself, it would be very easy for him to lurk around the needle exchange and pick people off. But that would defeat the whole object. So we had to put the word out – with very careful phrasing – not to pick on people going to the needle exchange.'

Dr Marks is absolutely clear that none of the early efforts of Harm Reduction would have got anywhere without the cooperation of the police. But, in fact, institutional support for Harm Reduction went much further than the Merseyside coppers. The 'Liverpool model' actually became a central plank in national policy.

'We published a paper in the *Lancet* in 1984 and it started building a head of steam,' John Marks recalls. 'Norman Fowler was Minister of Health, and he decided that if that's what the evidence says, that's what we're going to do. He was the one who had the courage to push it through. It was through him that the government decided, right, make Liverpool the model of good practice across the country – everybody must have a Harm Reduction service!'

* * *

This is particularly interesting as Norman Fowler had begun his career as a journalist with the *Sunday Times*, writing about the breakdown of the British System in the late 1960s.

And he wasn't the only name we might recognise among those trying to combat the spread of heroin in this era.

'Bing Spear was still Chief Inspector at the Home Office, and he was always strongly encouraging me,' Dr Marks continues.

'The Widnes model was meant to be rolled out across the country. It met a fair bit of resistance from psychiatrists with their usual, "I'm a proper doctor, I can cure you" attitude. They'd try and sabotage it with bureaucratic obstacles, but to our surprise, the Thatcher government went for the idea.'

In fact, most of the political resistance to Harm Reduction actually came from some elements of the far-left Liverpool local government. Pat O'Hare, who was Director of the Mersey Drug Training and Information Centre, recalls, 'The red Liverpool Council guys hated us. For them, drugs were getting in the way of the revolution and stopping class consciousness – the opiate of the people and all that. There were even rumours of threats going around – that boys were going to come round to burn our cars. It never happened, but that was the atmosphere of the time.'

But the official support for Harm Reduction on a national level was never driven by compassion for the plight of addicts. There was another, even darker, fear that drove the government to desperate measures – AIDS.

By the end of 1985 only seven cases of HIV had been reported to the Public Health Laboratory Service. Four of these were homosexual men; the other three were injecting drug users.[73] But the virus spread rapidly over the next two years, leaving terror in its wake.

And along with the spread of the disease went the hysteria in the press. The tabloids were filled with scare stories of a 'gay plague', with the *Sun* claiming that it could be caught from toilet seats and the *Daily Mail* warning that 'A million will have AIDS in six years'. This was the perfect storm of moral panics, with tabloid reporters openly bragging that 'AIDS sells more papers than bingo.'[74]

The HIV outbreak among drug users seemed to cluster – like addiction itself – around certain concentrated areas of infection. This localised epidemic effect may well have been caused by government policy – the classic example is Edinburgh.

'It's shite being Scottish,' claims the character Mark Renton in Irvine Welsh's *Trainspotting*. Whatever the truth or otherwise of that statement, Scotland has a long-standing association with substance abuse – particularly alcoholism and heroin addiction. But it was through the work of one Scottish doctor, Roy Robertson, and his studies of the '*Trainspotting* generation' of Edinburgh heroin addicts, that we came to discover much of what we know about how HIV spreads among drug-using populations.

What Dr Robertson found was that HIV almost exclusively affected drug users in the east coast cities of Edinburgh and Dundee. Glasgow, despite actually having a larger drug-using population, was virtually unaffected. Why was this the case?

The main reason was that throughout the late 1970s, there had been a UK-wide drive to restrict access to syringes and hypodermic needles – once again driven by the American-style abstinence approach to treating addiction. This was particularly successful in Edinburgh, where pharmacists had voluntarily agreed to refuse needles to anyone other than those with diabetes. The most important distributor in the city closed abruptly in 1982.

In that context, when HIV hit the city, it spread fast. Roy Robertson writes of shooting galleries where 20 to 30 addicts would share the same needles. He also records a fascinating interview with a low-level Edinburgh heroin user-dealer, speaking about the business he did when an American naval ship docked in Edinburgh.

the *J.F.K.* anchored in the Forth for a few weeks, with over a thousand men on board.

At that time, I was handling sales this side of Edinburgh for the 'Pharmacy Busters'. The more I sold, the more I could use myself. I made my way to the docks as soon as the crew landed. It was only minutes before I was leaving with a carload of Americans, all desperate for a hit of heroin, morphine, cocaine or anything else for that matter.

I take five of them back to my house to 'taste the wares'. There are two house 'sets of works' and five spikes, which have been in use for a couple of months. They use them because they don't have their own. The 'sets' then go on to be used for several more months by God knows everyone. (I had my own.)

I elected two guys to come and score for the rest of the users. They were buying up to 12 grams of 'H', 12 grams of cocaine and some other drugs. Enough for about 2,500 hits by my reckoning, every two or three days. I was told there were a few 'sets' on board, in covert places where the users could have a hit, then they would clean and replace the 'sets' for the next person.

There were hundreds of crewmen who went with the mostly 'H'-addicted prostitutes. They would ask the girls to get them bags of 'H' and share it with them, as well as sharing the girls' 'sets'. The men then went back aboard, and obviously had to use the 'covert' works for their share of the 'H' etc ... The girls in turn went home to share their 'sets' with their partners and friends.

The *J.F.K.* put in at Portsmouth around a year later and the guys were back on my doorstep again. 'Hi man, what you got for us?' They did not have their own 'sets' and told me that the 'covert' sets were brutally blunt and stiff and were in fact the same ones that had been there since they boarded!

The consequences of restricting access to clean needles was becoming horrifyingly obvious. In Edinburgh, around 50 per cent of regular injecting drug users were infected – almost exactly the same as in New York City, where similar restrictions had been put in place. In Widnes, with heroin-prescribing and a needle exchange, HIV infection was non-existent.

In 1988 the Advisory Council on the Misuse of Drugs issued a report that famously admitted that 'HIV is a greater threat to public and individual health than drug misuse.' With the general panic around the disease – and in the face of overwhelming evidence – the British government pragmatically endorsed the principles of Harm Reduction that the mavericks on Merseyside had pioneered.

So, what happened? Amid all the proven statistical success and support from police and government, how did this all come crashing down? Why aren't names like John Marks, Pat O'Hare and Russell Newcombe the ones we now associate with guiding national policy? The answer lies in a now wearily familiar pattern of the British War on Drugs.

'As soon as people found out what we were doing, the journalists started arriving,' says John Marks.

'At first it was tabloid fodder, all "Doctor for Junkies Hands Out Heroin", blah blah blah. But, actually, as people began to see it worked, most of the press came on board – even places like the *Daily Telegraph*. Eventually we had people coming in from all over the world, Germany, Switzerland, Australia, everywhere.'

Lisa also recalls doing countless rounds of interviews for journalists eager to meet one of the addicts on the programme, and Pat O'Hare recalls: 'My mission was to spread this around the world and be the public face of it. I was on television all the time. We were idealistic and wanted other people to benefit – but also, the more we spread the word, the more it strengthened what we were doing ourselves at home.'

It may well have been this active courting of publicity that brought the axe down.

'Eventually the Americans came,' says Marks with a sigh. 'Ed Sullivan did a whole documentary on the Merseyside programme for the *60 Minutes* programme over there.

'They ended with a shot of one patient of ours named Harry, smoking crack. Now, in all of Liverpool we had hundreds and hundreds of patients – and I think we had one single case of someone who was getting cocaine to smoke. We did that only because he had previously been injecting, and we were trying to shift him away from that.

'But the *60 Minutes* programme seized on this one outlying, unusual case. They didn't explain it, and that was aired all over prime-time American TV.

'Suddenly I got a panicked phone call from Bing Spear. "John, why didn't you tell us about the *60 Minutes* thing?"

'I just said, "Bing, we get television crews here from all over the world – I can't keep track of who they are. They just take their photographs and bugger off."

'But Bing was really upset, saying they were getting a lot of heat off the Americans about this programme. I tried to explain the whole thing, but that was the turning point. Word went out to the regional health authorities and they started pulling funding.'

Just as in the destruction of the British System in the late 1960s, though, there was no definitive crackdown. The torpedoing of the Merseyside model was done with another bureaucratic fudge, a subtle 'reallocation of resources'.

'They couldn't do anything about my personal practice, because it was perfectly legal,' Dr Marks says with a wry smile, 'so what they did was dissolve the whole local health authority, combine it with Warrington and set up a whole new authority. And this new one just happened to be stacked with born-again Christians, who immediately said they were removing the contract from our clinic, and giving it to some other lot, who were all gung-ho Just Say No-types.'

There was little a single doctor could do in the face of this bureau-cratic shutdown – even with the support of other experts and the local community. John Marks had to accept that the Merseyside experiment was effectively over.

Then he had to watch his former patients begin to die.

'Sid, the nice docker who'd survived for thirty-odd years with his loving family – he had to go back on the streets for his stuff. But he'd lost all his contacts and didn't know the strength of the street stuff. He died. The woman I told you about who looked at her reflection in the shop window, then cleaned herself up – she died nine months after we shut. It was all so unnecessary.'

In all, one in ten of Dr Marks's patients was dead within two years of the clinic closing.

Lisa considers herself lucky. Having worked in the clinic and needle exchange, she understood how the system operated. Even as other patients were dying around her, she was able to move from doctor to doctor, seeking out the surviving British System clinics. She has maintained her original prescription from Dr Marks to this day. She still works, and has been able to take care of her family and contribute to her community.

Danny's journey took a very different path.

'When I came out of prison I stayed clean for a few years,' he recalls.

'My wife had stopped using, but she had met someone else while I was inside, and they moved away. My whole focus was to get the relationship back and to have a life with my family. I sat in the job centre for three days straight, until I eventually saw a job at a factory in Buxton. I got that job, moved up there and did well with it.

'But my wife made it very clear she didn't want to see me – and made it very hard for me to see my daughter. Eventually it became so confusing for my daughter to have me half in her life and half out – that I had to make the decision to stay away. It was heartbreaking; you never get over that. She was my angel.

'Buxton was behind the wave of heroin by a few years – like a little island in the Pennines. But it got there eventually. One of the lads in the factory was into it, and he convinced me to come and score with him in Oldham.

'By that time crack had just arrived as well – and back then no one knew how to cut it, so it was absolutely pure. It was really strong stuff. I suppose I convinced myself that it was just a one-off, and wasn't going to lead me back into it. It had been three years, and I thought I was strong. Really, I was just stupid.

'That was what led me back into it. Heroin was the staple, and the crack was just a bonus. If the crack didn't come, I wasn't bothered – it was the gear I was really after.'

* * *

Danny had become swept up in the other so-called epidemic of the late 1980s – smokeable cocaine.

On 20 April 1989, the head of the US Drug Enforcement Administration's New York Division, Robert Stutman, flew to London to address Britain's top police chiefs. He told them a horror story. There was a new drug ravaging the inner cities of America, unlike anything that had come before. If the UK did not act fast, he warned, then within two years, ghettos like Toxteth and Moss Side would mimic those of Harlem and South Central LA.

He promised the wide-eyed British coppers there was 'a study that will be released in the next two to three weeks that will probably say that of all of those people who tried crack three or more times, 75 per cent will become physically addicted at the end of the third time ... We now know that crack is the single most addicting drug available in the United States of America today and certainly the most addicting drug available in Europe. Heroin is not even in the same ballpark.'

This was just what the tabloid press needed. THREE HITS CAN GET YOU HOOKED, thundered the *Sun*, setting off a spate of lurid moral panic scare stories around this new chemical menace.

But three weeks passed, and the study that Stutman had promised failed to materialise. Several months later, the *Independent* reported that senior British police officers 'attempted to trace the studies and the figures he quoted, and found they don't exist.'

Stutman's other headline statistic had been the terrifying claim that 73 per cent of New York's children killed by battering in 1988 were crimes perpetrated by crack-using parents. Later this was revealed to be based on just two such deaths, one of which also involved chronic alcoholism.[75] But by this time the damage had been done. The moral panic had taken hold.

In fact, crack wasn't even really a new drug at all, but simply a form of cocaine that you could smoke. The high is shorter and more intense, but it's ultimately the same drug.

However, the difference between cocaine and crack in the popular imagination is less to do with the product itself, than with who consumes it. Powder cocaine is seen as a 'white people's drug', and crack as a 'black people's drug'. In his speech, Bob Stutman used the term, 'the persistent poor'. The implication was unmistakable.

In fact, the nightmare wave of crack abuse that Stutman had so vividly warned about ultimately failed to break. Crack addiction in Britain has often been called 'the explosion that never happened'.

What did happen was that people who regularly used other drugs, primarily heroin, began to use crack alongside. In 2015, only 2 per cent of patients entering drug treatment for the first time listed crack as their primary drug of choice. However, 45 per cent of those presenting for treatment for heroin addiction also reported using crack as a secondary drug.[76]

In those concentrated pockets where crack did hit, however, it hit hard. Alex Wheadle, who spoke to us about the racism and brutality he suffered in 1970s Brixton, ended our chat by saying that it was the violence of the crack trade that destroyed the community spirit of the Frontline on Railton Road.

Another occasional crack user and petty criminal we spoke to, who wished to remain anonymous, remembered exactly how the south London scene shifted.

'Crack changed things not so much because of the people who used it, but because of the people who sold it. It's one thing if you're a dealer selling a bit of weed, but suddenly you had these Yardies with access to huge amounts of crack – and they would smoke it themselves. What do you think's gonna happen when these guys are smoking rocks all day – and they've got guns sitting there too. Suddenly any stupid little beef ends with blam blam blam. It was the business side of crack that made things get darker.'

In many ways, this process is an inevitable aspect of the War on Drugs. Everywhere that prohibition policies have been put in place, drugs get stronger and drug gangs more violent. But, despite what American law enforcement tried to project in the late 1980s, the vast majority of British users were just like Danny – they were addicted to heroin, and smoked cocaine on the side.

The British heroin epidemic of the 1980s, and the radical inno-vations it inspired, have redefined the War on Drugs ever since – not just in the United Kingdom, but around the world. This era defined two foundational visions of how addicts should be treated.

First, there is the abstinence-based model. This model orig-inates in the United States. It derives from the principle that drugs are a moral evil in themselves, and those who take them may be judged. The overriding priority must be to get the patient off drugs – even if they must be coerced. If they fail to stay 'clean', it can be called into question whether they even deserve the treatment at all.

Set against this is Harm Reduction. This school holds that drugs are simply chemicals; in and of themselves, they are morally neutral. Addiction can be awful, but those who suffer from it are seen as unfortunate rather than evil. They should be helped by the most pragmatic, non-judgemental methods possible – methods that are relevant to their actual needs.

For Harm Reductionists, the 'evils' of addiction might be things like poverty, violence, theft, sickness and enforced pros-titution. They argue that reducing these harms must take precedence over coercing an addict into abstinence.

Most of the individual elements of Harm Reduction had been tried at one point or another before the 1980s – but it was only then that they were collected and given a theoretical underpinning.

Harm Reduction as a school of thought is now recognised around the world. When activists in Vancouver hand out Naloxone kits to save people from overdosing, or the Swiss government sets up safe injection rooms, they are consciously practising Harm Reduction – and they proudly say so.

But, as global as it has become, Harm Reduction as a coherent set of ideas was born on the banks of the Mersey. It is a British idea, born of a uniquely British set of principles and historical circumstances. When the history of the global War on Drugs is finally written, the development of Harm Reduction will be presented as one of Britain's most essential contributions.

We can also learn a lot from thinking about the stories of the two long-term addicts, Danny and Lisa. Both of their lives fundamentally changed in a single instant – based on one encounter with law enforcement.

For Lisa it was the moment after her bust, when her probation officer happened to mention a doctor in Warrington with a novel approach to drug treatment. Meeting Dr Marks changed Lisa's life. She may still be a drug addict today but, having maintained her prescription for over 30 years, she is able to work, take care of her family and contribute to society.

For Danny, the decisive moment came in the butcher's shop when a drug squad officer picked up a cardboard tube with four micrograms of heroin residue. It was that one moment that led Danny to lose his job, lose his family, go to prison and begin his descent into the emerging British addict underclass. Like Lisa, Danny is also still a drug addict today – but he survives in the shadows, selling a bit of gear to get by, one eye always over his shoulder for an angry dealer or an arrest that could put him back in prison.

Danny and Lisa. Abstinence and Harm Reduction. Prohibition and the British System. All these people and ideas are still spinning in motion from the force of the Big Bang that was the heroin epidemic of the 1980s.

But, as the 1980s drew to a close, Britain was about to enter an entirely new era. A new generation was about to learn to take new drugs, and dance to a new beat. The UK was about to change the world once again. Britain was about to discover rave.

7

Revolutions

Transforming the World at
120 Beats Per Minute

Somewhere in Britain a group of teenagers walks into a night-club. They wait in line, check their bags at the cloakroom and head onto the dance floor. One of them looks around warily, then reaches into her pocket for the little bag of pills she has sneaked past the bouncers. Her friends gather round as she hands them out. For a moment their eyes lock in a mixture of anticipation, excitement and nerves. Then they knock back their pills and disappear together into the haze of flashing lights and thumping beats.

This could be any town in the UK – any weekend of the year. It is an instantly recognisable snapshot of British life. In fact, this scene would be familiar anywhere in the developed world. From Manchester to Manhattan, from Edinburgh to Estonia, groups of kids taking pills and dancing is perhaps the archetypal image that people hold of what youth culture means.

There's a very simple historical reason why this particular image of underground culture – which perhaps by this point has even become something of a self-perpetuating myth – is so universally recognisable: in the summer of 1987 four Englishmen went on holiday.

Youth culture in the mid-1980s was fairly desolate. The dying embers of the punk scene competed sullenly with the fey elitism of the New Romantics, and the time was ripe for a revolution. It was in this environment that Danny Rampling, Paul Oakenfold, Johnny Walker and Nicky Holloway went off to Ibiza for a summer break, and stumbled on acid house.

This was a version of the house music developed by obscure DJs in Detroit and Chicago, but given a thumping, psychedelic edge. The 'Ibiza Four' came back to the UK as acid house evangelists – inventing an entirely new form of underground culture that would soon conquer the country, and eventually the world.

By 1989, the movement had begun in earnest and Britain entered its 'Second Summer of Love'. All over the country kids would wait in their cars, calling semi-secret phone lines to receive carefully guarded details of where the party was at – then converge in their tens of thousands for hedonistic raves in the fields of middle England, much to the bemusement of those who actually lived there.

The police seemed powerless. If you've got 20,000 ravers going crazy in a field, then a couple of police vans turn up with 25 cops, there's little they can do except manage traffic. The Thatcher government, which had cut its teeth as the defenders of law and order, confronting striking miners and militant unions, began to attract criticism for its perceived failure to get to grips with a bunch of kids dancing in a field.

As if on cue, the tabloid press launched into a fresh convulsion of moral panic, and a wave of fake news crashed over the emerging dance music scene. To take just one famous example – in June 1989, a big rave for about 11,000 people was thrown in a disused Berkshire aircraft hangar. Amid the thumping tunes and psychedelic laser shows, the organisers released tiny scraps of shiny foil from the ceiling like confetti. The foil caught the lights as it fell, giving a kaleidoscopic, shimmering effect.

The following Monday, a pearl-clutching horror story was splashed over the front page of the *Sun* reporting that thousands of foil wrappers for wild new party drugs had littered the floor of this new type of illegal 'rave party'. It was an obvious nonsense, but it sold papers. In a later interview the then editor of the *Sun*, Kelvin MacKenzie, was brutally honest about why the tabloids loved rave stories so much.

> This was a great story for the tabloids for one important reason. You could either read it and say, 'Cor, wish I was there – I'm going to go to the next one.' Or the older readers could say, 'Bloody disgraceful ... something must be done!'
>
> Of course there are some people who say that ecstasy doesn't turn up in wrappers. Now, I'm slightly too old to know if that's true or not. All I can say is that if the *Sun* said it was true in 1989, then it was definitely true because we were selling 4.3 million copies per day.[77]

MacKenzie's brazenness is almost impressive. But that exploitative mix of prurient voyeurism, self-righteous condemnation and blatant disregard for truth is emblematic of how so much of the tabloid press have covered drug issues since well before the 1960s.

Fake news aside, though, there was a genuinely utopian, idealistic current to this new party scene. For those who went to them, raves were seen as great social levellers, attracting black and white, rich and poor in a way few other cultural movements ever had.

But all that loved-up euphoria didn't come from nowhere. Just as with the Mods of the early sixties, people rarely dance all night without some extra fuel to see them through. This was the era of MDMA. Nowhere in the history of popular culture – with the possible exception of reggae and marijuana – have a musical form and a particular drug been as irrevocably intertwined as rave music and ecstasy.

Rave didn't just revolutionise the music scene – it transformed the shape of British culture. Crucially, this was the era in which drug use went from being a niche interest to a national mania. Even in the depths of the 1980s heroin epidemics, with hundreds of thousands of skeletal addicts haunting inner-city council estates, there were corners of Britain where some people might still have been able to claim to 'not really know what this whole drugs thing was all about'.

After the rave generation, that naïvety would never be possible again. From the early 1990s on, drugs were threaded into the British psyche. Even those who might never actually touch a pill themselves would immediately know exactly what slang phrases like 'spliff', 'pill-head' or 'junkie' meant. Drugs had become part of the daily language and a feature of our national landscape.

But somebody needed to supply all the little coloured pills to keep the parties going. And the gangsters stepped right in.

Along with the transformation of popular culture, the rave era of the early 1990s saw an entirely new level of criminality and violence related to the drug trade. In fact, the scene produced an entirely new class of criminal figure, never before seen in this country. This new class of criminal was to shape both the development of the emerging dance music scene and the future structure of the British drug trade. The era of rave was also to become the era of the club doorman-turned-gangster.

'Whoever ran the door determined who sold the drugs in any club. If someone wasn't in with us, they got fucking battered. They got taxed for their money and drugs – and if they were working with their own firm, they could come see us and we'd fucking have it with them too. Simple as that – no fucking about. It's how we made our money.'

James finishes speaking, leans back in his armchair and takes a sip of tea. Considering the only work he's ever done has revolved around the application of extreme violence, James is actually a fairly pleasant guy. He's witty and charming, and never talks with even a hint of swagger or bluster. The opposite of the loudmouth hard-man down the pub, James speaks about brutally violent situations with the cheerful matter-of-factness of someone explaining how to fix a car engine.

'I went into the army at 16, and left at 20 – following a girl,' he continues. 'I got into working the doors because it was cash in hand, easy money. But, my first real work was with Paul Massey. That's where I learned the rules.

'Paul would make the arrangements, then his crew would come and tell me to leave certain dealers alone, because they were with us. Then, if one of ours spotted anyone else selling in the club, he'd let us know, and we'd drag the guy out the back, batter him and tax his gear.

'We'd go see whoever managed the club, give him an envelope of cash and tell them to shut the fuck up and stay out of it. In those days the lads on the door told the manager exactly what to do. If we needed anything – like deleting certain footage off CCTV or something – it just happened. But, then Paul went to prison for stabbing a fella, and I had to find new work.'

The Paul Massey that James is talking about was an infamous gangster who built his empire through 'security firms', before moving into drugs and essentially taking over Salford in the 1990s. Later in life he began acting as a mediator between different Manchester gangs, and became such a well-known community figure that in 2012 he ran for Mayor of Salford, and didn't finish last. But, in 2015 Massey was shot to death outside his home in Clifton, a small town within the City of Salford. The murder ignited an ongoing cycle of gang violence that continues to this day.

James continues, 'After Paul went away, I just joined another firm. By then I'd worked my way up, and was usually head doorman – that's when it all really kicked off.

'I ran doors all over Manchester and Ashton-under-Lyne, which was buzzing back in the nineties. Ashton was actually rougher than Manchester city centre. All round north Manchester they're all fucking bonkers.

'Early on, I was doing a club called Molly Malone's, which had a garage house night downstairs, which was a nightmare for security. So, this load of local scallies comes in one night and starts causing trouble. I get a shout and come down with our call-out team, and square up to one of them. He says, "We're not going." I say, "Yeah you are," – and straight away he pulls out a pistol.

'Now, I've got a bulletproof vest on. But they're quite short – and he sticks this gun into my stomach, right below where my vest ends. I was just thinking, "Of all the places to put it!"

'So, I have about two seconds to think what to do – and basically figure if he was going to shoot, he would have done it already. So, I just sort of walk him upstairs, get him outside and just go, "If you're gonna do it, do it." Obviously, he didn't. I had to hold my ground in that situation really – or it would have been a free-for-all from then on.

'Of course, we knew these lads. They were local drug dealers. Both Hattersley and Ashton have big gangs of dealers who fight it out. So, my bosses had to put in a call to the guys we knew they worked for – otherwise we might have these lads coming back with 40 of their firm. That happened regularly, so this had to be sorted out up the chain. This was the era when any drug dealer started to think they could get away with anything.'

There is something very modern about the scene James has just described. It's a long way from utopian LSD-dealing hippies at free festivals, or even small-time heroin pushers in 1980s Liverpool. This feels more like the British underworld we are familiar with today – dealers waving handguns in dingy nightclubs, desperate to project an air of violence to protect their patch. It was in the rave era of the 1990s that this new Britain emerged.

But James was also about to rub up against another innovation of the 1990s drug war – the organised British drug-dealing 'firm'.

The Noonans had started out as armed robbers in Manchester, before inevitably finding their way to the drug trade. The three brothers who headed the family, Damian, Desmond and Dominic, were suspected of responsibility in over 25 murders, though Dominic was never convicted for any killings.[78] They had battled Paul Massey for control of security at Manchester's famous Haçienda club, before going onto run an estimated 80 per cent of the nightclub doors in Manchester.

'I was the head doorman at Teasers on Peter Street. It was when that area was buzzing with the big clubs. Our place had all these girls dancing on the tables in little hot pants and boob tubes – it was proper buzzing,' sighs James with a hint of nostalgia.

'So, it's Friday night and this lad is selling something he shouldn't have been, so one of our lads bounced him down the stairs. And I mean bounced him. Only problem was, he was one of the Noonans' little cousins.

'So, Sunday morning I'm sat at home and I get a call from my two bosses asking what the fuck happened. I explain a bit, then they say, "Look, the Noonans want a proper meet-up with us at

Heaton Park. They want the head doorman there, so you've got to come."

'The deal was that we would come on our own, they'd come on their own – and we'd sort this out with no one bringing any firm. Well, you'd have to be an idiot to walk into that without backup – so we had two vanloads of lads, all armed, parked round the corner. But, we had to wait on our own in the park, just the three of us standing there.

'So, we see Damian Noonan come round the corner – and about five seconds later, 40 or so of his firm all came round following him, including these two Asian brothers who used to do a lot of their shooting for them. I was just thinking, "Fuck, fuck, fuck" – but we had to just stand there and hold our ground.

'Now, Damian was the brother who I actually got on with a bit. He was the one you could have a conversation with. He had a pistol on him, but we just had to stand there and explain what had gone on with the lad in the club. And, to be honest, we'd made him look a bit of a dickhead, because as far as everyone there could see, we'd stuck to the deal to meet on our own, while he'd shown up with this bloody army. Of course, none of them knew about our vanloads of tooled-up lads waiting round the corner.

'But then – just as this stand-off is getting a bit tense – these two cars screech up, and out jumps Dominic Noonan. Now, Dominic was just a fucking wrong 'un. He immediately starts shouting about how he'll have us all shot – and he demands to see the head doorman. So I step forward, and he gets right in my face. He says he wants the lad to get £1,000 compensation, replacement clothes and the doorman who leathered him to be sacked.

'Then, just as he's finishing he leans right in my face and hisses, "and I'll be raping your arse!"

'I wanted to hit him so hard you can't believe, but I would have been dead right there. All three of us just had to keep our mouths shut. Then he just jumps back in his car and fucks off.

'So we're left with Damian, and everyone's feeling a bit fucking weird now. So we say, "Look we'll replace the guy's clothes and phone – but the grand's compensation and our guy getting sacked ain't happening." And Damian said, "Yeah all right, leave it with me." See, him you could have a conversation with – whereas Dominic was just a fat, horrible bastard.

'They were just testing us really. If we'd given ground there it would never have stopped. Every club door in Manchester was worth a shitload in drugs money. That's what it was all about really.'

Dominic Noonan's rape threat was no idle bit of intimidation. During the 1990s, male rape was emerging in the drug world as a method of instilling terror and control in rival criminal enterprises. Men would be held down, raped and photographed – then the photos used for blackmail. This would barely have been thinkable in the criminal world ten years earlier. Once again, the arms race dynamic of the War on Drugs only ever leads in one direction.

In the end, Damian Noonan died in a motorcycle crash in Spain, Desmond was stabbed to death by a crackhead user-dealer and Dominic is serving 11 years for arson, blackmail and perverting the course of justice. Their territory has long since been overtaken by even more ruthless gangs, whose vicious drug wars throughout the late 1990s earned Manchester the nickname 'Gunchester'.

For the bouncers, though, it was only a matter of time before they realised they could make more money if they stopped providing protection for drug dealers, and just sold the product themselves. These were firms of 20 to 30 hard-as-nails doormen, many of whom brought an ex-military discipline to their operations. They saw a multimillion-pound market emerging and they wanted a piece of the action.

Across the country, firms of doormen gradually morphed into straight drug-dealing gangs. The competition was intense and violence began to spiral. Cities like Liverpool, Manchester and Nottingham began seeing convoys of blacked-out Range Rovers in their city centres, as different doorman firms tried to put on shows of strength and bravado.

James's firm in Manchester was no different. 'I started doing runs down to Liverpool to pick up cocaine for my bosses,' he recalls. 'They went with the cash, I went in a separate car and got the gear – probably about a kilo or two per trip. I just made sure it got back to Manchester safely and got 500 quid. Why wouldn't I do that? I know the higher-level guys were involved in much bigger stuff and making loads of money, but this was easy for me. It was just a few hours' driving.

'These guys we were seeing could get violent very easily, but with me they were always professionals. If there was a problem, we sorted it.

'Eventually, though, I actually got my own club. I part-owned it while still running other doors around town. That's when things really got going with the drugs business. We controlled the flow on the doors, and if anyone wanted to have it with us, we'd fucking have it. We were ruthless. If they stepped it up a level, we'd step it up a level. If I thought shit was really going to go down on a night, there were these two brothers I'd call, and they'd sit outside in a car, parked up with AK-47s just in case.

'We had some problems with other firms. One night another car followed us driving home from the club. It was fucking madness – they were chasing us and shooting at us down the M60. We just had to put our foot down and get away. Then we came back and sorted that crew over the next few days.

'The licensing officers were on it too with the clubs. If they had a problem, they got a nice envelope of cash to keep them quiet – not just from me, from every other club owner too. We were making so much money from the drugs business, who fucking cared?'

This progression from doorman to drug dealer, to full-blown gangster with the power to bribe officials, is perhaps the archetypal story of the British clubland underworld of the early 1990s. The booming black market in illegal drugs made this process virtually inevitable. But, the specific structure of the market – and the place of the doorman-turned-gangster within it – actually resulted partly from the police's own attempts to control and undermine the original anarchic rave scene of 1989's Second Summer of Love. To find out how, we have to go back to Brixton.

The man who first made rave legal was Simon Parkes – founder of the Brixton Academy music venue. Simon had opened the Academy in 1982, with Brixton still smouldering in the shadow of the riots. By the time rave broke in 1989, he had turned the former derelict cinema into the hottest venue on the British music scene.

Simon explains how he first encountered acid house:

'We used to put on our own club nights, and one of them ran a residency in the VIP area with this club called Shoom, which was run by Danny Rampling and is usually considered the first proper acid house club night. I very quickly saw that Shoom was becoming the coolest part of the night – it was where everyone wanted to get into. I was sort of fascinated by this new music, so I started getting interested in the whole rave world – the secret parties around the M25 and all that.

'I actually knew a lot the main rave promoters anyway, both from the music scene and because a lot of them had actually gone to posh schools and were a bit like me – the tearaway kids of quite well-off families.

'It was definitely exciting, but I'd had enough experience in Brixton to spot the bad guys in this scene a mile off. It was the guys selling ecstasy that really ran the show. A gang of dealers would attach themselves to a promoter – who definitely needed them in there to get the party going. But then they just took control. Who was going to really call the shots – the posh boy promoter or the hard drug-dealer gangsters?'

This pattern – the inexorable transfer of power from musicians and promoters to the dealers – is one we have heard repeated across the rave scene. Indeed, Neil Woods remembers witnessing it playing out many times while working under cover at nightclubs across the north of England. Simon, however, was about to get drawn deeper into this world than he ever anticipated.

'The whole thing really happened by accident,' he continues. 'Or, more accurately, I was set up. At the time I was looking for investors to do some repairs on the Academy. I approached a couple of quite posh guys I knew, and they invited me to dinner. I got sat next to this older guy, who turned out to be Sir David Stirling who founded the SAS back during the Second World War! I'd grown up on commando mags and all that at school, so I was dead impressed – and he was a seriously impressive guy.

'Of course, my mates never had any intention of investing in the Academy, and I'd been sat next to him on purpose. A few days later I get a phone call. "Hello, it's David Stirling, I wonder if you could pop into the office."

'So, I go down, and David Stirling isn't even there – but these two other guys are. They're part of this private security firm all made up of ex-SAS guys, and say they may or may not be working with "certain" government agencies. They're investigating the rave scene, and specifically some of the people getting involved with my mates. What they want me to do is to introduce them under cover, so they can infiltrate these big drug gangs.

'This was a real dilemma for me. I've never been a grass — and the last thing I ever want to do is mess with someone having a party. But, the new wave of gangsters coming up through the ecstasy business were a different league than anything we'd seen before.

'The SAS guys made clear they didn't have any interest in messing about with a bunch of ravers having a dance in a field. They called that "kiddies' stuff". They were interested in two things – the drug dealers and the security firms.

'Then they said something that really got me. Right now it might be raves out on the M25, but sooner rather than later these gangsters were going to hit Brixton. And when they did, it wouldn't just be E's they'd be selling, it would be crack. Brixton was my home turf. I love Brixton. I employed all the kids off the local estates. The year before, we'd done this anti-apartheid show with Public Enemy and Jesse Jackson – and Jackson had given this terrifying speech about what crack was doing to the inner cities in America. It was really that that made me agree to help.

'So, I knew one of the main rave promoters, Jeremy Taylor, through old-school-tie bollocks. He was having massive trouble with his so-called security team, who were all linked to the West Ham Inner City hooligan firm. They were now muscling in for more and more of the action and he was terrified. He called me saying, "I can't get out of this." So, I said, "Look, I can get you six personal bodyguards – all ex-SAS, and they'll protect you."

'So, I introduced this SAS lot in there, and to a few other people as well. They wanted more out of me, but I refused. Eventually the wrong person was going to figure out the common denominator here was my name.

'But, the SAS lot worked their way from Taylor to some of the other big promoters, and they did protect them from the bad guys. But suddenly things started going wrong at the raves themselves. A sound system that was meant to get picked up would get raided and impounded on the morning of the party, or a particular 0898 number would get shut down so a rave couldn't happen.

'I'll never really know how much of a role I played in shutting down those big underground raves, but my intention was only ever to protect what we'd built in Brixton. I have no regrets, because I saw what came next with the ecstasy trade – and it wasn't pretty.

'A bit later, though, when I had trouble with a few heavy Brixton gangsters, those SAS guys offered to "take care of them for me". They said they'd grab them, take them to a barn in Kent – and it might take one day or it might take five, but from then on every time they heard my name they'd shit their pants. I very politely said no thank you. These were not guys to whom I wanted to be owing favours. If a few bouncers in Brixton are after you, you can move out of the area – these SAS guys will track you down to a jungle in Borneo.'

Whether or not it was down to Simon's undercover intro-ductions, as the summer of 1989 turned to autumn, the big underground raves were indeed running into problems – both with the police and with the gangsters who ran the ecstasy supply. As it happened, though, it was exactly these problems that propelled Simon to his central place in the history of the rave scene.

'I saw that some of the raves were getting shut down, but elsewhere the police were still struggling to deal with them – and the tabloids were having an absolute field day. So, I had an idea. I went to the police higher-ups in Brixton and just said,

"Look, let me legalise this. Give me a licence till 6am and we'll do the raves at the Academy. They'll all be in one place, contained – and you can stop getting all these complaints from farmers in Kent."

'And, to my total surprise, they went for it. Maybe it was some kind of reward for my previous cooperation, I'll never know. But whatever it was, I got the UK's first 6am licence and started doing the country's first legal raves.'

The decision to make the rave scene legal and bring it into commercial venues was completely transformative. What had been an underground movement flooded into the mainstream. Acid house beats were suddenly heard on *Top of the Pops*, DJs became superstars and the experience of going to a nightclub would never be the same again.

At that moment, however, the rave scene essentially split in two. The hardcore edge of the movement went deeper underground, into squats, warehouses and free festivals. The more mainstream branch became subsumed into general nightlife culture, watering down its original utopian idealism in favour of massive commercial clubs, celebrity DJs and corporate-sponsored summer festivals. The one thing that remained constant, however, was the demand for pills and powders. And that meant organised crime.

Simon Parkes's brainwave in getting that first 6am licence may have put him at the forefront of a pop culture revolution – but he never counted on the fact that it also meant bringing the War on Drugs into his own venue.

'Bringing rave to the Academy changed everything,' he says, rolling his eyes.

'We were ahead of everyone else on this, so it was really exciting – but on the other hand, the level of criminality just went through the roof.

'Previously we'd had to deal with all sorts of problems from local Brixton gangsters. But the really big organised crime firms in London had always seen Brixton as just too chaotic – it was too much hassle for them to get involved. That all changed with the ecstasy.

'We had 5,000 capacity, eight weekend nights a month, and they're each spending £20 a night on pills. You're basically talking a million-pound-a-month ecstasy market – and that's just our one venue. With numbers like that, there's no way the big guys weren't going to muscle in.

'From that moment of doing the first legal rave, I basically spent the next six years chasing pill dealers around the Academy. But these new guys were a different breed than anything we'd dealt with before – these were proper gangsters. You'd catch them and take their bag of pills off them, but they'd say right to your face, "I'm coming right back, and you're getting shot." And about half the time they really meant it. They had serious backup from major criminal families. I was put under police protection several times, and had to start wearing a bulletproof vest to work.

'Obviously, the key to any venue is controlling the door. If you control the flow of drugs, then you basically control the club. I was very lucky at the Academy, because I had found my own security early on. They were connected to proper south London firms, and had a sort of old-school mentality of intense loyalty. I'm sure a few of them had arrangements with dealers, but they never turned on me. But the guys who ran clubs like Haçienda or Cream up north, or my mate who ran the Fridge down the road in Brixton, got totally fucked by their own security teams.

'But when the drug gangs saw that they couldn't scare us at the Academy, they just tried to buy us. I got a visit from a heavy geezer called Tony Tucker and one of his mates. These were the "Essex Boys", who a couple of years later were found shot dead in a Range Rover somewhere near Rettendon – they made a movie about them.

'They wanted to book the Academy for six Saturdays – the first of each month over a half-year period. We sorted the deal, then, just before we shake on it, Tucker turns to me and says point blank, "What's your stance on drugs?"

'I told him that I'm not an idiot, I know what goes on, but my staff don't get involved and any pills we find we confiscate. He just goes, "Right then," flips open a briefcase and slides it over.

'I say, "What's this?" And he goes, "That's your cut – £100,000 for keeping your guys off our backs."

'It's quite a thing to look down at 100 grand, there for the taking for essentially doing nothing. But I just closed the case and slid the money back. Once you start making deals with these people, you become one of them – and eventually they own you. I could have been a lot richer had I got involved in that sort of business, but seeing how that lot ended up, I think I made the right choice.'

Simon's position at the Academy, however, got even more complicated. The gangsters weren't the only side in the drug war trying to use the venue for their own ends.

'We developed an arrangement with the local police. When their budgets were being decided, they sometimes would need a little spike in the statistics. So, they'd give me a call and for the next few nights if we caught a mid-level dealer we'd say, "Right, we're going to let you off this time. We're not calling the police, and we're going to let you keep your gear as well – just don't do it again." Off they'd go thinking it was a total result, and we got to look like we were showing "respect" to whatever big firm they were working for.

'But, we'd always let them out of a specific prearranged exit, which the cops would be watching. Then, when the dealer's a few streets away – bang, the cops swoop in and pick him up. If you do five or six of those over a weekend, that's a statistically significant increase for the police, and their department gets their budgets sorted.'

That local police commanders were willing to manipulate statistics like this is an indication that political pressure was coming down the chain of command. It shows that drugs were clearly becoming a much higher priority in policing. The pressure to manipulate and inflate stats – to charge users as dealers or overestimate the street value of drugs seized – was a constant fact of life for Neil Woods in his years as a detective. It will be an all-too-familiar dynamic for any cop who's ever worked on a drug squad. In fact, during this era the War on Drugs was producing a revolution in law enforcement just as seismic as that in the criminal world. But for Simon Parkes at the Brixton Academy, the change was more prosaic.

'Obviously, when we were chasing pill dealers around the venue we had to try and figure out their systems. The guy who takes a punter's money is never the one actually holding the drugs, so we had to follow them and discover how they worked. Most of the time it was just impossible – if you busted one, a hundred more would immediately take their place.

'We also had to have paramedics on standby, and a hotline to St Thomas' Hospital down the road. We never had a death, which is something I'm very proud of – but as time went on, the dealers started putting all kinds of shit in their drugs to cut them. We had people passing out or reacting badly, and we'd have to look after them.

'We were always a responsible venue and took care of anyone who came through our door. What's happened in clubbing recently though is that they've brought in new licensing laws, so if there are too many calls to a particular venue, the police can just shut it down.

'Obviously, the idea is to get clubs to crack down on drugs. But, what actually happens is when someone gets sick, the operator just thinks, "If I call an ambulance, it will mean another mark on my record." So, instead of actually helping them, the doorman will just push a drug casualty out the back door, and dump them by the wheelie bins. I've seen this happen so many times – some new rule comes into protect people, but it actually makes the situation so much worse.'

The cynicism Simon is describing is a world away from the idealism of the early acid house movement. But, that original utopian energy wasn't wiped out completely. When 1989's Second Summer of Love came to an end, the rave scene split in two. The commercial end of the circuit mutated into nightclubs, and brought organised crime with it. The real hardcore ravers, however, just went deeper underground and threw even wilder parties. It was pandemonium. In fact, it was Bedlam.

Steve Bedlam gives us a cheeky grin. 'Yeah, I suppose when you've been part of getting 50,000 people to the biggest free rave in British history, it is quite an amazing feeling, actually.'

For a decade and a half Steve ran the Bedlam Sound System, one of the central party crews of the 1990s underground rave scene. Bedlam were key players behind the Castlemorton Common Free Festival in 1992, the most iconic of all the 1990s free raves – but also the one that spelt the beginning of the end for the movement. Steve's story is emblematic of how the rave scene developed, the effect it had on British drug culture and the reaction against it by the authorities.

'I'm a council estate kid from Hackney – so I grew up in the reggae sound system culture of the seventies and eighties. Me and my mates started smoking marijuana from about 10 years old – then from around 12 we were sneaking out to the Four Aces

Club and all the blues dances. We were estate kids, and we got into mischief – a bit of street robbery and things like that. But we were mainly just into listening to reggae and the Beatles and Jimi Hendrix and smoking pot.

'Then, in 1988, I'm about 17 and my sister starts going out with this guy – and all of a sudden they're rolling in on a Sunday afternoon, still off their heads, talking about this new rave scene. They went to all of the original M25 circuit parties like Biology, Karma, Sunrise, Back to the Future and all that lot.

'The first rave I went to was life-changing. Me and my best mate blagged some money for the tickets, picked up a bit of hash and hitched a lift with some other ravers in a VW van. I took my first half a trip and danced like I never had before. It wasn't like the blues dances I knew in Hackney – there was no violence, no fights, no one mugging you. Everyone was smiling and I met all these amazing people who actually wanted to talk to you.

'From then on we went to raves every weekend, Friday night to Sunday daytime. That became my life, and the drugs went with it. The pills were so good back then, all the Pink New Yorkers and White Burgers – the classic old-school pills that would send you off your tits for hours just dancing. I was working at a clothing factory at the time – doing ironing for 50 quid a week. Raving was my only outlet. I listened to pirate radio all week at work and couldn't wait for the weekend.'

But, like many enterprising kids of the era, it didn't take Steve long to realise that the illicit drug market might offer opportunities that low-paid menial work never could.

'I went to Glastonbury for the first time in 1989. We jumped over the fence and had an absolutely incredible time. And that's where I met the new age traveller lot. Their whole lifestyle blew my mind, not just because of the drugs – there was a sense of community that was like nothing else I'd ever seen. They made their own acid, and after I'd hung out with them a bit they offered it to me at three trips for £5, when they sold for a fiver each in London.

'So, I got into selling acid and ecstasy – never cocaine or heroin or anything like that. At first you do it just to fund your own nights out, but you soon realise that this is actually a really good earner. It did eventually get quite big for me – but never as a long-term thing.'

In fact, Steve's career as a drug dealer, and even as a drug user, was fairly short-lived. He was destined to play a different role on the underground scene.

'That experience with the travellers really stuck with me. I soon moved out of my mum's place and onto the Hackney squatting circuit. Then, in 1991, we started the Bedlam Sound System.

'Our first rave was on Holloway Road with about 1,200 people. We hired a sound system, broke into an industrial estate and squatted a warehouse. There was thumping house and techno music, everyone was high and dancing – it was just the greatest feeling you could ever have.

'After that we took the bit of money we'd made, and people chipped in their giros and drug money, and we put together our own sound system. After that we were doing parties all the time, anything from a few hundred people up to 5,000. All our parties were free, but you were sort of expected to leave a donation in the bucket.

'We never did DJ line-ups or anything – people would just come because they knew we did good stuff. We did actually get some of the big names coming down too, but all totally impromptu. Guys like Fabio and Grooverider or L.T.J. Bukem would do their sets in the clubs – then turn up at ours and want to burn it up a bit.

'On our scene, we even looked at the early M25 acid house raves as a bit commercial. They did great shows and all that, but 25 quid to get in? Fuck off. The squat party scene was never about that. We did amazing things with our warehouses too. There was always art, sculpture, performances – it was all really creative, mind-bending stuff. But we never did it to make money; it was just something we believed in.

'And the funny thing is, I personally stopped taking drugs in 1992. They were still a major part of the scene I moved in, but I got off on putting on the parties rather than the drugs themselves. I still smoked pot, but I haven't touched any harder drugs at all since then.'

The Bedlam crew were putting on their anarchic, hedonistic raves at exactly the same time that James the Manchester bouncer was facing off with the Noonan crime family, and Simon Parkes was being offered briefcases full of cash at the Brixton Academy. One might assume that, if anything, the violence and criminality would be worse on the underground circuit than in the clubs with their 'professionalised security teams'. In fact, it was the exact opposite.

'Sure, some of our crew sold drugs at the parties – but there were only one or two confrontations,' Steve explains. 'There was one guy called Fridge Man who used to literally drive into raves with these huge fridges and start selling beer to the punters. Of course, that was just a front for his real game, which was selling ecstasy, speed, cocaine and crack.

'He tried it on with us, and I had to face off with him. The only problem was he had a crew of 15 heavy crack-smoking geezers with him. So, we had to get a bigger posse together and shut his bar down. But then he went off to his car and comes back waving this pistol – and I was just thinking, "Now it's crackheads with guns – great!"

'But we were 20 years old and stupid, so we just stood our ground. They kept coming back, though, so eventually I had to sit down for a beer with him and make a deal. When our bar ran out – which it often did – he was allowed to set up his fridges, and sell whatever he wanted. But, he had to stop his boys from smoking crack at the parties, because that creates a really negative vibe. And he did actually stick to the deal, and he'd always put a big donation in the bucket.

'We never had formal security at our events – just some mates on the door. It was a sort of self-regulating system and it worked almost all the time. There was only one incident where a group of gangsters took over our door – and that was actually at a ticketed party at a club. We just let them get on with it for a few hours, then they just fucked off. They took a few grand, which should have gone to us – but it just wasn't worth kicking off over.

'Everything we did was word of mouth. I think we were just too much hassle for the whole organised crime thing. That was more part of the commercial club raves that were all ticketed and on the radio.

'We actually did business with serious organised crime people, but only on the drugs side of things. Some of our lot would go over to Holland and bring stupid amounts back. So, serious geezers connected to the Adams family and the Reillys would buy and sell with us. But none of them ever gave us any trouble at the parties. To them we were just a bunch of hippies.

'To be honest, the main thing with the raves is that the football hooligan firms stopped fighting. All those guys came to our parties – Chelsea fans, West Ham fans, Millwall fans. I had to stop a massive fight between the Chelsea and Millwall firms, and just basically said, "Look, if you're going to fight you can fuck off, that's not what this place is about." And within a few weeks of them coming to the parties, they'd all become mates.

That was down to the drugs and the free environment that they were now in. Some of those guys are still my friends today.

'The commercial raves were different. I remember listening to Centreforce Radio, which was one of the major pirate stations, and suddenly there was this big commotion and it went off the air. We all assumed it had been raided by the cops – but actually what happened was it was taken over by the West Ham Inner City Firm. They wanted to find out who the rave organisers were, control the info and take over the drug sales.'

The image of football hooligans suddenly becoming friends under the spiritually opening influence of ecstasy is one of the central myths of the acid house era. And it's partly true. The hooligan era, Britain's great national embarrassment for decades, did largely end in the early 1990s as rave took over.

But that's only half the story. While the vast majority of hooligans did indeed give up fighting for raving, it still left a hardcore contingent of the most truly committed criminal sociopaths. Seeing that they could no longer raise their armies for mass brawls on the terraces, this hardcore faction simply did what every other serious criminal of the era was doing – they became drug dealers.

Undoubtedly, there must have been some crossover between organised crime and the underground rave scene; the market for drugs is simply too big for there not to have been. But Steve's account broadly corresponds to what we found elsewhere. By and large, the serious gangsters were involved in the more stable world of commercial clubland. The underground squat party and free festival circuit was largely viewed as just too much of a chaotic mess to get mixed up in.

The same could not be said for the police.

'Of course we had the police trying to shut us down,' says Steve with a smirk. 'Half the time it was the nightclubs that called the cops on us because we were taking their business. I mean, what would you want – an expensive club with an aggressive, coked-up bouncer, or a party for a fiver where you have the freedom to do what you want?

'But, actually, it was our mates Spiral Tribe who got it worst from the police. They were another party crew who very much became the public face of the whole movement. They really believed in the spirit of it, and were sort of geniuses. They shaved their heads and wore all black, so they always looked amazing – and they had a real sense of purpose about everything they did.

'The media loved reporting on Spiral Tribe. Between the papers and the police, they got turned into these kind of rave bogeymen. To be honest, we were quite happy for them to be the guys out front – it meant they took most of the heat. We used to laugh about it with them all the time.

'There was one Spiral Tribe party where the police came in through the wall with a bloody JCB. It was insane. They'd laid on a proper siege outside this warehouse for hours. We were all trapped inside, playing "The Bouncer" by Kicks Like a Mule on repeat. The main line of that song goes, "If your name's not down, you're not coming in." We thought it was hilarious until – crash! The bloody wall comes down and this JCB comes through, followed by some very hyped-up coppers.

'The police really could get seriously rough, though. I got properly battered by them many times. But, most of the time when they turned up at a party, there actually wasn't a hell of a lot they could do. Nine times out of ten they just had to bugger off and pretend it wasn't happening.'

Little did Steve know, however, that his real confrontation with the authorities was only just beginning. When summer came, Bedlam and the other big party crews hit the road, following the old hippy free festival circuit. Eventually, that road led straight to the biggest free rave in British history – and the change in the law that all but destroyed the movement.

'The biggest festival every year was always the Avon Festival at Chipping Sodbury Common,' Steve explains. 'So, we're all on our way there, but then the police blockade us in a lay-by near Gloucester. There are about 200 vehicles in our convoy, and the police are telling us that Chipping Sodbury is closed, there'll be no festival this year and we're not allowed to leave. Of course we're like, "What do you mean we can't leave? We're not prisoners!" To which they reply, "Well, how many of those vehicles are legal? You can leave, but as soon as you do, we'll stop you and do a licence and MOT check." So, we were properly screwed.

'We ended up staying in this lay-by for about four or five days. There were hundreds of people; it was like a mini-festival in itself.

'But there was this one woman named Moe, who actually did have a legal car. So she drove all over England, finding all the different convoys of travellers and communicating between them. Obviously this was before everyone had mobile phones.

'Eventually she came back and said, "Right, I've found a group at this place called Castlemorton Common, and I think we should all go there." So, this one brilliant woman, Moe – who I never saw again after – was basically responsible for the entire Castlemorton Festival.

'We decide to go for it, so I find a high-ranking cop and say, "Look, we're going – if you want to arrest us, you'll have to arrest all of us."

'He replies, "Are you planning to leave Gloucestershire?"

"Yeah."

"Okay, in that case we'll not just let you go, we'll escort you to the next county."

'So, the police literally shut down the roads, and got a team of outriders on motorbikes to escort us to the county border, like we were a foreign government or something.

'So, then we all rock up at Castlemorton Common, we were the second crew there. We got a beautiful spot, up on this big ridge overlooking the whole thing. Then all the other crews show up – Spiral Tribe, LSDiesel, Circus Warp – the whole scene.

'Now, this would have been a completely normal festival, but the BBC and Capital Radio both decided to do massive pieces going, "Police Lose Control of Hippy Festival". It was the most insane advertising we'd ever had. People just flooded in, and it was absolutely glorious. It was the pinnacle – 50,000 people for a week, with 50 sound systems and maybe 5,000 travelling vehicles. It was amazingly anarchic, fun and peaceful.

'There was one story that became famous about people shooting flares at police helicopters. That was one guy, and he got a proper talking-to – because that's not what we were about. In any group that big, there's always going to be a few who want to balaclava up and cause trouble. Another group came up from London and started robbing people. We caught them, and let's just say by the end of the weekend they weren't fans of ketamine. They had to march around the festival with a sign saying, "I am a mugger". But the trouble really was minuscule. The scene had a sense of internal discipline.

'For the most part the cops seemed all right too. We played football matches with them in the field behind our tent. But, the whole time they were filling the place with undercovers, photographing everyone and taking down licence plate numbers.

'They let us do the festival – then just busted everyone on the way out. They had the plates of every vehicle transporting a sound system. Our system got confiscated, as did Spiral Tribe's and loads of others. It took about six months to get them back.

'Of course they came down hardest on Spiral Tribe. There was a trial that got loads of publicity. The cops tried to make out that Spiral Tribe was just a front for some massive drug-dealing ring. I know every single one of that lot and the idea is completely ridiculous. The Spiral Tribe guys consumed so much drugs, they would have been the worst dealers in the world. But cops tell themselves funny things when they get overexcited.

'Obviously though, the main fallout from Castlemorton was the Criminal Justice Act. The protests around that were hilarious. There were all the ravers, anarchists and Romany travellers – but then the bloody Ramblers also showed up in the middle of it. They were trying to preserve their freedom to go walking where they wanted – and in a way, so were we.'

The Criminal Justice Act of 1994 is one of the stranger and more complex pieces of modern British legislation, but essentially it was a sweeping law solidifying land rights and empowering landlords. It made evicting tenants easier, and largely erased both the duty and the funding for local authorities to provide space for traveller communities.

The Ramblers objected because it eroded ancient common law privileges to wander across grand country estates, but really, this was very clearly understood as an 'anti-rave' Act – specifically drafted in response to the media furore around Castlemorton. Perhaps the oddest part of the Act was Section 63, forbidding gatherings of more than 12 people playing music, 'characterised by the emission of a succession of repetitive beats.' Young people of the time – with some justification – took this to mean that it was fine for posh folk to sit in a field listening to Beethoven, but working-class kids having a dance could be arrested.

For their own part, the police themselves largely viewed the Act as somewhat ridiculous. Neil Woods recalls the chat in police station canteens across the country being that this was strictly an affair between the politicians and the tabloids.

The Act was largely unenforceable for a number of reasons – not least because raves tend to happen at night. If you're a duty inspector covering the night shift in, say, north Cheshire, you might have two patrol cars to cover the entire area. If you get reports of an illegal rave going on, you'll have to pull resources from all over, leaving the people your force is meant to be protecting vulnerable to muggings, robberies and worse. But, while this law may have been rarely enforced, its symbolic power was unmistakable.

'We just left,' declares Steve Bedlam, with a touch of anger. 'We said fuck this, and went to France. Spiral Tribe went first and the other crews followed. We spent years touring all round Europe doing festivals, then on to America and Australia. The police in Europe were just as bad, if not worse than the police in the UK – but we had glorious times.'

Steve eventually returned to the UK after years on the road, and started his own successful business making sound systems. Then, in 2015, the European refugee crisis hit. With waves of migrants drowning in the Mediterranean, and shanty towns developing in Calais, Steve decided to do something.

'Our community were always creative, altruistic people – and we know how to get things done on our own. We put out a thing on Facebook, and within a few days had raised enough to found the Refugee Community Kitchen. It was all characters from the original rave generation that put it together, and it's grown and grown. We now have a full-time kitchen set-up in the Calais Jungle, and cook 2,500 meals a day – all done by volunteers from our little scene. It's the same spirit with which we approached our parties back then – we do it ourselves, and it's about community.'

* * *

In the 1990s, the Criminal Justice Act drove the underground ravers – the kind who found community kitchens – into exile. Of course, what that left was the commercial club scene, and the organised crime that went with it. For James the Manchester doorman, as for so many others, the career path from bouncer to full-time drug dealer was inevitable.

'I started really making money from drugs when I started growing cannabis,' James picks up his story. 'My mate had just got out of prison, and he approached me. He knew what he was doing, so I gave him the money for the first grow. Then I realised I could make serious money out of this.

'Eventually I had seven different grows up and running. We didn't mess about with small quantities, we only did serious weights – and everyone paid, because they knew what would happen if they didn't.

'We'd get people to set it up in their houses, and we'd go by once a week to check on things and pay the electric. If people did well, they made money – if they messed about, they got a kicking. That's just the nature of the business.

'We'd rob other people's grows as well – we'd just tool up and burst in. The trick was always to time it right, so the plants were just ready when you robbed them. One of our own grows got robbed too. I suspected the guy I was working with was in on it and had to give him a battering.

'I'm not proud of any of this, but it is what it is. I don't even smoke the stuff– it makes me sick. But that Blue Cheese skunk was just a massive seller. I made good money off it. And now it's everywhere; I reckon there's a grow on every street in the UK.

'The whole drugs scene is so much darker than it was. Basically, the pills in the nineties were good, then they gradually got shite. That's when it all shifted, and then cocaine came in and took over. Northern people love coke as much as London people now. It grew from this one subculture of pill-heads to just fucking everyone. Office workers, plumbers, firemen, soldiers – suddenly everyone was on coke. On the same night I'd catch 15-year-olds and 65-year-old granddads doing lines in the toilets. I've caught off-duty coppers doing coke plenty of times. And if cops and granddads are on it, and so are the kids – then it really is every-where, isn't it?'

The universalisation of the drugs scene that James is describing is a result of what happened in the 1990s. Britain became drugs aware, and would never be the same again. What had started as an underground subculture ended up completely transforming mainstream society. Getting high was no longer the exotic interest of bohemian subcultures or an urban underclass; drugs were now woven into the fabric of our national life.

In fact, the revolution that started in Britain had reverber-ations all over the world. House music may have been invented in Detroit, but in America it had always been a tiny subculture, largely among the gay and African-American communities. It was only when it hit the UK that rave really took over. It was British DJs and British crowds that propelled dance music to dominance. Eventually, that sound crossed back over the Atlantic, and came to dominate the entire global music industry. In many ways, the world still dances to a British beat.

But, in terms of the British War on Drugs, the 1990s symbol-ised a much deeper shift than just kids popping pills and doormen becoming gangsters. This was the moment when the first generation of the drug war ended, and the second began.

It wasn't just drug culture that would never be the same – the entire structure of British criminality and policing was about to be profoundly transformed. The story of the War on Drugs is not about the constant cycle of headline-generating drug raids, or even new laws coming into force – it is the story of change over decades. It is the story of generations.

8

Generations

A Vision of Change Over Time

The British War on Drugs is now well into its third generation. Most of the people fighting it – on both sides of the conflict – barely realise that these are battles that have been fought and refought in different guises over the last 50-odd years.

The drug war generates a constant stream of headlines, crises and minor hysterias. While this dynamic sells papers and generates social media clicks, it rarely ever allows for a sense of change over time. Amid all the noise, we are almost never able to take a step back and establish a vision of how this conflict has changed and mutated over the past five decades.

The city of Liverpool plays a central role in this story. The Scouse firms were the first to recognise the economic potential of the drug market, and even today there are probably more drug dealers per capita on Merseyside than anywhere else in the United Kingdom.

Contrary to the bile of certain red-top newspapers, there is nothing uniquely criminal about Liverpool or the people who live there. Gangsters from London, Manchester, Birmingham and Glasgow are every bit as brutal and violent. The 'grafters' from Liverpool just happened to be a bit quicker on the draw in the early 1970s. They were the first to spot that creating a market in illegal drugs meant enormous potential profits, and organised crime networks in the rest of the country have been following in their wake ever since. As one Manchester gang boss from the late 1980s admitted, 'they're miles ahead of us – while we were fighting over territory, they were doing multimillion pound deals.'[79]

In order to get a vision of how the War on Drugs has developed over time, we spoke to three generations of Liverpool drug dealers. Each of these men has experienced the violence of the drug war at first hand. Each represents a vision of how the War on Drugs has grown from a relatively obscure, niche area of criminality to become one of the defining aspects of British society.

'Look at my hands. Look at them. They're fucked.' Patrick leans forward in his seat and extends his arms. His hands are massive, but are pitted and craggy like chunks of rock in a quarry – a testament to the damage they've done over the years.

Patrick stands around six-foot-six, and carries himself like a heavyweight boxer. Now in his fifties, he still works out five hours a day in the gym just to burn off the excess energy and keep himself level. Like his hands, Patrick's face carries a spidery roadmap of scars. He's been shot three times.

This is another drug-war figure whose life has been defined by violence. Today he's calm, keeping his volcanic energy in check with incessant exercise and 12-step programmes – but it doesn't take much to imagine just how terrifying he must once have been.

When he walks into the flat on the rough estate in north Liverpool we've rented for our interviews, he immediately gives the place the once-over – as if instinctively checking for surveillance and back doors. He eventually seems to decide we're kosher, and lowers himself into a chair that seems far too small for his massive frame. Only then does he begin to open up, telling his story in a thick Scouse rasp.

'We all grew up in care homes. My dad was on the ale, so I got smashed up, my mum got smashed up. Then I got nicked for stealing and got a care order. But I just escaped and basically lived on the streets from the age of ten. I just had it in me to be defiant. In this area there was no work, no jobs – we were getting fucking nowhere, so of course we started on the graft.

'By 1976, when I was around 14, I was stealing all over Europe. Their security was so loose – we'd run rings round them. We'd sneak into supermarkets, hide in a cupboard or somewhere till it was closed, then steal all the wages. We'd smash jewellery shops all over Germany, Norway, Holland, Switzerland, wherever. We'd find out when the football was on, go over a few days before – then come back with all the fans, with a Liverpool FC hat on and all the stuff in our bag.

'Then I got into more serious robbery stuff – security vans and building societies. Sometimes we went armed, most of the time we didn't even fucking have to. We were hard enough, so why get nicked with a gun? We'd just smash the guard onto his arse and take the bloody bag. I was in and out of prison, but I didn't fucking care. Honestly, I felt more at home in there than I did outside.

'Obviously, then the eighties came and heroin hit. We knew how to graft it before anyone else. I used to get it for £100 a gram, and had four guys out on the street selling it in £5 deals. We had busloads of people coming in from all over to buy it – I was doing about £800 a day, but that was still just kids' stuff really.

'Then I went down for a long stretch for robberies – and inside it was totally different. Prison is where you get your schooling,

and I was in Category A prisons with real serious old criminals –
Charles Bronson, the lot. The drugs were taking off outside, but
inside the old-schoolers said, "We don't want any of that fucking
heroin in this jail." Quite a few people got stabbed because the
old boys didn't want it inside.

'But the whole time I was in, I already knew what I was
coming home to because my mate Curtis Warren came up to see
me in jail. We were best mates from growing up together. He let
me know what was going on outside.'

Curtis Warren is the wealthiest British criminal ever caught.
After a meteoric rise from a rough background in Toxteth, by the
mid-1990s he was Interpol's number one most wanted criminal,
and even appeared on the *Sunday Times* Rich List. He's a living
symbol of how the Liverpool drug firms dominate the European
black market.

'When I got out of prison, it was Curtis who explained to me
how everything was different now – how it was all about drugs,'
Patrick continues.

'There were loads of different firms wanting me to work with
them – but then Curtis brought in the first ever ton of charlie to
the country, and that was that.

'I'd only been out maybe six months, and there I was on this
big shipment with Curtis. We stayed out all night watching this
customs yard where they had all the stuff just sitting there
hidden in lead ingots. We watched them all night, and there
were only two guards in the whole place. I said we should just
smash the guards up and take the stuff – but Curtis said they
were all marked with mercury anyway.

'Curtis had set this whole deal up with Mario, who lived in
Venezuela and worked for the Cali Cartel. They'd set up this
whole thing with smuggling charlie in lead ingots. I used to run
Mario around in the car when he was over here.

'So, we left the ingots on the customs yard, but everyone got arrested anyway – everyone except me. That morning, our other mate Colin Smith phoned me to come pick him up – but by the time I got there the customs lot were already all over him with their guns out.

'As soon as I saw that I went to go warn Curtis – I knew the bird's house where he was laying up. But when I got there, Curtis was in the corridor already in the cuffs, with the customs all pointing guns at him. He gave me this look, like, "Best fuck off, mate" – so I fucked right off. I wasn't listed on the conspiracy charge, because the whole thing actually went back to a previous shipment they'd done while I was still in prison.'

The names Patrick has just dropped are a who's who of the top echelon of the British drug trade. And the particular shipment he is describing, with the cocaine hidden in lead ingots, is in fact one of the most famous and controversial drug busts in British history.

In late 1991, Curtis Warren and Brian Charrington, a Middlesbrough-based trafficker, travelled to Venezuela to meet their contact Mario Halley. It was a watershed moment – they were finally going to cut out all the middlemen separating British drug dealers from the South American cartels.

Their first shipment was 600kg of cocaine sealed in lead ingots – a record-breaking haul for the era. Warren reportedly knew the exact length of the longest drill bit used by HM Customs, and the load went through. For their second load, the team were even bolder – they went for a ton.

This time, however, the operation hit a snag. Another Cali shipment in lead ingots was busted in Holland, and the cartel warned Curtis to stay away. Losing £160 million worth of coke was a small cost of doing business, if it meant their new British contacts avoided prison.

Curtis left the load sitting on the customs yard for days, just watching it. Unfortunately, another of his partners, the Ghanaian businessman Joseph Kassar, couldn't resist the temptation, and moved the ingots off the lot to an industrial estate. This triggered HM Customs, who launched Operation Singer, and 26 people were arrested.

But then things started to go wrong. It emerged that Brian Charrington had been a police informant for the North East Regional Crime Squad the entire time. Customs decided to push forward with his prosecution anyway, despite loud protests and political interventions from NERCS. But the prosecution's case fell apart. The judge ordered that Curtis Warren be found not guilty – at which point he reportedly strode up to the shell-shocked customs officers and told them, 'I'm off to spend my £87 million from the first shipment and you can't fucking touch me.'

Then, several months after the trial, one of Brian Charrington's police handlers at the North East Regional Crime Squad was reportedly found driving a £70,000 BMW registered to none other than – Brian Charrington. Today, Charrington himself is in prison for drug trafficking. The other 'friend' Patrick mentioned seeing on the morning of the bust, Colin 'King Cocaine' Smith, was shot to death in 2007.

The very public failure of Operation Singer signified Curtis Warren's ascension to become the most important drug smuggler in Europe. It was also the moment he became a marked man for both the British and Dutch police.

Hearing Patrick casually drop that he was intimately involved in this landmark moment in British policing history is fascinating. For Patrick himself, though, this was only the beginning of his own rise in the world of the 1990s drug war.

'After that we got hold of the heroin trade in the UK – our first order was a ton. It came through Afghanistan, northern Turkey, the Balkans and all that. I'd have someone in London and they'd get a message on their pager in code – most of the time he wouldn't even know what he was picking up.

'After the robberies I'd done, this was so easy. It didn't even feel like real grafting – it felt like drugs were legal. The police were miles behind us; they didn't have a fucking clue. We never used phones – we'd have meets face to face or in the crowds at the football. No other firms would fuck with us, because we had the reputation from the real, proper grafting before. We had this fucking city locked down.

'Most of the Liverpool lads weren't even grafting here. We'd been in jails all over the country and were connected all over. To be honest, even this thing of calling it a "firm" is sort of bollocks. People call it a firm, but it's just people grafting. In Liverpool everyone knows everyone, and everyone works with everyone.

'You have to maintain your reputation, but most of the time I wouldn't use a gun – I'd just smash people up. But, say, there's one firm that still runs Glasgow today that used to come down every week to buy 250 kilos or so. So, one time, just to let them know, I had my mate come by and offer to sell them some MAC-10s, Uzis, grenades and silencers. We said, "It's no bother, you don't have to take it now – we can always send someone up on a motorbike."

'We were never going to actually sell them any of that stuff – they might come back and use it on us. I just wanted to let them know what we could do.

'Another time we had problems with the Turks we got our gear through in north London. They sent us some stuff and it was shite, so we had to go and kidnap one of them. Even then I didn't use a gun – I just smashed him up and took him. They were all threatening to come up to Liverpool and burn our houses – but we were just like, "Fuck off, we'll be down in London in three hours and deal with the rest of you." I was ready to take the guy's feet off, but eventually a deal was made through another south London firm – the money was sorted, I think it was about 200 grand, and we sent the lad back down.'

This is an image of the modern British drug war as it emerged in the 1990s. Armed robbers making the transition to drug dealing; shipments of heroin and cocaine numbered in tons; British firms creating global networks with South American and Turkish suppliers – all backed up with the threat of extreme violence. What's interesting, though, is that Patrick maintained enough of his roots in the 'old-school' pre-drug war criminal mentality to still rely primarily on his fists, rather than a gun – even when he himself got shot.

'If we wanted an area back then, we fucking fought for it,' he explains.

'I was about 15-stone, fit as fuck – doing five-mile runs, in the gym all the time, squatting quarter tons, 180-kilo bench-presses and all that. When we were growing up around here every garden had a punchbag – we were all in the fighting clubs. It goes back in history in this area.

'So, this lad called me on for a straightener – but I just went and smashed his whole crew up. I found these four guys and just blitzed them in about two minutes, shattered their faces. Then Curtis and another lad, Johnny Philips, showed up to back me – but I didn't need them.

'I ran about four miles down to where I knew the main fella was, just to be nice and warm when I got there. But this lad backed out and never showed up. He lost face over that. So, then I'm coming home and see some bloke in a mask. I thought he had a baseball bat on him, so I thought I'd take it off him and smash him up with it. Turns out it was a shotgun. I threw my hand across my chest, but got blasted from about five feet away. I was in the hospital for a few months, but I rolled out of there and just went right back on it. I had about

30 more fights with this lot afterwards, I wouldn't give them an inch.

'I could have used guns if I wanted. We had safe houses all over the country – not for drugs, just to stash guns. We had them everywhere, just in case we needed them on the graft. We had automatic weapons, everything – Desert Eagles that could shoot through a fucking wall. But I didn't like that. I didn't like having guns around me.

'Back in the 1980s if we needed a gun we'd have to go and see someone and ask permission – and they'd bloody say no. Some older head would be like, "Why would you want to bring heat on these areas by using a gun? Go have a fight with the lad – knock fuck out of each other for ten minutes, then shake hands." It's the drugs thing that's changed that now.

'I've got nephews of 14 right now who'll take your life without a second thought. Their mum's a heroin addict, that's what they've seen all their lives.

'We call them PlayStation Gangsters now. They think the world is fucking *Grand Theft Auto* or whatever. In my day it was organised violence, now it's all about front – kids are tooled up at 13 or 14. It was a long road for me to get away from that life after my last daughter was born, but I look around me now, and things have got much, much worse.'

When Patrick talks about his 14-year-old nephew and his friends, there is genuine concern in his voice. To watch a man who has seen and done the things that Patrick has wringing his hands over what today's child gangsters are capable of is acutely disturbing.

In fact, though, there is a clear path that leads from Patrick's old-school world of straighteners and criminal hierarchies maintaining order to the chaos of today. It's a path that lies at the heart of the British drug war's second generation.

* * *

'Of course all the armed robbers became drug dealers – of course they bloody did,' exclaims Will. 'Especially a kid like me – basically a working-class smart kid with a bit of a brain. Why go around security vans with a sawn-off shotgun when you can make more money with less risk? It's just basic risk and reward, isn't it?'

Will is several years younger than Patrick. He also comes from a rough neighbourhood in north Liverpool, but whereas Patrick was an old-school bruiser who had to learn his way around the drug trade, Will's entire criminal career has been defined by it. He is a figure of the British drug war's second generation – and at his peak, he was Britain's most wanted criminal fugitive.

Prior to the late 1980s, the aristocracy of the criminal world were the armed robbers. They earned the most money and commanded the greatest respect. Then came the revolution of the 1990s, and within a few years the old-school hard-men had been completely wiped out by the drug gangs. The profits involved in the drug trade were like nothing the British criminal world had ever seen, and it has turned the entire underworld hierarchy on its head.

Sometimes the effects of a government policy can take a generation to become apparent. It was only in the 1990s that the legacy of creating a black market for drugs was becoming clear. This was a gold rush for British organised crime. Soon, the only reason anyone would bother undertaking an armed robbery was to raise the capital to get into the drug trade.

'It was the ecstasy that brought us all together,' says Will. 'Before that you'd barely talk to someone from the next estate, let alone a different neighbourhood. It was a gang mentality. But with ecstasy the barriers started to fall – starting with the criminal barriers. People started to network. Before, a lad from Norris Green would never work with a lad from Halewood or Croxteth. It was just after Hillsborough as well, with 96 dead and the whole city being accused of being murderers and scum-bags – of course it just exploded. There were people who would never dream of getting into proper grafting, suddenly becoming drug dealers.

'I'd done a bit of graft before, obviously, stealing from factories and that – but the pills just changed the whole game. I started out selling in the clubs, and I was bloody good at it. There was an older grafter who was sort of funding me. He'd lay on 200 tablets – sale or return – and I'd give him the money later. I was only making three quid a tablet, but that's £600 a night, four nights a week. For an 18-year-old in the early nineties, with no proper work about, that's a good wage. I wasn't partying myself – I'd save myself one pill, then go home and iron the money totally buzzing.

'Then, when I'd made myself a little bit of money, I go on my first proper holiday to Ibiza. And that's where it all changes. I start chatting to these cockney lads – just being social over a beer – but it turns out they're from a serious north London firm. So, I say to them, "I'm going to come and see you with proper money and we'll get things done."

'They probably thought I was chatting shite – but I went straight back to my older mate in Liverpool, who was well respected on the estate. He asked if I was really confident in this lot – I said yes, and 24 hours later I was on my way to London with 250 grand in a rucksack.

'I wasn't even nervous or anything. I was just a good networker, that's what I do. I'm Scouse – I know how to talk to people. We all just had that confidence. So, in six months I've gone from £600 a night to carrying 25,000 pills back to Liverpool. I sold them all in a week – I did 20,000 in bulk, and kept 5,000 for myself to sell. After that it just went off – I started doing wholesale to all the different estates. I knew who to talk to all over the city and just sorted it. This was all in the space of a few months.'

* * *

No criminal enterprise in history has ever offered this sort of meteoric rise. The drug market represented such a massive expansion in potential profits that new talent flooded in. The old-guard gangsters were as powerless as the police. They faced a simple choice – become dealers themselves, or be swallowed up. Will was just one of the young grafters caught up in the gold rush.

'I started with this firm of lads when I was about 17, and stayed with them about ten years. We got into bringing in heroin – 100- or 200-kilo loads at a time – usually through Turkey, but some other places as well. One of our lads made the arrangements with the Turks, and my remit was sorting the route this side.

'I could spot opportunities and I could network. I worked out the transportation and the logistics and came up with ways to get the stuff in and out. That was my thing. It grew so fast – heroin, cocaine and black hash in ridiculous amounts. Tons and tons of the stuff – five tons at a time.

'We weren't idiots. It was an organised business – the logistics were broken down into single-cell structures, like a jigsaw puzzle. If anyone was busted, they didn't know about the whole system, and couldn't tell the bizzies anything.

'We used to read autobiographies of drug lords, terrorist groups and paramilitary organisations to get their methodology. Then we'd use their methods to stay ahead of the police. I always figured that any top football player will always be watching footie, any top writer will always read books – so, anyone in the drug game should be the best they can be.

'I remember one Birmingham firm refusing to deal with someone because they said he had a "council estate mentality". We were the opposite. We properly educated ourselves in this graft. We had all our vehicles modified – you'd have to take them away to a garage and take them apart to find anything. The cops didn't have a fucking chance. The codes I created have gone to the FBI, and they've still never cracked them.

'Of course there was violence as well. There always is in this game – but we used controlled violence. It had a point. If we had a problem with someone, we'd pick them up in a van, take them to a side street, stick a gun in their mouth and let them know the score. But really, the power came from not having to use violence, but everyone knowing you could.

'And yeah, sometimes it got a bit fucking scary. There were times when I thought the South Americans were going to kill me – I said bye to my ma and everything. Then I went over to Amsterdam to meet a paramilitary group we were dealing with, and I walk into this house and it's all covered with plastic sheeting. I just think, "Shit, I'm gone here." Then I go in the bedroom, and this guy pulls out a big .45 – and I think, "Fuck, I'm definitely going." Then he just goes, "Here, have a look at that," and hands it to me!

'But you can't get anywhere in that game without the confidence to just ride shit like that out. When I was just starting out, I was on the way back from London once with 250,000 pills – a couple of million quid's worth – and the bloody car broke down on the M6. I look in my rear-view mirror and see two traffic cops walking towards me. Well, they ended up giving me a lift to a taxi rank, with the pills still in the rucksack.'

This is a brand new type of criminal. No previous underworld generation would be reading biographies of terrorists to learn how to break their operations into single-cell units. This was purely a development of the drug war's second generation. Yet, even this only scratches the surface of how professionalised the drug trade was becoming.

'I eventually worked out that we were only making three grand a kilo on charlie,' explains Will. 'We were laying out 30,000 and taking on massive risk – just to make three grand per key. It didn't make sense. So, we had a meeting round the table – the top five firms in the country – cockneys, Scousers and Mancs. And we just said, "Right, nothing's going anywhere – we're going to keep everything here, let the price go up, then send it out."

'So, we all held our shipments back for about two and a half months. We just sat and watched the price go up from £35,000 to £50,000 – and only then we sent it. I'm not claiming to have been a senior player at this meeting or anything – but it was a serious deal.'

This small anecdote is as crucial and fascinating as anything else we have heard. There is almost universal consensus among criminologists that the illicit drug trade tends towards monopolisation. It's a simple Darwinian process – the big fish with more power, money and weapons swallow the little fish, making them even more rich, powerful and able to wield violence. This is one of the key dynamics of the War on Drugs, but no one we've come across has ever had as clear an example of how this process works in practice.

It was with the second generation of the drug war, around the mid-1990s, that British organised crime groups finally achieved this level of monopolisation. A meeting like the one Will describes – determining the supply and fixing the price on a national level – would simply have been impossible for the gangsters of any previous generation.

It was only in this era that organised crime groups developed the heft, infrastructure and capacity for violence to achieve this sort of monopolisation.

It was here that the British War on Drugs could be said to have reached its mature phase. The drug war was growing up.

The process of monopolisation that Will describes has had a profound influence on how the War on Drugs is fought – not least in enabling the gangsters to achieve enough power and wealth to begin corrupting the police themselves. We'll explore that process in more detail, but as Will continues, his story is a reminder that it wasn't just the gangsters who 'grew up' in the mid-1990s – it was also the police themselves.

'I remember the moment clear as day,' he recalls. 'I was sitting there with some of my crew, flipping through the *Liverpool Echo*. I opened it up, read the main story, then just turned to the others and went, "That's it lads, we're fucked."

'The report I read was that in response to a string of shootings we'd had in Liverpool the police had gone over to New York to learn their zero tolerance policing. They were getting armed and were going to come down hard and decapitate every firm in the city. I really remember that moment – reading that and just thinking, we're fucked now.'

Zero tolerance is a controversial school of policing, essentially meaning that the police crack down on 'minor' infractions, like graffiti or petty vandalism, in order to deter more serious crime. Pioneered in New York City under Mayor Rudy Giuliani in the early 1990s, it was first championed in Britain by Ray Mallon, Detective Superintendent of Cleveland Police, who earned the nickname 'Robocop' for his efforts.

Zero tolerance was one of a raft of new tactics and strategies the police scrambled to develop in the face of the drug war's second generation. More significant in the case of Liverpool – and quite possibly what Will is actually referring to – were the 'disruption tactics' adopted in the wake of the murder of David Ungi.

Ungi was a Liverpool family man, shot to death with an automatic weapon in Toxteth, on 1 May 1995. The killing sent shockwaves through the city. The chief constable of Merseyside Police promised his officers would 'fight fire with fire'.[80] That night he ordered Merseyside's armoured estate cars out in force, each with a team of police carrying Heckler & Koch semi-automatic carbines. It was the first time routine armed patrols, as opposed to armed teams coming out for specific operations, had been deployed on the streets of mainland Britain in peacetime.[81] Military-style checkpoints were set up at key locations, and major suspects were stopped and searched with extreme force several times a day.

The idea was to forcibly disrupt the gangsters' operations at every turn. But, while it may have shaken up some mid-level grafters, the real players in the drug game were by now far removed from this sort of street-level drama. As Will insists:

'At my peak I wouldn't go home for five weeks at a time. I'd live out the way in hotels and only come home when the work was done. All the guys were heavy, but they were family men, and we knew from the books we read that that's how they get you – through your family. If you're at home, they know where to pick you up for surveillance. If there's no starting point for them, there's no surveillance.'

These were drug war professionals with networks all over the country, developed through business and prison. They did their work away from home. Roadblocks in Liverpool were a bother, but not a threat to their real operations. Far more worrying was the emergence of intelligence-led policing (ILP).

ILP was pioneered by Kent Constabulary, then exported across the country and eventually around the world. In very broad strokes, in the 1990s the police realised that under 5 per cent of the population was causing over 50 per cent of the crime. This was true from high-end drug dealers, violently defending their territory, to the gutter, with addicts stealing to support their habit. The police labelled these priority prolific offenders (PPOs) and made them their key targets.

Traditional policing is inherently reactive. An incident occurs, then you gather the evidence, piece together what happened and go after your suspect. Obviously, this approach was inadequate for the new world of the drug war. Drug offences are, by definition, unreported crime. There's no victim to call in the police, as there is in a robbery or assault. You have to go looking for the crime. And since by now drugs underpinned virtually all other forms of criminality, this new law enforcement doctrine called for a 'strategic, future-oriented and targeted approach to crime control, focusing upon the identification, analysis and "management" of persisting and developing problems or risks.'[82]

This was a new world of policing – a world of long-term surveillance, of building pictures of complex criminal operations, of confidential, paid informants grassing on their own bosses. This was the birth of the high-level War on Drugs that we recognise today. If gangsters like Will were beginning to act like multinational CEOs and structure their operations like terrorist networks, then to catch them the cops were going to have to act more like spies.

One can trace this progression clearly in the 'alphabet spaghetti' of British policing agencies. In 1965 nine individual police forces joined up to form Regional Crime Squads (RCS). This was followed in the late 1970s by the creation of the tiny and ineffectual National Drugs Intelligence Unit (NDIU). In 1992, the NDIU became the National Crime Intelligence Service (NCIS); then the NCIS and the nine RCSs merged, and eventually became the Serious Organised Crime Agency (SOCA) – which in turn transformed into the National Crime Agency (NCA). Intelligence-led policing was supplemented by the Proceeds of Crime Act (PCA) and the Regulation of Investigatory Powers Act (RIPA), among many, many others.

Each one of these developments, along with their irritating acronyms, was a response to how the criminal networks of the drug war's second generation were becoming more integrated and sophisticated.

In a way this makes perfect sense. Just as a new generation of gangsters had emerged, so had a new generation of cops. When the Misuse of Drugs Act was passed in 1971, most high-ranking police officers had come of age before the Second World War. Many were ex-military, having served in Malay or Suez. This generation simply didn't understand drugs. But by the 1990s the old guard were retiring, and the officers advancing through the ranks to replace them had all earned their stripes in the 1970s and 1980s. They were just as much products of the drug war as the criminals they were chasing.

And, just as the aristocracy of the criminal world shifted from the armed robbers to the drug lords, an analogous shift took place among the cops. This process was immediately noticed by Peter Bleksley, the officer we interviewed about the Brixton riots, as his own career progressed.

'As I was coming up loads of other detectives were saying, come join the Flying Squad – come chase armed robbers. I was just like, bollocks to that! I could see what was happening. I knew where the growth was coming from.

'I knew what the gangsters were moving into. They were all getting into selling drugs – there's more money in it, and they're not going to get shot by the cops.

'I could see where the government was going to be ploughing money and resources, so I went on the drug squad. Over the next few years, if you were an undercover with the DS at Scotland Yard, you were a rock star. And now the bloody Flying Squad are dealing with kebab-shop robberies.'

* * *

With the coming of age of its second generation, the War on Drugs had fundamentally transformed not just British criminality, but also British policing. From this moment one had to act under the assumption that there was simply no aspect of organised criminality that *was not* underpinned by the drug trade. In terms of sheer profitability you can take every other form of criminal activity, add them together and you'll still be nowhere close.

In university physics classes lecturers will demonstrate how gravity can warp the structure of space-time by placing a heavy steel ball onto a stretched rubber sheet. The steel ball is the War on Drugs. It has fundamentally warped the entire structure of criminal justice in Britain, giving it an entirely new centre of gravity. There is now no organised crime that is not, ultimately, a facet of the War on Drugs. And the point at which this process reached critical velocity was sometime around the moment in May 1995 when Will opened the *Liverpool Echo*, turned to his mates and said, 'That's it lads, we're fucked.'

But, like everything else in the story of the War on Drugs, the mid-1990s revolution in policing had vast, unintended consequences. Will clearly recalls the immediate reaction of his firm – and every other firm in Liverpool – to the events of May 1995.

'What did we do?' he says with a shrug.

'We got armed. We had to, it was the only option. If they're getting armed, we need to get armed. Every firm did – because if one firm tools up, we all have to. We don't want to get shot by either the police or other gangsters. What would you do? From that moment the violence went way up. That's when guns really started to be everywhere.'

This is the arms race dynamic of the War on Drugs, rendered with brutal clarity. The police get smarter, so the only option the gangsters have is to get more violent. The police realise they need to use community intelligence and turn low-level players into informants against their bosses, so the gangsters have to make sure everyone is more scared of them than they are of the police. As ever, it is the most vulnerable who are caught in the crossfire. It is a dystopian negative image of the Peelian Principles that should underlie policing. The insidious effects of that mid-1990s moment are still being played out today.

'The police made a decision to hit all the big firms – and they did start to get some results.' Will continues. 'They were getting rid of the higher echelon – either arresting them, or just disturbing them and shaking them up. They were shaking the tree and seeing what would fall.

'But the real players all had money, so all they did was fuck off out of the country. They went to Spain, Amsterdam, wherever. They were still importing drugs, but were just staying out of the police's way.

'So, really all the police did was to get rid of the people who controlled the drug scene. Like I said, we used "controlled violence" – that was because there were high-up people controlling it. Suddenly that control went.

'You could see some of the effects right away – everyone got tooled up and things got way more violent. But, some aspects take 20 years to develop. Now you've got the 14- and 15-year-old kids riding around on Scrambler bikes shooting each other. And they have no sort of control whatsoever. Kids now don't even fight, they just say, "I'm going to your ma's" – meaning "I'm going to shoot your family." And it's usually over nothing – just front.

'1995 was like a climate change moment. You can trace that forward to 2005, then to 2015, and we're just seeing the effects now – it takes a generation. The cops decided to shake the tree, but they didn't realise that when they shook the tree they were going to disturb the roots.'

* * *

What is going on here? Patrick and Will – two men who have spent their lives in the drug war and are well used to the extreme violence it demands – have both expressed horror at what today's teenagers are capable of. What has changed to make even these hard-men take a step back? What is happening to the third generation of the British drug war?

'I've been carrying a knife since I was 13,' Alex says matter-of-factly.

'I was going to drop off a ten bag of weed, and these other lads robbed me – so I decided I wasn't going to get robbed no more, and started carrying the blade.

'To be honest though, I've only had to stab someone once, when I was grafting crack and heroin out in Stoke. Some crack-head and his bird tried to rob me – so I stabbed him in the arse with a screwdriver and screamed, "You'll be next, you fucking slag" at the woman. That was about a year ago when I was 15.'

Alex has just turned 16. He's slightly chubby, with a mop of messy hair and the gangly awkwardness of most adolescent males. He doesn't come off as particularly threatening, yet Alex has already seen and done things that would terrify and appal most adults.

'I started smoking skunk at nine years old. That's about normal where we're from, it's everywhere really. Weed's the easiest thing to get. That's how the dealers first got to know me when I was a kid.

'Then my mate introduced me and I started selling weed for this 16-year-old lad. He'd give us a quarter to sell on tick, then it went up to an ounce – then I was doing an ounce or two a day. There's no beef over weed really, no one's arsed about a weed graft – it's everywhere anyway. I know loads of people running their own grows.

'The real graft is in heroin and crack. I'd already been kicked out of regular school when I was around 11, just for fighting and smoking weed – so, my mate who knew some olders introduced me, and I started selling crack around my area. But it only got really serious when I went country.'

'Going country' is the practice of big-city drug gangs sending people out to small towns and villages to take over the local drug market. The police refer to this as 'county lines'. It is considered one of the most concerning developments of the contemporary War on Drugs, creating a parallel economy to that of the traditional user-dealer pyramid scheme.

'I've been everywhere, all round the country,' continues Alex. 'I started in Mold in Wales when I was 14. Since then I've been in Queensferry, Devon, Cumbria, Stoke, Middlewich, Crewe, all over – selling crack and heroin. You tend to go to the same places again and again, but a few months apart.

'My boss would have someone take us down there, and I'd do the serving up. I'd go meet the smackheads while they were gouching or rattling. We'd take over a crackhead's flat, pay him three rocks a day – and I sleep on the couch. Honestly, they're usually fucking nasty, disgusting places – fucking plants growing out the wall.

'The head boss was probably around 45 years old, and there were maybe ten people working around him, including my boss who was maybe 22 – he gave me the gear to sell.

'My boss would rent a phone from someone on his level. And that phone would have the numbers for all the addicts in that town saved on it. So, from that we'd just set up right away. On a good week we could do £1,500 a day, so maybe six or seven grand over a week – and out of every £100, I get a tenner. And, by the time the cops even realise you're there, you've already gone on to the next place.

'You also get a bit of cash for food, and free weed while you're grafting. So, we'd just sit there and smoke weed and serve the junkies. It was okay when there was an Xbox to play – otherwise it's a bit fucking boring and the only thing to do is laugh at the crackheads. It was doing county lines in Stoke that I stabbed that crackhead in the arse. I've probably done county lines over a hundred times. There was over a year where I was away basically every week.'

It seems almost a point of pride with Alex, and with many of the other Liverpool grafters we spoke to, that the Scouse firms have a 'business mentality'. While young people in towns like Stoke or Queensferry might be messing about, causing trouble and distracting the police, the Liverpool lads are serious criminals, there to make money – even at 14 years old. But while this may be the rule when they are out in the 'country', the same does not hold true in Liverpool itself, where violence among young people in certain areas is endemic, anarchic and chaotic.

'I could get a gun in an hour,' says Alex with that same banal, matter-of-fact tone.

'At the most it would take an afternoon. It's easy for anyone to get a gun. My old boss would just call his mate who gets them in from Albania and places like that – they even come with the red tip still on, so you know it's not been fired before.

'People my age wouldn't really go for a straightener – they'll just carry a knife or a gun. There's stupid beefs all the time, and people get stabbed or shot over them. It always starts over drug territory – but then it gets to be about any stupid stuff, or just about what postcode you're from. Kids from Toxteth tried to come down and sell in our area, so we had to chase them off – my friend got blasted with a shotgun. He was 14, and the kid who shot him was the same.

'And if they can't do you, they'll go after your family. When I was 15, I was working with this other grafter, and he had a beef with these other lads. It was a graft thing over money and territory. But, because I was with him, it came onto me.

'So, my house got "ran through" – that's what we call it. They smashed the windows and ran in – three at the front, three at the back. I wasn't even at home, but my dad was. They slashed him right across the face with a knife. He almost lost an eye, but he moved his head back just at the last second.

'Of course, I knew who it was – so I called my boss for a gun. But his were all hot, so he said all he had was a grenade. So I took that. I kept the grenade in my room for six months, waiting for my chance. Eventually, though, my boss needed it back, and I was always away, going country anyway. So I gave it back to him and I think he sold it on.

'No one here would ever call the police about something like that. Even when my dad got slashed in the face, it just wasn't an option. I went for the grenade. If you call the police over a grafting thing, then you'd be a grass. No one would ever do that. Not ever. You never call the bizzies on other people grafting.'

Mistrust of the police is nothing new in the sprawling, neglected suburbs of north Liverpool. But 15-year-olds with grenades having their families targeted over minor drug beefs is. This is a different universe from the 'controlled violence' of Patrick and Will's eras. This is a world where 14-year-olds are sent across the country to sell crack and heroin for weeks at a time. This is a world where teenagers ride around on Scrambler motorcycles, smoking skunk and blasting each other with shotguns over petty insults. This is a world where violence is random, brutal and senseless.

But while this new era may be chaotic and incomprehensible, the historical logic behind it is not. There is a very clear reason why this world has taken the shape it has. The War on Drugs has entered its third generation.

'Most kids I know who start grafting either have a dead parent, or a parent in jail,' Alex explains. 'I'd say out of my friends over 80 per cent are single-parent families, and more than a quarter have a parent inside. My boss even had a beef with a father-and-son team who were selling together on our turf. He had to solve that problem.

'All my mates smoke weed, but only one has got into crack – and his dad is a crackhead. He was sniffing coke from about 13 or 14, and around 17 he's got into the crack and heroin. He's just gone now.'

When Patrick talked about his 14-year-old nephew who would 'take your life without a second thought', the first thing he mentioned was that the child's mother was a heroin addict.

Today, a whole generation has grown up with parents either absent, addicted or in prison. The War on Drugs is all this generation has ever known. They have never been socialised outside of the drug war's rules. It has shaped almost every aspect of their lives. Is it any wonder that the violence has become so brutal and chaotic that even the most hardened criminals of previous generations are taken aback?

In fact, the bigger picture of the drug war's third generation is, if anything, even more alarming. The chaotic violence Alex describes is largely prevalent only at his level of the trade. He and his friends sell the product, but they do not import it. At the higher end, the illicit drug market still follows its age-old pattern – it tends towards monopolisation.

What this means is that Alex's little gang might be stabbing and shooting a rival gang from a few streets over. But, ultimately, both gangs will likely be buying their gear from the same importer. This importer will be part of a serious organised crime group, sitting high up the supply chain, far removed from petty street violence.

These high-level gangsters are thriving. The street-level violence keeps the headlines buzzing and the police busy chasing low- and mid-level dealers. The serious Organised Crime Groups (OCGs) sell to all sides, and rake in profits never even dreamed of by previous criminal generations. And, as will be explored in the next chapter, part of what they spend this money on is protecting themselves by corrupting the law enforcement system from within.

The first generation of the drug war was the generation of discovery. Grafters like Patrick had to learn that the old era of cops and robbers was over, and the new era of narco barons had begun. The second generation was the generation of monopolisation. Professional criminals like Will transformed the drug game from a lucrative cottage industry into a mega-business, fundamentally shifting the centre of gravity of British criminal justice – and, indeed, British society.

The third generation is something new entirely. It is a perfect storm, combining the vast profits of a massive multinational industry with the nihilistic brutality of a dystopian novel. The high-level gangsters enjoy their monopoly, while teenagers shoot each other on the streets. When we are finally able to step back and envision the War on Drugs as a process of change over time, this is the picture that emerges.

Perhaps the most chilling part of our conversation with Will was when he told us the story of one young man from his area.

'This lad is 16, and his main graft is robbing drug dealers. Well, the dealers caught him and snatched him up, and all he said was, "Yeah, kill me. Just kill me. Whatever." And he absolutely meant it. For the kids now, death is just another option. It's just there as another thing that might happen, and it doesn't matter.'

* * *

At this point Will, formerly Britain's most wanted criminal fugitive, stops and shakes his head in pity and disgust. 'How have we got to that? Who's accountable for all this? We have to be accountable to a judge for our actions, but who's accountable for the state of this situation now?'

Another crucial point Will insists we take note of is that the effects of the step-change he witnessed in 1995 are only just being played out today. As he puts it, 'it takes a generation'. It took a generation from the Misuse of Drugs Act in 1971 for Will and his crew to build the drug trade into a global empire. It took another generation from the moment in 1995 when Will opened the newspaper to learn about the escalation of police tactics, for the perfect storm of the drug war's third generation to come of age.

Now, picture that 16-year-old saying, 'Yeah, kill me. Just kill me. Whatever.' Picture a generation for whom 'death is just another option'. And now picture what this nihilism might look like 25 years in the future if we follow the same course. Between Patrick, Will and Alex you've seen a vision of the first three generations of the British War on Drugs. Whether or not you see a fourth is up to the moral courage of those who write the nation's laws – and those who vote for them.

9

Corrupting the System

The People Who Don't Exist

Darren A. and Kevin P. don't officially exist. Both are living, breathing people. Both are born-and-bred British citizens. Both still live in the United Kingdom. But neither uses the identity with which they were born.

Both of these men are protected witnesses. They are criminals who made a choice to betray their accomplices, give evidence to the police and go into hiding.

Betraying high-level criminals is a dangerous career move. In return, the police 'vanished' them – taking them across the country and providing new names, new homes, new official documents. Darren A. and Kevin P. disappeared into the witness protection system.

Talking to people who don't officially exist is a curious experience. To sit in a living room and sip tea with people who have spent years living off the books, with the ever-present gnawing fear that their former criminal friends might track them down, is a glimpse into a shadowy aspect of the human experience.

It also gives a crucial insight into a key dynamic of how the War on Drugs has developed – and how it has fundamentally warped British policing. This is an entire realm of how law enforcement works that has never been properly explored.

The range of evidence the police can use to convict a criminal is fairly narrow. Unless a suspect is caught bang to rights, the police essentially have two methods available: forensics and witnesses.

Drug crime is even more complicated. A top-level gangster may never even be in the same room as the drugs he is trading. There is no victim to report the crime, or to interview after. Police or customs can undertake surveillance – but to break the codes, conduct a successful investigation and secure a conviction is incredibly difficult. More often than not, the case will still rely on being able to 'turn' a witness – convincing them to give evidence in order to save themselves prison time.

This system is separate from but related to the use of registered informants – moles within criminal organisations who funnel the police intelligence, but who won't necessarily be the ones actually giving evidence in court. The War on Drugs has transformed how both of these crucial systems work in British criminal justice.

We've seen how the drug war functions as an arms race. How, as the police get smarter and develop new tactics – surveillance, undercover operations, intelligence networks, etc. – the criminals only ever have one response: to get nastier and more violent.

All too often, this arms race comes down to one simple scene: A mid-level drug dealer is caught by the police. He's bang to rights and facing five years inside. The police, however, offer him a deal. If he will become a witness against the higher-level gangsters he buys his gear from, they'll knock three years off his sentence. He'll be sentenced to 24 months, and be out in 12.

It's a tempting offer. And his gangster bosses know it. The only option they have is to make sure that, as he sits in his cell weighing up his options, the dealer fears them more than the time inside. Every single person in the boss's network of suppliers, enforcers, dealers, user-dealers and addicts has to live without any doubt that – should they become an informant or a witness – they will be tortured or killed.

So, the police respond to this threat by offering the suspect protection. 'We'll give you a new identity, in a different part of the country – out of the reach of your former mates.' Their entire investigation now rests completely on that dealer sitting in his cell weighing up the options. What does he fear more – prison, or the gangsters?

Of course, law enforcement relied on evidence from witnesses long before the drug war kicked off. Informants have also long been a part of how the police have gathered intelligence on criminal networks.

But the War on Drugs has changed how these systems operate at their most fundamental level. Like the steel ball on the rubber mat in the physics lecture, the drug war has warped the centre of gravity in the relationship between the police and the informant. It was into this warped system that Darren A. and Kevin P. – the people who don't exist – were drawn.

'When you're selling heroin you have serious control over people,' Darren says with a reflective air. 'It's a very strange feeling. I think I only ever abused that power once – and I regretted it immediately, and tried to make up for it in my own way.

'There was a guy called Rob and his missus, a couple of serious shoplifters who used to buy off me. She'd just turned up at my door after a weekend in the cells. I only had a tiny bit, less than a bag – but she was in a bad way after being in the nick, so she started going off her head and screaming at me.

'I got annoyed – so I took that little bit I had, and very slowly tipped it out on the floor in front of her. That little thing was everything she wanted in the world, and I tipped it out on purpose – just to make her feel like nothing.

'I felt terrible immediately. So, when my new supply come in two hours later, I gave her a free bag to make up for it. Honestly, it's probably not the worst thing a drug dealer has ever done – but it stayed with me. I do have a conscience. Though, heroin does have a real knack of bypassing that.'

Darren is in his mid-forties. He's intelligent, perceptive and funny – cracking jokes about even the most difficult episodes of his life. But there's also something injured about him – a sadness and anger behind the banter and northern stoicism.

'I was a teenager when the man I'd always called Dad turned round in the middle of an argument and shouted, "Well, I'm not your fucking father anyway!" That came as a bit of a shock.

'He was a massive guy and everyone on the estate was shit scared of him. I respect the fact that he brought up three kids that weren't his, but basically he liked to psychologically torture people. He only ever hit my mum once, but he degraded all of us constantly. We'd get the belt as punishment – which I actually think is fair enough – but it was the constant psychological degrading that was hard. I think that's probably what started my mum drinking. By the time we were grown she was a serious alcoholic, with bottles hidden all over the estate.

'Then, when I was 18, the whole early-nineties rave thing basically took over my life. I hate violence, and no one at the raves was looking for a fight. A friend gave me some speed, and that was that really – it was speed and pills for me. All my friends smoked hash, but I never liked it at all. I was working silly hours at a factory, and the raves just blew all that away.

'I got into selling drugs by accident, really. I was buying for myself, but because I knew a dealer all my mates started asking me to get some for them too. So, one day this dealer turns to me and says, you know you've been up and down these stairs about 30 times today – you could've sold an ounce yourself!

'As soon as I started selling, the bigger dealers in Buxton all started offering me their stuff at silly prices, just to get me on their books. But it only really took off when I started selling heroin.

'My mate Howard had family in Ireland who used to come over to steal cars. They'd nick one – and by the time it's reported, it would already be over in Ireland on the ferry. But, then this lot ask Howard if he can get them heroin, because they'll make a killing over there.

'So he came to me and I sorted him two ounces. It was good little deal, and we did it quite a few times. Then the lads over in Ireland get a visit from the IRA, saying if you're going to be selling, we want our cut – or face the consequences. So that was the end of them selling over there.

'So now Howard's stuck with two ounces of smack that he doesn't know what to do with. From there, it basically took us about three weeks to take over the heroin trade in Buxton.

'My thing was that I never used to cut it and I gave people fair wraps. So, of course the smackheads came to me. And I always paid cash up front and never took anything on credit – so the bigger dealers liked me too.

'The whole heroin thing was quite new to Buxton – it hadn't got really violent yet. All the dealers sort of knew each other, and there was enough business to go round. I was buying it at £800 an ounce, and selling in £10 bags – making quite serious money. But, then I got linked in with this guy called Junior in Manchester and things started to get a bit more serious.

'I first actually tried heroin on Boxing Day 1997. We'd had some ketamine and I just thought, "Fuck it, why not?" I was terrified of needles, and my mate told me that as long as you only smoke it two days in a row, then stop for five, you'll be all right. It's funny, the things you tell yourself will work.

'Then one week I start getting these calls from my mate Howard – bugging me for a nine-bar of weed and a load of pills. He was calling me every day, really pushing me for it. So, eventually I went and got it – but when he came over, he suddenly said all he wanted was a half-ounce and a few of the pills.

'That didn't feel right to me, so I watched him through the window as he walked away. Just as he gets to the top of the road, he gives this little wave to this other guy – who immediately starts running towards the house.

'My girlfriend and I immediately panic and throw the gear out the window, but it's too late. The cops bust in, find everything and we're taken off to the station. Howard had completely set me up.

'To be honest, I might have been able to blag it, but what the cops said was that they didn't have my fingerprints on the gear, but they did have my girlfriend's. So I immediately just told them the whole lot was mine. They did me for possession with intent to supply and I was looking at five years. That's when I decided to do my first bit of grassing.

'I made a deal. I gave them a load of info on Junior, my Manchester dealer, and got my sentence knocked down to 21 months. The only problem was, as soon as they nicked Junior, he found out it was me who'd grassed him up.

'I was just a few weeks in at Lincoln Prison, and my padmate suddenly just scarpers as soon as association starts. Then these two massive guys just barge in and kick the absolute fuck out of me.

'I don't know how Junior found out. It could have been either through a solicitor or the police themselves. Either way, I got taken to the hospital wing, and then put onto the protected wing with all the nonces and serial killers.

'Eventually I volunteered for transfer to Stafford Prison – which is the slash-up capital of the British prison system. Usually you only go there if you've been kicked out of Lincoln. I'm probably the only person who's ever actually *asked* to go there.

'There's a prison mindset that you learn inside. Time just means something else. It grinds you down. Why do you think they come up with so much ingenious shit in prison? They're just so fucking bored. That's why it's a training school for criminals. I settled into that prison mindset pretty well though. I reckon that later on, that's what got me through the whole protected witness thing.'

So far, Darren's story is a standard drug war progression. A young man from a troubled home, with few prospects other than working long hours at a factory, realises he can actually make proper money as a dealer. He gets caught, turns grass and takes a kicking inside.

In fact, it's only when he gets out of prison that Darren's story takes its real downwards spiral – a spiral that mirrors the wider developments that were taking place in the War on Drugs across the country.

'When I came out of the nick, the only people I knew were smackheads anyway,' he continues.

'My girlfriend had left me while I was inside. I stayed out of the game for almost a year, but when these are the only people you know, it's not easy.

'Junior came up to Buxton with a few heads looking for me – but he didn't find me. One of my so-called mates drove around with him pointing out where I might be. He got paid a bag for it. That's the thing about smack – it replaces loyalty.

'At this point a guy named Peanut was running the show in Buxton. He wouldn't deal with me because he said I was a grass.

It can be quite scary having that stigma. You're dealing with very unpredictable people in that world – things can go sideways very quickly. I was also using again. I started out with the "two days on, five days off" thing. But of course I got cocky and lost track. No one wins out in the end. It was about this time that I progressed to injecting because smoking was just costing too much.

'My brother was a heroin addict too. I hadn't seen him for years, but I tracked him down and went to stay with him in Sheffield for a bit. While I was there he found my bottle of methadone, swigged it – and died of an overdose. I found him. I think that's when I really took a "fuck everything" attitude to life.

'So, I just kept using and selling – and eventually I was sort of accepted back into the fold with Peanut and everyone. But then Peanut and a few others got nicked. And that's when Kenny came and took over the entire Buxton scene.

'We'd had gangs from Manchester try and take over before, but it had never really stuck. But this was on a totally different level. Kenny was linked in with Arran Coghlan, who had basically taken over all of north Manchester. Everyone had heard the stories about Coghlan. He was called "Az" on the street – and it's not a name you wanted to hear.

'See – originally the Quality Street group had run Manchester, then there was the era of Paul Massey and his type of gangster. Then Chris Little came along and wiped all that generation out. But Chris Little got shot in the face and now Coghlan was in charge. And he sent Kenny up to take over New Mills and Buxton and all the towns up that way.*

'Everything changed when Kenny came in. He was a ruthless fucker and he had serious backup. The first thing he did was

---

* Arran Coghlan has never actually been convicted of drug dealing. He has also been cleared of all three murders of which he has been charged – earning him the nickname, the 'Teflon Don'. However, in 2016, his £450,000 house was seized under the Proceeds of Crime Act.

kick fuck out of a few people just to make a point. One couple were pissing him off, so he got the bloke, held an axe over him – and told him to choose between his hand and his knee. The guy just froze and couldn't say anything. So Kenny took the back of the axe and smashed the guy's hand again and again. His hand was totally disfigured – it never really recovered. That was just Kenny making a point.

'One by one, he took over all the independent dealers in town. Word went out that if anyone went outside to score in Manchester or Sheffield, he'd kick their doors through.

'I got picked up by Kenny like everyone else, and worked for him for about two years – using and dealing. The market was massively expanding and we had people coming from all the surrounding towns to buy. I went from selling 15 bags a day to selling 60 or so. Kenny forced me to cut the gear with Mannitol, which I'd never done before. I always wanted to sell good product, and keep people coming back. He didn't give a fuck – he just wanted more money.

'At the same time, I had so much access to heroin that my own use just exploded. I became the typical emaciated junkie – just selling all the time to keep my own supply going – it was just more and more, more and more, all the time.'

Darren has just laid out a typical story of drug war monopolisation. The police arrested Buxton's independent dealers, which opened the door for the serious Manchester gangsters to move in. The heroin market massively expanded – and violence rocketed. When the big fish eats the little fish, there's always blood in the water.

But the arms race of the War on Drugs never stops. Just as Kenny was violently consolidating his position at the top of the food chain, the police were developing new tactics of their own.

'A couple of undercover cops got into our crowd,' Darren explains.

'I spotted one immediately. He just felt wrong. I warned all my mates too, but they ignored me and I could see him getting into them – and that meant he would inevitably get information on me as well.

'But to be honest, I was too far gone at this point – I just didn't care. I could see everything crumbling around me. There were people dying left and right from overdoses. I actually think that in my head I'd already made my decision. I knew if I got busted again I was going to make a deal. I was so fucked up on gear that there was nothing else I could do.

'So, eventually one night, just after I'd just scored from Kenny, the police bust down my door. It was a big team all in their balaclavas – and I obviously shit myself.

'But, when they cuffed my hands behind my back, I still managed to wriggle into my pocket and slip the SIM card out of my phone. Then, when they transferred the cuffs to the front, I swallowed the SIM while no one was looking. I'd got that line off a mate who'd been busted, and he'd told me there were 19 charges attached to that phone number.

'They got me down the nick and made me wait eight hours, so that just as I was interviewed I was also starting my rattle. I used the solicitor that everyone involved with Kenny did. I knew I was fucked anyway though. As soon as they tell you you've been seen selling drugs to an undercover you know you're done.

'I made the decision to do the witness thing then and there. I knew that if I didn't get out of that scene I was dead – either killed by Kenny, or just through my own drug abuse. I was using eight or nine bags a day – people were dying all around me. It was only a matter of time.

'Even if they put me away for a couple of years, I'd be using inside, and then I'd just be hanging around with the same people when I got out. So, when the police said, "Go into witness protection and we can vanish you" – I just made my mind up.

'Obviously, this wasn't like grassing on Junior. With Kenny it wouldn't be a kicking on the prison wing – if he caught me as a witness I was dead. I'd lost a brother to heroin already. I knew I'd never get a second shot at life in Buxton, Sheffield, Manchester or anywhere round here – I knew every fucker that sold drugs in an 80-mile radius.

'But while it was all getting sorted, I still needed to go on remand – there was no way I was getting bail. The prisons around us were all full, so I eventually got sent to Nottingham – now properly into my rattle and having a rough time.

'So, I get in there, and who's the first fucking person I see? Only fucking Peanut from Buxton. Prisons are supposed to get lists of people who aren't meant to be put together – but the first thing Peanut does is walk up and say, "What's all this I hear about you giving a statement?"

'I immediately freeze. Because how the fuck did he know that? This is all meant to be completely secret, and I'm supposed to be being protected.

'I now know that what had happened was that someone on my team also worked for Kenny – but he was really owned by the people Kenny worked for in Manchester. So, as soon as I agreed to be a witness, he's put a word in someone's ear.

'I just had to blag it. I said I didn't know what he was on about, and I'd been busted like anyone else. Peanut obviously didn't believe me. He'd already had his association that evening – but he told me to meet him the next morning on the exercise yard and he'd sort me out some baccy. I knew immediately he was setting me up to get knifed.

'So, I get back to my cell – and of course I'm going totally scatty. Then the senior officer for the wing wanders in and breezily goes, "I understand we can't keep you and this other prisoner together. I thought I'd come see you first, because you're on the first floor."

'I went absolutely mad. Not only were me and Peanut not meant to be in the same nick, but if Peanut had happened to have been the one on the first floor, this guy would have gone to see him first!

'So, I went off at this guy, and they immediately took me onto E Wing for protection. I did the rest of my rattle in prison, which is serious agony. Then, when I came out, I started the proper witness protection thing.

'The first thing they did when I got down here was to drive me around the area doing PNC checks on all the licence plates to make sure they're not putting me down the street from some drug dealer who might have connections with the lot back home.

'But, after that I was on my own. I was stuck in this new place with no family, no friends. I had to completely start again. I sat in the job centre day after day, cold-calling companies and offering to work for free. Finally someone gave me a go, and I actually did well with it. When I do something, I really do it – whether that's taking gear, or working.

'Living like this is really strange though. For at least the first year any time a car comes by and slows down near you, you're terrified. You're staring, frozen, wondering if you should run, or just act normal.

'Then, after a year or two you settle down, but tiny things can still trigger that response – a story about a drug raid in the local paper or something. I used to monitor the *Buxton Advertiser* online, just to keep track of who was doing what – because every major crime they reported was my mates up to something.

'The way I think about it, it's probably not worth their effort to actively come looking for me. But if someone were to hand me over on a plate – give them my new identity and address – they'd probably take the drive down. Because if I turned up in the paper mutilated or killed, it would get the message out. These guys have a reputation for fear to uphold. They trade in terror, and it fucking works.

'But honestly, the fear isn't the worst bit. I was arrested two days before my mum's birthday. I had to phone her and tell her I wouldn't be able to make it – then I didn't see her for nine years. She knew I was alive, and I spoke to her on the phone, but she couldn't know where I was. Once you make this choice, you're cut off from everything you know – family, friends, everything.

'It's hard for me, but it's also hard for them. I lost my nieces and nephews in a really tragic fire, and I couldn't go back to support my family through that. I can't tell you how difficult that was. There isn't a day that goes by that I don't think about the choice I made.

'On the other hand, I'm alive. And I've been off the gear since I got here. I can still spot a smackhead or a drug dealer a mile off, you never lose that instinct – but I've binned it completely.

'So, you can call me a chickenshit or a grass or whatever – but I'm alive, and I'm clean. Of course I've got regrets. If I had the option to just do the time in prison and still think I'd survive, I would have done it in a second. I can handle prison. But I knew I would be dead – so I did what I had to do to save my own life.

'It's a very strange life, this witness protection thing. I can see how it's become necessary, though. Between the first time I grassed on Junior and the second with Kenny, the whole scene totally changed. It's not enough for the police to offer someone six months off their sentence any more, because now the alternative is a bullet in the head.'

Darren is correct. The growth of witness protection is a direct result of the War on Drugs arms race. As it ramped up in the late 1990s, intelligence-led policing began leading to some high-profile arrests. The gangsters responded by becoming ever-more violent to further intimidate potential witnesses. The police's response, in turn, was to offer witnesses a new life.

Darren is clearly traumatised by having had to completely leave behind his entire life. But this is what the police must now ask of anyone brave enough to give them the evidence they need. These are the sacrifices the drug war demands of those who fight it. Based partly on Darren's evidence, Kenny was convicted and sent down for ten years.

And in Darren's case, the system can at least be said to have worked – in its way. For everything he gave up, Darren, as he says, also got a second chance at life. He would almost certainly not be alive today without the witness protection programme.

But the arms race never stops. The profits generated by the drug trade are so vast that even the system of witness protection itself can be corrupted. So what happens when the system breaks down?

Kevin P.'s life changed with one phone call.

'I picked up the phone and it was Jimmy. He says to me, "Kev, I think we've got a problem – do you know a guy named Michael Derby?" In that second my blood went completely cold. There was no second thoughts or anything, I just knew I had to get out.'

Kevin was right to be terrified. He was a police informant, embedded in a major south London organised crime group. Michael Derby was the codename he used to pass on information. The only people who should have known that name were Kevin himself and his police handler.

Now his underworld boss, Jimmy, was on the phone, asking if he knew who Michael Derby was. Something had gone very, very wrong.

'Jimmy's crew paid someone in the police to find out their informants – it happens a lot,' Kevin explains.

'They find some copper on the force and take him out to the strip clubs and all that. They give him a bit of money and a flash of the lifestyle – and he gives them any information they want. I used to hear them discussing it a lot.

'Jimmy didn't know that I was really Michael Derby, or I'd be dead already. But he'd got inside the cops enough to find out that name – and I know somewhere there will be a link between "Michael Derby" and my own name. That's why I had to disappear into witness protection.

'Jimmy was dangerous. He was a drug dealer – a serious villain. What his lot would do was – if they were going to shoot someone, they'd cover a flat in black and white vinyl sheeting to protect for blood and DNA and all that. Then just roll the guy up in it.

'There were a few times when I would walk into flats to do a pick-up, and that sheeting would be on the walls. I'd shit myself every time – like, is this for me? But every time I just walked out, which meant I knew some other geezer was going to get it.'

Today, Kevin lives in a small, run-down house set in the suburban sprawl outside a large English town. He is a very sick man. He has suffered heart attacks, strokes and numerous other conditions that he blames on the stresses of living as an informant. His erratic criminal lifestyle meant he was unable to properly manage his diabetes, which led to him developing a condition called gastroparesis. He now can't take solid food and has to feed through a tube in his stomach. Throughout our interview this tube occasionally pops out from under his shirt as he slouches on a sofa.

Kevin doesn't have friends. He is sick, lonely and almost penniless. Trapped far away from anyone he has ever known, he is one of the War on Drugs' walking wounded.

The vast majority of people who become police informants are criminals looking to save their own skin. Kevin, however, is highly unusual. He became a criminal specifically to become an informant.

'I hate drug dealers,' he practically spits.

'My sister has been on the gear for years, and I hate them for it. She got into it through her fella, Stevie, who was an armed robber. I always hated him for getting her on to it, but I hung around him and helped his crew out when they were doing the robberies. They would knock over security vans and use the money to buy drugs that they would sell on.

'But then, I went on holiday to Greece, and at the bar of some ferry, I end up having a drink with this bloke named Dave. It turns out Dave is a copper back in England – doing undercover detective stuff. But he's a really good bloke, and we become friends. So, we're chatting away and I start telling him about my brother-in-law Stevie and some of the villains I know. I reckoned Dave thought I was bullshitting, so when I got back to London, I phoned him up and started giving him information about a security van job that the crew were about to do in Balham.

'They stopped that robbery, though Stevie got away. So, after that I start doing more stuff with that crew – just so I can feed more information about it to Dave. Through that I get involved with other villains, and I give Dave information about them too. Dave became my best friend really – and I tried to get more involved with the crime scene in order to give him the information.'

Undercover police are manipulative by definition; it's the essence of the job. But, for this character 'Dave' to meet someone by chance in the bar of a Greek ferry, and within a week have him passing on information about armed robberies, is impressive opportunism even by those Machiavellian standards.

And yet, when Kevin speaks of his detective mate Dave, he does so with real affection. The two did become genuine friends, and Dave cultivated Kevin as an informant for years. But it only began to get really serious when Kevin got involved with Jimmy.

'Jimmy was connected to the Richardsons – but also loads of other people,' Kevin explains. 'He had so much respect – people called him the Don. He brought me in to work at a taxi firm he owned as a front, to explain the money coming in. But that was also a safe place for them to talk. That's how I started meeting all Jimmy's mates.

'It took a long time to gain these people's trust. These were proper professionals, they were very careful about who they spoke to. So, whenever they started talking business, I'd walk away. I did that on purpose – and that showed so much respect that they liked it, and they started trusting me.

'Jimmy's crew were fucking violent. Gummidge was a bloke who was famous for biting people's noses off. I saw people he'd done that to – he was a scary bloody psychopath.

'Then there was Jerry, who was Frankie Fraser's mate. He started taking me under his wing, but his son got jealous – and he was seriously violent, so I had to step back a bit. So, then I put the son up to the police on a car theft thing and he got nicked – and then I could get into his dad's business even more.

'But also, because I don't take drugs, I got a different sort of respect. They knew they could trust me with handling money – if they gave me ten kilos, they'll get ten kilos back. So, they started giving me little jobs – driving something here, picking something up there. It took a long time, but I started to gain their trust.'

Kevin's story is already extremely unusual – getting involved with dangerous gangsters specifically in order to feed information to the police. Yet, though Kevin may have been careful about observing gangster etiquette, his real rise through the criminal ranks was fuelled by something else entirely.

'I've always been into swinging – you know, the sex clubs,' he explains.

'I've never been out with a girl that I didn't get into that. It's a fantastic life. I never get jealous, so it suits me. I've had really good times with it all through my life.

'So, these gangsters find out I'm into this swinging lark, and suddenly they all want to come. Guys like Gummidge – really hard drug dealers – would bring their girls down and have a great time. They'd fuck every bird in the place. And, because I was the one who got them into the clubs, that was sort of my entry into the whole gangster life. My only rule was that I never went with my friends' birds, and my wife never went with my gangster mates.

'From there, I was accepted and we started going down to all the boxing matches – we'd go gambling and down the dogs. We'd hang around the nightclubs with all the actors off *EastEnders*. I did like that life, I have to say – but the real reason I did it was always to give the information to Dave.

'Eventually, I started driving Jimmy around, taking him to his meetings and all that. Then they start getting me to carry money for them – 40 grand, 50 grand – they were making a fortune.

'The drugs were always the main earner. I'd drive stuff all over the country – loads at a time. I'd drop off the cocaine, pick up 50 grand and bring it back down. I was also hiding 30 kilos of speed at a time in my own flat, and looking after all their cannabis growing.

'They were making masses of money, but they only gave me £250 a week as a wage. I was tempted to rob them actually, but I wanted to stay in their circle and keep passing on the information to Dave. That's why I never asked for more – I wanted to keep them sweet. I just got £250, and then another £100 from the police as a "consultancy fee". I became a drug dealer in order to take down the bigger drug dealers. It was my own sort of crusade.

'And I did get some of them properly nicked. One proper geezer we called Uncle John – I got him done for kilos of coke and guns. He got proper time inside for that, and I know he's still out there looking for me. And I got all my sister's dealers nicked too. I used to stand there and watch them get taken away and think, "I done that."

'The thing is, the police would officially tell me I wasn't allowed to do certain things – but then on the side, they'd tell me in secret to go and do it. They all knew I was carrying drugs around – and I wasn't meant to do that. But you try and do my job without being able to drive drugs around. It's a joke.

'I was always encouraged to break the rules – but on the quiet. But, because of that, I never knew if I actually would be protected if anyone found out. These were scary geezers I was dealing with – I saw other people getting beaten up all the time, I knew they'd had people killed.'

The use of informants is supposed to be governed by strict regulations. But, as will become clear, the erosion of ethical standards between the police and informants has been just more collateral damage of the War on Drugs. The grey area that Kevin describes, with the police unofficially encouraging informants to bend the rules, is another dynamic that Neil Woods remembers growing steadily throughout his time on the force. It is almost entirely a function of the drug war arms race – and, for Kevin, the blurring of these lines was just beginning.

'The main thing that got me in with Jimmy was that I spotted another informant. I was getting info from both ends – the gangsters and the police. I picked up from the coppers that there was another informant somewhere in our circle, but I didn't know who it was.

'Then I notice this one geezer from Gravesend who does some of our coke imports for us. We're talking big loads – 100 kilos at a time. I watch this geezer, and eventually work out that he's bringing it in, getting paid for it – then putting it up to the cops, who will follow it and bust it way down the line. So, he still gets his money and it can't be connected back.

'Of course, he only tells the police about the ones he wants to get caught. 99 per cent of them are fine, then every so often he throws the police one to keep them off his back. And from that he gets protection for all his other business. I thought, "You clever cunt." But, I pointed him out to Jimmy, and told him not to work with that geezer.

'There was another bloke called Dave Courtney who was an informant too. Everyone knew he was a grass and wouldn't deal with him, so in the end he fucked off and wrote some book about what a hard gangster he was. But everyone just thought he was a tosser. He was always on about how he knew the Krays – and I'd always say, "Who fucking doesn't know the Krays round here? Who fucking cares about the Krays?" There are people selling drugs now who've killed more people than the Krays by the time they're 25.

'But spotting informants made Jimmy trust me enough that I was actually able to introduce Dave and his partner under cover. We all went down to a caravan on Leysdown-on-Sea, where a lot of the London drug dealers have caravans.

'Dave and Jimmy really got on – they were getting pissed and smoking puff. Dave bought a Porsche Boxster off Jimmy, and then they started doing weed deals, and buying guns off the back of a car lot that the Richardsons owned.

'The only scary thing was when Jimmy and Dave went off somewhere without me. That made me nervous because usually

I was controlling the information – I knew exactly what I'd said and what each one knew. But if I wasn't there, it could get messy.

'But then Dave went and brought in this whole other squad under cover. They came down from up north, and we all ended up at the swingers club. That was mad – the coppers and the gangsters all together, with all these naked birds everywhere.

'There was one inspector we all called Roger Rabbit – because as soon as he got in there he was into this blond bird. It was all legs everywhere. Then as soon as that was done, bang – straight into another one. Most of the cops didn't actually go with the girls, but there was no stopping Roger. And I'm sitting there, looking at these hard gangsters, just thinking, "Fucking hell, if you only knew that was a copper there fucking your wife."'

At this, Kevin gives a raspy laugh and leans back on the sofa with a self-satisfied grin. And it is a funny scene – the cops and the gangsters all bound up in a suburban English orgy. One wonders whether the inspector in question was able to claim those hours as overtime?

Much more serious, though, is the generalised blurring of boundaries in the relationship between informants and their police handlers. This is just one small, absurd example of a corruption that would eventually spread all the way through the police. And this corruption would fundamentally alter the course of Kevin's life.

'When I heard Jimmy that day on the phone say the name "Michael Derby" I just froze up,' he recalls. 'Jimmy should never, ever have known that name. And if he could find that name, he could find me. He was selling lorryloads of cocaine – he could pay as many coppers as he wanted. I put down the phone, called Dave, and he immediately linked me with the witness protection people at the Met.'

* * *

This is what the money generated by the drug trade ultimately does – it corrupts the very systems the police have put in place to combat it. That Jimmy was ever able to penetrate the police deeply enough to discover Kevin's codename should be profoundly worrying, but what happened to him afterwards is just as dispiriting.

'I was passed over to the witness protection team and assigned these two handlers. The first thing they did was steal from me. They had me in this house and were supposed to be buying me food and stuff – but we'd go shopping and half of it would go straight into their car as presents for their wives.

'The whole system was a shambles. I kept being introduced to new people from the police – when the whole point was meant to be that no one knew who I was. I knew that Jimmy had his own guys inside the cops, so I was terrified all the time. I couldn't trust anyone – but I had no choice. It was either that, or stay where I was and get killed.

'We had to give up everything about ourselves – my wife as well. She had to leave behind all her family and friends. She can't even use her maiden name. The hardest part is the hospitals – I have to see all these specialists, but they somehow aren't supposed to know my real identity. I've had to let doctors know who I am so they can get my records – but I know for a fact that Jimmy was going to hospitals up and down the country looking for me. If someone can pay the police, they can get medical records, can't they?

'I thought witness protection was meant to look after you, but they don't. You get a bus ticket, that's about it. They're meant to find you a job, or training, or anything – but none of that ever really happens. I had nothing. I was penniless. I wasn't even getting my £100 from the police every week any more. What was I supposed to do?'

This is a bleak picture. Kevin was unable to trust even his own handlers, knowing that Jimmy's cocaine profits enabled him to corrupt the witness protection system. There isn't even the slight redemption offered by Darren's story of being given a second chance at life.

Kevin couldn't find work, as Darren had. He'd only ever been trained for one type of business. So, broke and abandoned by the force that was meant to be looking after him, Kevin turned to the only way of making money he knew.

'There was this bloke, Martin, who ran a swingers club up in Walthamstow,' he explains.

'I could tell he was a drug dealer right away. He was always that bit flash and lairy. So, I ask him for a half an ounce of speed, just to test him out – and we start talking about swinging a bit, and get to be mates.

'Martin was connected to the King brothers, who were gangsters in south London. He was a violent guy – almost mental. You could be sitting there, and suddenly he'd throw someone against the wall and just start battering them.

'But I got on with him, so he took me down to Dunstable where they mixed all the gear up and did the cutting and the bagging. He owned a brothel down there as well, where they used to store some of the drugs. There were good swingers clubs in Dunstable and St Albans, so we used go down there a lot.

'So, I started working for him bringing in drugs – while I was living in witness protection. We were always driving over to France or Amsterdam to buy gear. We'd bring in 30 kilos of coke at a time – or we'd buy 100,000 pills, then have to sit up all night putting them into wine bottles. Then, once it was back, I'd sit up in this garage in Dunstable and knock it together. We'd cut it with Novocain or benzocaine, sometimes Epsom salts – whatever we could get on the cheap. Then we'd re-press it using a big hydraulic press.

'I actually told the police I was doing this, because I wanted to take Martin down as well. But they couldn't officially put me on the books as an informant, because I was in witness protection.

'We even did robberies on other drug dealers. We drove out to France with this other geezer – and this bloke takes his shotgun, walks straight up to their car and sticks it in the guy's face. We made 300 grand in euros off of that – all while I was officially in witness protection.'

Witness protection is a creation of the War on Drugs. The development of these tactics only became necessary through the grimly inevitable arms race of the drug war. The result is stories like Kevin's – and thousands of others like it across the country.

Kevin has known nothing other than the drug war. His family were drug users – he became a drug dealer. It was almost inevitable that, even in witness protection, he would go back to the only trade he ever knew. The system was not set up to provide other options. Kevin himself looks back on his own choices with real bitterness:

'To be honest, I miss that gangster life. I've literally lived the last years just sitting indoors. I don't go out; I don't see anyone; I don't go to swinging clubs. I just vegetate here. I would honestly be much happier if I was carrying kilos of coke around. At least then I'd be going on holiday.

'And they never even nicked Jimmy. He was always too clever for them. And he knew too much. If they nicked him, he'd tell about all the coppers he was paying.

'They never nicked Martin either. I thought I was informing on him so he would get his comeuppance. Now he's sitting in a 500-grand house with a swimming pool and I'm here. I made him all that money, and I've got nothing. I've had two strokes, I've had heart attacks, I can't eat food – my liver and kidneys are all fucked. The other day the doctor was talking about me losing my feet.

'You know how I feel about the police? I feel raped. I feel raped and dumped. There are things I know about the police and what they got up to that I can't even tell you. They're supposed to help you, but really they just take what they can and leave you to rot.'

As we leave Kevin, the final image we have of him is of a dying man, sitting in an empty house, with the tube he eats through poking out of the bottom of his shirt. But the bleakness and tragedy of Kevin's story is very simply the bleakness and tragedy of the War on Drugs. In his own morally confused way, Kevin has fought the drug war from both sides – and now he is paying the price.

In Darren's story we saw the trauma of how witness protection rips someone from their home, family and everything they know. In Kevin's story – in that one moment when he picked up the phone and heard his gangster boss use his own police codename – we saw the beginnings of how the informant system can be corrupted by drug money.

In the following chapter we will see just how far the corruption of the War on Drugs can go.

10

Endgame

The Crisis at the Heart of British Policing

Frank Matthews does exist. You can follow him on Twitter. He is quoted in newspaper articles and TV documentaries. But, as with Darren A. and Kevin P., 'Frank' is not the name he was born with.

Frank is also a protected witness. However, there is a key difference between him, Darren and Kevin – Frank used to be a cop. He had a highly commended, 25-year police career – working complex investigations and running ultra-high-level informants. Then he became a whistleblower, calling out endemic corruption and racism within the Met.

Frank had to be placed under witness protection out of the fear that his corrupt former colleagues – and the criminal informants with whom they had formed relationships – might carry out reprisal attacks. Through his story it becomes clear just how far the corruption of the War on Drugs has warped British policing.

'Here's the problem,' Frank explains, 'the police start off running the informant – but before long it's the informant that's running the police.

'Take something like Operation Tiberius, right? That investigation just focused on north and north-east London – and it named something like 55 corrupt officers. Now, 30 of those officers were people I worked closely with. Some I was surprised to see named in there, some I definitely was not – and some who should have been named, weren't. Tiberius is a dangerous document because it names informants – some informants that I myself was running. Reading that report, I can see how so many operations were sabotaged.

'But the main thing about Tiberius is the stuff that isn't there – especially the drugs stuff. I know exactly why it was suppressed. No one's ever really reported on it properly – if they did it could bring the whole system crashing down.'

The 'Operation Tiberius' that Frank is talking about is perhaps the most important internal investigation into police corruption in British history. Created in 2002, the report was immediately suppressed by the Metropolitan Police. It wasn't until 2014 that the document was leaked to the press.

We obtained a rare un-redacted copy of Tiberius – 163 pages detailing incident after incident of prolonged, high-level police corruption. The report's explicit conclusion is that corruption within the police is 'endemic', and organised crime is able to infiltrate the Met 'at will'.

These are extraordinary charges, particularly for an internal investigation that might have been expected to give the police an easier ride. Small wonder the document was suppressed.

A full analysis of Operation Tiberius would require a book in itself, but there are two key points to take away. The first is that, while there have always been corrupt coppers, there is only one reason why it has now escalated to the point where organised crime can infiltrate the police 'at will' – the War on Drugs. The second is that if Frank Matthews personally worked with over

half the detectives named in Tiberius, then his story can illumi-
nate a crucial lost narrative of modern policing.

'I joined the police as a cadet in 1975,' Frank begins. 'At that
age I absolutely felt the adrenaline of kicking in doors and
making arrests. But what I quickly learned was that my real
skill as a police officer lay in simply being able to talk to
people.

'My first posting with CID was in Kentish Town, north
London. This was the mid-1980s and the area was properly
rough. Especially bad was one particular block on Kentish Town
Road, where the flats had all been squatted and were full of drug
users. We were constantly in and out of there, chasing dealers,
burglars and all other sorts of criminals.

'What I learned there is that instead of nicking every drug
user for a small bit of gear, it was far more useful to just talk
to them. There was one guy – an ex-Royal Fusilier – a user, but
fairly stable and happy with his life. I used to go down there and
have a cup of tea with him, just to have a chat about what was
going on. So, when there was a murder in that block – I immediately knew who to speak to.

'There was a Scottish guy who worked on the oil rigs, but also
supplied heroin. He used to hide his gear behind an old fireplace
– but one day he takes the marble mantelpiece from it, and beats
someone to death with it over a drug debt.

'Because I had developed this informant inside the block, we
cracked that case very quickly. We knew exactly how he'd done
it, where he'd dumped the body and even what colour rug the
victim was wrapped in. That was just accomplished by talking
to people and treating them like human beings.

'From there, cultivating and working informants really
became my speciality as a detective. I'm not being arrogant, but
I was very successful with it.

'The main thing is to treat the informant fairly. So many coppers treat informants as a one-hit wonder – they do one bust, and they're burnt out. I thought that was crazy. You put so much effort into cultivating an informant, you want to keep them – because as they rise through the criminal hierarchy, their information is going to keep getting better and better. An informant is like a good bottle of wine – they just get better as the years go by.

'From very early on I found that drug people often make the best informants. Drug people are into everything – so you might start off by talking about drugs, but then also pick up information about stolen goods, robberies, guns – anything! Obviously, they'll never give you their current supplier – but if someone upsets them a few months down the road, you never know what you'll pick up.

'In my early days, senior management weren't interested in drugs at all. They came from a different time – the priorities were murder, burglary, robbery, car theft – crimes where you could see the victim. But, as the drugs thing grew and grew, so did the importance of running long-term informants, which meant I did better and better.

'All through the early 1990s it just kept getting bigger, until I was working really serious high-level informants spread all over the world. At my peak I had 18 active registered informants. That's slightly crazy – usually a detective would have no more than a handful at any one time. And these were all quality high-level sources as well.

'It actually became sort of a running joke – I could be halfway up a mountain in Wales and my phone would go off: "There's been a shooting, do any of your guys know anything?" It was 24 hours a day, 365 days a year. I think it's fair to say I became one of the Met's top people in this.'

Frank's description of his early years is essentially a picture of how policing under Peel's Principles should work. People trust the police enough that when a serious crime, like a murder or an assault, occurs, their first instinct is to help the police solve the case. It's the essence of policing by consent.

The drug war poisons this relationship. Frank goes on to describe just how easily the exchange between police and informant can become toxic.

'As I advanced I could also see the problems creeping in – and they were serious. It could start with something as simple as being asked to do a car check. Your informant asks you a simple favour – to check up on a certain car. Now, this guy is giving you masses of intel on drugs, cocaine shipments, guns, whatever – and he may need this information to give you more intel on a certain job. Not only do you want to keep him sweet – but it's actually in your interests to advance his career in the criminal world, because then he'll get you even better intelligence.

'So, what develops is this mutually reinforcing arrangement of interests. The cop wants the informant to rise through the criminal ranks – and on his side, the criminal also wants his handler to rise through the police, so he can offer better protection. So he keeps feeding the cop intelligence – usually on rival criminals – so that the cop gets good busts, and makes a name for himself.

'But then it gets even muddier, because of how the force is structured. Let's say you're a copper with a Regional Crime Squad, working an informant – formally, that informant is the property of the Regional Crime Squad. But then your five years on the RCS finishes, and you move on to the Flying Squad. Of course you hand over the informant to your successor on the crime squad – but it's not like you just stop knowing him. You've developed a relationship over years.

'So now, this informant has suddenly got connections in the Regional Crime Squad *and* the Flying Squad. If he's clever, he can now start playing one off against the other. All it takes is one corrupt detective on a squad to seriously sabotage any number of investigations. So, all you need is a few corrupt cops dotted through the force – all advancing up the ranks – and it can seriously, seriously disrupt what the police are able to do.

'And that's just talking about what the police call "noble cause" corruption – where you break the rules in order to ultimately catch the bad guys. But, in the 1990s when the drugs market exploded, an astronomical amount of money just poured into the criminal world. From there you could see how fast the police corruption spread around you – you could watch it happening right in front of your eyes.

'People at the top of the criminal food chain are incredibly manipulative. They can run rings round most coppers. And, if it's not just basic greed, everyone has vices which can make them vulnerable. These informants are people who can get you anything – officers get sucked into this world of champagne, elite clubs, women, drugs – the whole lifestyle. But, once they've crossed that line, the informant owns them. Now the informant is running the cop, not the cop running the informant.

'There was one informant I tracked – a big player in the drug world who has since been murdered. He was in the system for decades, and had gone through handlers in every section of the force – some of whom had reached senior management level.

'This informant set one of his handlers up with a girl – and got it on film. From then on the cop was working for him. This officer kept climbing through the ranks, overseeing several high-level investigations. But all the time he was passing on information to this informant – including about other police informants.

'Once an officer has been corrupted, he literally becomes a currency in the underworld. The informant who owns him can sell his services. "Oh, you need something checked out? I've got a copper who can do that – for a price."

'But – the real problem is Funny Firm. That's what regular coppers call Professional Standards – the guys who are meant to internally investigate police corruption. Inevitably, corrupt officers will find their way in there – so the guys meant to be investigating corruption are massively corrupted themselves. The whole thing becomes a complete dog's dinner.'

This is the effect that the War on Drugs has on policing. It was the drug war that spurred the growth of intelligence-led policing, leading to a massive expansion in the use of informants. It was also the drug war that sowed corruption into this very process.

The effects are not just seen at street level, but extend right into the higher ranks of the force itself. Frank saw this dynamic play out in his own career. His story is like nothing we have ever heard – offering a window into a hidden crisis that would come to infect the very heart of British policing.

'Corruption can start on a very small scale, but if you follow it, you never know where you'll end up. There was one squad I had to work with frequently, led by a particular detective who was a thorn in my side for years. Everyone secretly knew he was up to his neck in it – but our conflict actually started over a very low-level form of corruption.

'Through my informants, I was putting up jobs to forces across the country. But, with this particular squad, people were messing with the paperwork. They were adding their own informants to the logs and changing the dates around so it looked like their lot were the primary sources of info.

'That meant that when the time came to divvy up the money their informants would get the lion's share. One assumes the coppers would then get a kickback.

'This isn't uncommon – but it was happening so much with this particular squad that I started to get pissed off. Sometimes it was thousands of pounds, sometimes only a few hundred. Funnily enough, the straw that broke the camel's back was actually a stolen £400 Ford Escort that we were watching as part of a much bigger operation.

'I just snapped, and marched into my chief superintendent's office and accused this detective straight out of being corrupt. I could see the chief rolling his eyes – because in the police this is just "not done". But they'd pushed me too far.

'So, he calls in this detective – and his boss, and a few of the higher-ups – and I'm asked to repeat my allegations in front of everyone. Maybe they thought I would back down – but I just fucking went for it. I only actually laid out a tiny bit of what I knew, but it was enough.

'The detective was absolutely fuming – and then, about a week later, another detective comes and tells me that this guy is openly saying that I'm going to be found with a kilo of coke in my car.

'Framing someone up with drugs is common enough with bent coppers – but eventually I decide he's bluffing. If he was going to do it, he would just bloody do it and not bother with the warning. But, what he actually did was to move against me in a much more subtle way. He used the system itself.

'There was another team I worked with on high-level stuff – and this detective instructed a contact there to stop processing my logs. Now, this might seem like some little procedure thing – but it is actually incredibly serious.

'At that point I was working heavily with one particular top-level informant who dealt with international drug cartels all over the world. This guy was unique in that he dealt with the product, but also with cleaning the money. In the drug world it's extremely rare that you'll get access to someone who's into both sides of the game. He was giving me information about the top echelons of the entire drug world – South America, Holland, Spain – everywhere. This was specific intelligence on shipments by the biggest drug dealers in Europe, the very top of the food chain. He really was the crème de la crème.

'Me and this guy were in daily contact – several times a day. And, every time we spoke, I meticulously filled in my logs and got them to the operational contact I had for the relevant operation. But, then this corrupt detective got this one particular operational team to stop processing those logs.

'The first I hear of it is I get a tap on the shoulder one day and called into the chief superintendent's office. He says, "I need to take your mobile phone off you" – then a couple of detectives from Funny Firm turn up.

'I get escorted straight to the commander's office. I'd known this commander all my service, and the first thing he says is, "Listen, I don't believe one word of this, but apparently you've been picked up on various recordings throughout the world talking about serious deliveries of drugs and huge amounts of cash."

'I immediately tell the commander that I've got nothing to hide, and that I was talking to a registered informant. They ask me who the informant is, and I refuse to say – which they immediately accept, because that's completely within my rights. I will never, ever disclose the identity of an informant, because you never know who's listening – even within the police.

'It turned out the Dutch and Spanish police forces, as well as a few from South America, had all been bugging my informant's phone. I'd always assumed he was being monitored – which is also why I was so ultra-meticulous about filling in my logs. But the second those logs stop going in, it starts looking like I'm not a copper, but I'm actually involved in the deals this guy is making.

'Suddenly all these international police forces think I'm some sort of kingpin, importing tons of cocaine and millions of ecstasy tablets. There'd been an entire Funny Firm investigation going on for months.

'But I just stood my ground and told them that they had my phone – all they needed to do was match those records with the recordings and my own paperwork. It very quickly became obvious that the whole thing was a farce. And in the end, the operational link from that team admitted that he'd been specifically told not to process my logs.

'So, then attention turns back onto the corrupt detective – but he passed it off as not wanting to alert customs to particular operations. This actually isn't uncommon. Customs and the police have a massive rivalry. Customs always want to bust shipments at the ports, so they get the glory. The police will often want to let a shipment run through, so they can follow it and see where it goes. So, sometimes logs will "temporarily go missing", so that customs don't get alerted to sensitive operations.

'The detective dressed it up as one of these situations, and everyone had no choice but to accept that. But, several people knew what he was up to – and this incident was the trigger for how we then moved against him.

'We knew most of this detective's corruption was enabled by his long-term relationship with a specific high-level informant named Alun B. Alun had been an informant for years. He'd passed from section to section in the police and had corrupt officers all over the force – and by now some of those officers had risen to serious rank.

'So, my chief superintendent calls me in and asks if I want to be part of a covert operation to neutralise this detective by going after Alun.

'The chief superintendent had come out of Flying Squad – so he picked a guy there he knew we could trust, and we put together a team. This all had to be done completely off the books, because Alun had several other high-up guys in the Flying Squad under his thumb. If anyone else there knew about it, word would almost definitely get back to Alun, and then to the detective.

'So, we begin covertly investigating Alun. The off-the-books Flying Squad team are out in the field, but they come back to me for info from my informants. It was informants informing on other informants, in order to help police investigating other police.

'And, when we eventually busted Alun, we brought in the biggest haul of firearms the Met had ever taken. This was an insane load of guns – every kind you can think of – with the ammunition to go with them. It was all bound for drug gangs up and down the county. The shit absolutely hit the fan when we brought in that arrest.

'But, the interesting thing is, though we definitely hurt the detective who tried to frame me, I don't think Alun himself ever actually saw the inside of a prison cell. I went to my informants, and none of them could even pick up any rumours about him in the prison networks – and usually these guys can find someone in a matter of minutes.

'My theory – and of course I can't prove this – is that Alun himself was taken over as an informant by Funny Firm – to inform on the corrupt cops he knew about. Very soon after our covert operation, our guy from the Flying Squad went to work for Funny Firm. That's very rare, because Funny Firm usually avoid people from the Flying Squad, because they have such a reputation for corruption.

'I reckon our guy brought Alun with him, and they went to Funny Firm as a pair – handler and informant. So, Alun now had access to the cops who know which other cops are corrupt – which is about as valuable as you can get in the criminal world.

'Alun himself then went a bit dark on the criminal networks. He dropped off the radar – which is to be expected from someone involved with Funny Firm. Then, six years later, he resurfaces – and is immediately machine-gunned to death in central London.

'I'll leave you to think about the significance of that. Alun had been informing on other high-level criminals for decades – and had broadly been getting along just fine. But, the moment he starts informing on corrupt cops, he gets gunned down.

'I certainly don't think a cop killed him. But did someone arrange it through their own network of informants and contacts? Was someone being protected? We'll probably never know, but one thing's for sure – once you start informing on corrupt cops, you really are in danger.

'And the really mad part is – the whole story didn't even end there. When that corrupt detective first stopped my logs going through, it wasn't only the Dutch police who picked up on my conversations – it was UK Customs as well.

'Customs actually had me under surveillance for months. I'd obviously learned to spot surveillance, and could shake them off fairly easily, so I didn't pay it too much mind. But then, in order to get to me, they actually went after my own informant and nicked him.

'The second I heard about this I went straight to my boss and told him I needed to do a prison visit. Bear in mind, my day job throughout all this is working murders and major enquiries – and we're up to our necks in complex cases. But, somehow, instead of kicking up a fuss, my boss just says all right, off you go then.

'That made me suspicious right away. Usually if you try and get a couple of days off from a murder enquiry, the higher-ups will give you hell for it.

'Then, when I get to the prison, instead of being mucked about by customs as usual, I'm whisked straight into this specially arranged interview suite. By now I'm pretty certain something is going on. And sure enough, the first thing my informant says when we're left alone is that customs have asked him to record me – and if he can get me to incriminate myself, he'll get time off.

'Obviously, he doesn't trust customs because he knows they're probably as bent as the police. He also knows his own solicitors are probably reporting back to his OCG. But he and I have known each other a long time – he knows I play straight. I suppose he thought I was his best chance.

'I just said, "Look, if you want to record me, go right ahead. I've got nothing to hide. So, on you go."

'Of course, customs didn't have any sort of case. They were just having a go – trying to get my own informant to inform on me. So, they just hold him for a few weeks – and then release him, and have to return the 250 grand he'd been nicked with, with 6 per cent interest.

'So, for all that effort, for all those hours of work, what had we achieved? Nothing. The whole time that we're busy investigating each other, the drugs are still pouring into the country, and the money is still flowing out.

'All that's happened is my informant has become a bit compromised, so he has to move more to the drugs side of things and leave the money-laundering. So, we lose a bit of useful future intelligence.

'In the end, that detective was actually busted for corruption. It was part of the famous Ghost Squad investigation years later.[83] But, despite all the money and access that squad had, they investigated him so badly that the charges wouldn't stick. They eventually put him on suspension and just left him there until he went over retirement age. It was a way of keeping him quiet, because if he'd started talking about everything he knew, the entire Met might have been in trouble.'

If Frank's story seems intricate, mind-bending and profoundly disturbing, that's because it is. It is also a snapshot image of what the War on Drugs has done to high-level policing in Britain.

It is the drug war that has elevated the use of informants to such an essential element of policing practice. It is the drug war that has flooded the underworld with money. This has created opportunities for corruption on a scale never before seen in Britain. Perhaps the key phrase in what Frank has told us so far was when he spoke of 'informants informing on other informants to help police investigating other police'.

This is not policing as Robert Peel envisioned it. It is law enforcement forced to stray from its original moral purpose.

'In my entire career in the police I was always focused on catching the top dog – the big-time gangsters who really profit from crime,' Frank continues. 'But, eventually, I was forced into the realisation that this was simply not going to happen. The corruption of the informant system was just too widespread.

'In the old days, informants were an incredibly useful tool. The drug money has changed all that – to the point where a lot of criminals are now becoming informants specifically in order to manipulate the police. Having a corrupt officer in their pocket has become just another tool for any serious gangster.

'Eventually, it got to the stage with me where so many of the top echelons of any OCG were all registered informants, that it became impossible to properly investigate anyone – because they all have their own high-level cops protecting them. Becoming an informant is now just an insurance policy for gangsters.

'So, for any real detective trying to investigate organised crime, you don't know which criminal is under the protection of which of your bosses. Suddenly your investigation is getting sabotaged from above, because you're poking your nose into areas that might threaten someone else's informant.

'This means you can't actually solve cases – and if you push too hard it will harm your own career advancement. So any talented, ambitious detective looking at the drug trade is now hobbled from the start.

'If there are corrupt officers above you – and by now you have to assume there are – you don't know what they are hearing about you from their own informants. This is where it gets dangerous.

'You might find it's not just your work being sabotaged – you might find yourself under investigation. Because of the way information flows, one corrupt officer high enough up the chain can manipulate the whole system in very serious ways. They can turn it round on you.

'And one person can never put it all together. You only ever have one piece of the puzzle. But, unless everyone sits round the table and shows all their pieces, the picture never comes together. But – no one round that table trusts each other, because the others might be corrupt as well. So the full picture never forms, and the corruption just grows.

'So I realise I'm never going to catch the really top guys, because they're all protected. I also realise that I was never going to get into the likes of the Flying Squad or the National Crime Squad, because the brass considered me a troublemaker and I wouldn't play the game.

'But then a job came up at SO10 – the people who do witness protection. I'd already done a bit of that on an area level, and I thought this might be a bit of a break – a chance to get away from the 24-hour, 365-day life I was living.

'SO10 was massively expanding at that point several people joined at the same time as I did. Witness protection was seen as a growing part of policing. Because of all the drugs stuff and informants getting targeted – more witnesses needed protecting!

'But, if I thought SO10 was going to be any better than what I'd experienced before, I couldn't have been more wrong.

'The first partner I was assigned at SO10 was obviously corrupt. He was ex-Flying Squad and I knew from the off I couldn't trust him. By now I had learned to spot the signs, but I'd also learned not to dig too deep too quickly.

'I made it very clear that we weren't going to work together, which perhaps got people's backs up. So, they did what in their minds they must have thought was a punishment – they partnered me with the one Asian guy on the squad.

'I come into work one day and all my files have been moved off my desk. So I'm like, "Yeah, funny fuckers – where's all my stuff?" And the response was, "Oh, you're partnered with the Paki now."

'My instinct was to tell these idiots to fuck off right there. But I never knew when these might be the people I had to count on to keep me alive. So I bit my tongue and got on as best I could.

'In fact – in over 20 years on the force, this new partner I'd been assigned was one of the most conscientious, intelligent and committed detectives I ever worked with. But he was Muslim and non-drinking – and simply the wrong colour for some of the idiots on the squad.

'They'd call food he ate "smelly shit" to his face. They'd talk loudly about holidays in Goa, where they'd click their fingers and all the Indian boys would come running. It was constant – and it was disgusting. But he had been dealing with this nonsense his whole service, so he always stayed absolutely professional.

'We were both ostracised – him because of his race, and me because I wouldn't go along with the constant corruption of the unit.

'There was a safe in the office where we kept the cash we used for all our operations. Our covert identities all had fake credit cards, but that leaves a trail – so wherever possible, we tried to do things in cash.

'This team used that safe as their personal piggy bank. They'd grab wodges of cash to go on the piss. And I don't mean down the pub – I mean gangster lifestyle on the piss, champagne, elite bars – all the rest of it. I never personally saw cocaine use, but I wouldn't doubt it for a second.

'And they were complete blabbermouths. They'd introduce supposedly secret witnesses to other departments as a favour to higher-ups. At the end of their five years at SO10, they want to get onto the Regional Crime Squad – so a favour here and there is their ticket to their next posting. I was tapped up by other people, looking for me to locate protected witnesses for them. They acted as if that was just "how things were done". But obviously, that completely undermines the entire system – all it takes is for the wrong bit of information to pass through the wrong set of hands, and your witness can get killed.

'Now, if the system is working properly I should have been able to go to somebody and say that people were attempting to compromise the unit. But, of course the people I'd be complaining to would be in on it as well. So then I'd be at risk.

'But, despite all the hassle, my partner and I quickly became one of the more successful teams in the unit – which made the others resent us even more.

'It gradually moved from snide comments to actively sabotaging our work. We'd request certain bits of kit and they'd make problems for us requisitioning it – all sorts of minor things to undermine us. Today they'd call this stuff workplace bullying – but it actually became dangerous, because this is stuff we really did need to do the job safely. What really worried me, though, was how the whole system itself was being corrupted.

'For instance, I was in charge of looking after a particular drug dealer-turned-witness, and needed to go and see him to drop off some money. I always parked well away from any safe house, and I always got there early, just to check everything looked okay before going in. So, that night I'm sitting there, observing – then the door opens. A group of people from the ops team walks out the door.

'Now, that team shouldn't have been there. They shouldn't have even known where the safe house was. No one outside our unit should have known of its existence.

'They don't see me – and they get in their car and drive off. So, now I'm in two minds whether to even go in or not, but I had to give this witness this money and he'd have gone ballistic if I didn't.

'So I knock on the door, and he obviously thinks it's the ops team who've forgotten something, because he swings open the door with a big smile. The second he sees me he goes white. He immediately gets really defensive and doesn't want to let me in.

'But eventually I get past him – and there, sitting on the table, is a professional-grade set of scales and all this other paraphernalia. He was selling coke out of a police safe house – with the full knowledge of the police ops team. The funniest thing was, he actually tried to pass it off by saying his missus had been doing some baking. It was embarrassing actually – like a teenager trying to lie to his parents.

'Another time was much more serious. I was leading a case connected to a major south London gangster named Kenneth Noye, who was involved in everything from the Brink's-Mat robbery on down. This was a seriously high-level witness – we'd actually taken him out of prison to a rented place, under constant armed guard by SO19.

'So, my partner and I come out of that safe house one day. We walk back to our car, and have to circle back past the house on our way home. As we're coming up the street, we see another car creeping along outside, obviously giving the safe house the once-over. We pass this car slowly, and clearly see a guy off our ops team – along with a bunch of other guys we don't even know.

'My partner and I both look at each other like, "Did you see who the fuck that was?" It was clear as day. And again, no one should have even known about that place. It wasn't even one of ours – we'd rented a place, to keep it even further off the books.

'But then a guy turns up at that safe house with a gun. He literally turns up and knocks on the door holding a shooter. Inside are all these SO19 guards, armed to the teeth – but their orders are not to engage unless the house itself is breached.

'There was a safe zone created in the back of this flat, so the procedure is to get the witness in there – and only start shooting if someone actually gets in. But they never go out and confront anyone. With SO19 it's "No matter what you see, no matter what happens outside – you do not open that door."

'So, they don't open up and the guy eventually buggers off. But, now the safe house is obviously compromised – and the witness is terrified. He now knows that the OCG can find him – that they've penetrated the police enough that they can even track him down to a supposed safe house.

'We then have to move the guy in a panic. The only safe place we could find to put him was actually an army barracks outside of London. But even then, the OCG tracked down his family – just to send an extra message.

'This guy's brother and mother weren't involved in any sort of crime, but they were in danger as well, so we'd helped them sell their house and get set up with new identities on the other side of the country. Then they got a visit. It wasn't violent – a guy just called round to have a word with them, concerned that this witness would "do the right thing".

'That's all it takes. In this country it's easier for people to undermine the witness, rather than shoot them. They just demonstrate that they can't be protected – that no matter what, they can be tracked down. All it takes is having someone from their old life give them a wave from across the street. The witness now knows the police can't really hide him, because they've been corrupted.[84]

'Even after all that drama with the gun, though, when we were meant to go up and take care of this family, our boss suddenly insisted that my partner go alone. This is completely against procedure – never mind that it was an 800-mile round trip on a demanding case involving witnesses who had already come under threat.

'We argued back, and eventually he was allowed to take along a civilian clerk. Again, this is against all the rules, as this clerk should never have known where this family was being kept. It was just sheer bullying.

'But the final straw came when a witness got shot in Brixton.

'It was an organised drugs hit – and word immediately went out all over the area. We had 19 other witnesses, all of whom needed to be checked on immediately. But, when I call for backup, I get told that it's December, everyone else is out on the piss and we have to handle it on our own.

'This meant going into some of the worst estates in south London with no support, when we know there is a shooter actively targeting witnesses. The witnesses themselves are hostile because they don't trust the police – and we're often visiting them in crack houses and brothels where they're up to their necks in stuff they shouldn't be.

'Each one has their own complex set of needs and demands. This means repeated visits, hour after hour. It took days – with no support at all. It was obvious we were being deliberately frozen out by our own team.

'For me this was just too much. I'd had enough, and went off sick for a while. Then, when I'd recharged my batteries a bit, that's when my partner and I decided to take the fight back to the Met.

'The first thing we did was to go to our DCI and run him through the basics of the problems we had experienced. He rolled his eyes and immediately said, "You do know what you're doing, right?"

'We knew it was risky – but this had gone too far. It was now jeopardising important cases. The DCI convened an office meeting, which only made us more alienated from the rest of the unit. So, then he says the best thing is for us to work from home – indefinitely.

'I reckon he would have been happy for us to stay at home twiddling our thumbs and just keep getting paid until we reached retirement. That's a classic police strategy – move problems off to the side until they go away quietly.

'But that's not what either of us had put in our service for. We had jumped through all the hoops and nothing had worked. So, we decided to take out a race relations claim, which set us on a rollercoaster that lasted two and a half years.

'First off, we were assessed by an outside force for our own safety. Obviously we couldn't use the Met – because the Met were the ones we needed protection from. A superintendent from Hertfordshire went over the details, and immediately said, "Right, you both need to go into top-level witness protection right now."

'We were a threat to the whole corrupt system – a system that protected these guys and earned them money. These were people with their own network of high-level informants – people who knew contract killers. I scared a lot of people in the police because of my own experience with informants. I held a big piece of the puzzle. I may not have been able to do much with it on my own – but what happens down the road if I get together with someone else who holds another piece?

'Our claim was based on race relations, but there was enough corruption stuff in our statements to seriously worry people. We did that on purpose, to show we meant business. So, from working in witness protection, we were forced to go into witness protection ourselves for fear of reprisals from other cops.

'Our witness protection people wanted to completely relocate us to the other side of the country. But of course we knew the system was so bent that they'd find us anywhere. So, we chose to have our own homes reinforced instead. I had steel doors, bomb-proof windows, a panic room and buttons to call a 24-hour armed response if we were attacked.

'That's how we lived for two and a half years. Eventually, our case was taken on by Imran Khan and Michael Mansfield, the lawyers who represented the family of Stephen Lawrence. That just raised the temperature even more, because that case was still very fresh in people's minds.

'We also got assigned two extremely high-up detectives from Special Branch. They said they were there for our welfare, but of course we suspected that they were there to monitor us – to see if they could dig up any dirt to sabotage our case before it had even begun. That's how these things are done.

'Our houses were both rigged with surveillance equipment – supposedly for our own protection, but we had to assume they were also using it as a monitoring system. That's not uncommon when dealing with a protected witness – I've done it myself. We also knew we were under surveillance because we had a mole on the inside. It was all over the grapevine that they were gunning for us.

'So, after two decades on the force – having stayed absolutely straight – I'm forced to live in constant worry about how corrupt people higher up might manipulate the system against me. And this wasn't paranoia – we caught them in the act.

'We knew we couldn't talk openly on the phone, because we'd had Special Branch in there doing the wiring. So we arranged to meet and go over some papers in Walthamstow market.

'Within minutes we realise we're under surveillance. We've done this day-in day-out for years – we know the techniques, we've been trained to spot them. It really does become habit – you go down the shops on a Saturday afternoon and you don't even realise you're doing it.

'We both made the guy at the same time. I looked at my partner, he looked at me – and we both automatically went into counter-surveillance mode.

'You walk one way, then another – then double back on yourself. You duck in and out of shops. If the guy had been a bit cuter, he should have dropped off and let someone else take over – but he stuck right with us all over the market.

'So, we both go up to a cash machine and make sure he follows. Then, the second I take the cash I spin round before he can do anything and loudly ask, "Have you got the time?"

'He just goes, "What?"

'"The time! Have you got the time?" I get deliberately confrontational, just to see his reaction. But he was frozen like a rabbit in headlights.

'So I just snap. "Look, all coppers know the time. If you want to know the time – you ask a copper."

'Now, you say that to any tough-looking geezer on Walthamstow market, and they'll either smack you or think you're a nutter and walk away. But this guy just stands there, looking like a kid who's been caught stealing from a sweetshop.

'So, I turn to my partner and say as loud as I can, "Right, we've got one." And off we walk, as fast as possible.

'We were both annoyed – but we still have this paperwork to go over, so we decide to head down a few stops on the tube to Finsbury Park. At least there we'd be in a wide-open space, so it would be hard for anyone to follow us around.

'We get to the park and sit up on the ridge of this little hill, and almost immediately we see this guy who just doesn't fit. Once you know what to look for, it really stands out. This guy isn't even trying – he's walking alone, but openly speaking. So, he's either on a radio, or having an intense conversation with himself. They'd obviously followed us all the way down from Walthamstow.

'So we figure we'll take a walk ourselves – we'll go find their backup team and get some vehicle registrations to report. We go through this little clearing – and bang – we stumble on a full surveillance team all parked up – motorbikes, cars, the works. They had a bloody van with a guy on a mountain bike in the back, all kitted up. This was top-level stuff.

'I go marching over to take down a registration number, but as I'm scribbling, a bloke sprints up and throws his jacket over it. So they obviously know we're on to them.

'So, we end up in this awkward stand-off, just eyeing each other. But then I start to get worried, because this is beginning to feel like some sort of set-up. So my partner and I start heading back towards the tube station.

'But, just as we're getting to the exit of the park, a police car screeches up – blue lights and sirens on. It stops right in front of us and out jump a couple of cops who say, "We need to search you."

'They didn't say who they were, or give any grounds for the search – which is really basic procedure. So I ask, 'Well, why do you need to search us?"

'"We'll tell you about that later."'

'"No, you'll tell us about it now."'

'Then a couple of the Special Branch lot sidle up behind us – so I immediately say to the PCs, "Keep those people away from us!"

'And to their credit, the PCs did put themselves between us. This felt too much like a classic situation where someone gets drugs planted on them. I'd been around enough to know how it's done.

'So the PCs and Special Branch go off in a little huddle – and then the PC comes back and says they've been informed we are in possession of drugs. One of them lunges for my pocket and pulls out my warrant card.

'The second she opens it, she turns absolutely white. Suddenly she realises she's wandered into something much bigger that she doesn't understand.

'Of course, she then lets us go – and we head straight over to Holloway police station to make a formal complaint. And funnily enough, the Special Branch lot walk straight in after us, having obviously gone there to fill in their notes.

'Now, the following day all I want to do is get out of London. I don't feel safe in my flat. I don't know what kind of surveillance they have in there. How did they know I was going to Walthamstow market? Were they following me? Were they monitoring my communications? I've seen how far these people can go when they feel threatened.

'So, I decide to go to Wales – just to get out of the Met's orbit. I get in my car and start driving towards Tottenham Hale. I'm just coming up towards Ferry Lane, and I notice a car behind me. There's something about this that catches my eye. I think it was that the two guys inside were talking, but not looking at each other. Again, after years of running surveillance you get a sixth sense.

'On the other hand, I know I'm still on edge. I don't want to be paranoid – so I do some little manoeuvres, just to see what they'll do. They're still right behind me.

'Now I'm beginning to really not like this. Are they really that mad to put more surveillance on me? And if so – what else are they mad enough to do? Is there already a kilo of coke in the back of my car? I didn't check it before I left, and they've had all night to do whatever they want.

'So I come to a red light – and I see they're stuck a few cars behind me. All these thoughts are spinning through my head, and I just think "Fuck it."

'I shoot straight through the red light and down onto Ferry Lane. But, then I spin round, go on the outside lane – and drive the wrong way, going against the traffic. I weave in and out, going from lane to lane, as you would on an urgent distress call.

'Eventually I decide I must have lost them, so I slowly rejoin the traffic and start creeping forward again. In my head I'm still wondering if I'm getting paranoid and not thinking straight. Then – what do I see in my rear-view mirror? An all-black, high-powered Kawasaki motorbike speeding straight towards me.

'I freeze – a million thoughts going through my head in a split second. This is exactly how professional hits are done. If there had been two riders on that bike, I would have bolted from the car then and there.

'But there's only one rider, so I figure it must be 42 – which is the code we use for surveillance bikes. So I let the guy pull past me, and immediately scribble down his registration. He very obviously sees me writing it down, and immediately peels off.

'I immediately shoot straight onto Lordship Lane, screech over, jump out and tear the whole car apart. I was still watching out for surveillance, I was sure they could see me – but I just didn't care. They really had me scared now – I didn't know what they were capable of.

'I went straight to our lawyers with the motorbike's registration. They put in an information request to Funny Firm, who came back that no such registration existed, and "I must be mistaken" – of course with the heavy implication that I'm making the whole thing up.

'But, our lawyers made other enquiries, and they come back right away that the registration matches a black Kawasaki, exactly as I described – and that the bike is only registered to a P.O. box in north London. This is exactly how vehicles used for covert policing are organised. Funnily enough, not long after that, the Met offered to settle our claim.

'I don't think anyone truly understands how far this sort of corruption has gone in the police. I saw how it grew over my own career.

'In the old days, when the armed robbers were in charge, the corruption would be a tip-off here and there – getting someone to look the other way. It was a wink and a nod down the local boozer. It was old-fashioned noble-cause corruption – you tell me about the next robbery, and we'll nick them and give you a bit of leeway. But, at least the public get something back from that – even if there's a few hundred quid or a good time with a girl for the copper.

'But drugs changed everything. It turned the whole game upside down. Even from the early 1990s, I could see this massive change with my own eyes. The money was suddenly astronomical. Suddenly it's not your local copper getting corrupted – it's senior management.

'There's just no way to control that. If they admit that there are 250 corrupt officers at the Met and try to take them out, each one of them knows five more, and suddenly the whole force is finished.

'The world of the protected witnesses is definitely overdue scrutiny. That grew in the 1990s with the drugs thing – as a protection against the violence.

'You look at what the National Crime Agency do now – they take out the odd shipload. It looks great for the headlines; there's some good pictures in it. But those jobs are easy. You can catch a couple of muppets coming over with a few tons of coke all day long – but all you've done is catch a couple of muppets. You haven't learned anything about how the market actually works.

'And it's such a tiny, tiny drop in an ocean that's basically limitless. The gangsters just say, "Let them have the headline, if it keeps them off our back."

'For those guys it's a 1 per cent business loss.

'The whole current method is a scam. It's a sham. It doesn't really deal with the problem. And, at some point – someday – someone is going to be forced to finally just be honest with the public.'

Frank's story offers a disturbing vision of a crisis eating away at the bedrock of British criminal justice – but it is also a warning. If left unchecked, this rot will spread right into the roots of the system. And once the roots are infected, any new scandal might send the entire underlying integrity of British policing into existential crisis.

Looking at how fiercely Operation Tiberius was suppressed – a report that only dealt with two sections of a single police force – it becomes clear that the top brass are terrified of the scale of this problem being fully revealed.

How did it get to the point of cops using their network of criminal informants to undermine and threaten other cops? How did it get to the point where an officer seeing a black motorbike in his rear-view mirror would automatically assume that his corrupt colleagues had organised a hit? How is that even thinkable?

The answer is that this is a product of the War on Drugs. During the 1990s, the entire structure of criminality, and criminal justice, underwent a profound transformation. It happened between the headlines, so subtly that no one even noticed what was taking place.

There have always been corrupt coppers. But one doesn't respond to the threat of nuclear weapons by shrugging that there have always been wars. Sometimes a technology arises that changes the fundamental nature of an existing phenomenon. This is what the money generated by the illicit drug trade has done – not just to crime, but also to policing itself.

A comprehensive look into how the drug war has reshaped police corruption would take several books on its own. This is a vast, complex and shadowy story – and one that is actively suppressed by the authorities. But, it is worth taking a glance back at a few of the themes we have covered, to get just a glimpse of how far this corruption has spread.

In the chapter 'Generations', we discussed the idea of 'zero tolerance' policing – and the unpredictable effects of its introduction into Britain. Zero tolerance was pioneered in the UK by Middlesbrough Police – and in particular by the charismatic detective superintendent, Ray Mallon.

Mallon pumped iron at the gym, wore sharp suits and actively cultivated his tough-guy image, earning the nickname Robocop. He flew to New York to appear in fawning documentaries with the original champion of zero tolerance in the US, New York City Police Commissioner William Bratton.

Though its ultimate effects were simply to ramp up the War on Drugs arms race, zero tolerance did have some initial successes. Ray Mallon was a rising star, celebrated by the then Home Secretary Jack Straw and doing photo ops with Tony Blair.

Then it all came crashing down. In February 2001, after two extensive internal investigations, Mallon pleaded guilty to 14 counts of misconduct, 12 of which were serious enough to result in immediate dismissal.

This was classic drugs corruption. Detectives under Mallon's command had been protecting a notorious Middlesbrough dealer. They would tip him off about raids, ruining long and complex investigations. And the protection this dealer bought didn't end there. This dealer's ex-girlfriend turned up sobbing at the police station, accusing him of beating and raping her. She also claimed she had seen Middlesbrough detectives supply him with police-issue CS gas canisters to use against rival dealers, and arrange to have addicts who owed him money arrested. Mallon sabotaged the case to protect his own corrupt officers – and the dealer never even saw a cell for this abuse.

Middlesbrough detectives were found to be using cocaine themselves, and supplying suspects with drugs in order to elicit confessions – drugs supplied by that very same local dealer. When this corruption became the subject of an internal investigation, Mallon used his own position higher up the chain of command to subvert the probe.

In his own confession, Mallon admitted that he 'lied, deliberately withheld evidence from senior officers and turned a blind eye to detectives who took and dealt hard drugs, and supplied them to vulnerable suspects in custody.'[85]

This was the corrupt manipulating the system to protect the corrupt. This is what the War on Drugs eventually does, even to its most militant warriors.

In 'Generations' we also looked at the Liverpool drug scene, and its pride of place at the top end of British criminality. When speaking to Patrick, we touched briefly on the career of his childhood friend, Curtis Warren – the most successful British criminal ever caught.

Central to the case that finally brought Warren down was the involvement of Detective Chief Inspector Elmore Davies. Another charismatic, larger-than-life character, Davies had been deputy head of Merseyside Police's Drugs Squad before ascending to DCI. But, when he was passed over for further promotion, Davies began marketing his skills and access to information to the other side.

He passed Warren lists of witnesses, and confidential information used to disrupt major cases. He used police intelligence to warn Warren about moves other drug barons were making against him, and to tip him off that his phone was being tapped in prison in Holland. He regularly registered criminal contacts as informants, as an excuse for them to meet.

The operation that eventually brought Davies down involved 13 detectives. A covert video camera was hidden in the smoke detector of his office. That a major British police force should bug its own offices is almost unprecedented.

Davies was eventually arrested, imprisoned for five years and stripped of his pension. Curtis Warren himself is serving a sentence in Holland. When he is released he may well have to face fresh charges in Britain over his role in Davies's corruption. However, there are strong voices behind the scenes warning that sleeping dogs should be let lie – that if Warren started telling all he knew about corruption in both the police and customs, it could spark a genuine crisis of confidence in law enforcement.[86]

Perhaps even more curious is the case of Curtis Warren's friend, and sometime rival Liverpool drug dealer, John Haase.

What Warren was to cocaine, Haase was to heroin – bringing in tons at a time through his connections with various Turkish gangs. In 1992 Haase was arrested and sentenced to 12 years.

He then approached the authorities and offered to name the locations of various firearms caches, in exchange for a full pardon. A deal was struck and the Home Secretary Michael Howard himself granted the pardon.

Many of the weapons caches were duly found, containing everything from AK-47 and M16 assault rifles to Semtex explosives. The only problem was that Haase himself had organised those weapons to be placed there to be found. Sitting in his prison cell, he had perpetrated a major perversion of justice, which eventually involved police forces all over the country. Such is the power and reach that only drugs money can provide.

In the chapter 'Riots', we saw how closely drug policing was entwined with race relations in the run-up to the Brixton riots – pointing out the massive blind spot in the Scarman Report

The next seismic moment in the discussion around race and British policing came with the Macpherson Report following the racist murder of Stephen Lawrence in 1993. The Macpherson Report was the first time a major British police force had been officially called 'institutionally racist'. It shook Britain to its core.

A thorough examination of the Lawrence case and its aftermath could also fill several books. The Macpherson Report is a crucial document – but once again, there is a blind spot. What wasn't revealed at the time, and only came to light years later, was that Clifford Norris, the father of one of the defendants, David Norris, was a successful mid-level drug dealer – and a police informant.

Norris had his hooks in several police officers, including DS John Davidson – who was central to sabotaging the Lawrence investigation. Neil Putnam, the police supergrass who exposed the corruption, explicitly stated that Davidson admitted shielding David Norris on behalf of his father.[87]

While this case was raging, Frank Matthews was still a high-level detective with the Met. He personally knew many of the names involved and can offer an inside look at how the Lawrence investigation went so badly wrong.

'Again, this was an issue of the treatment of witnesses,' insists Frank.

'The main witness for the case was Duwayne Brooks, Stephen's friend who was with him when he was murdered.

'Duwayne requested witness protection, but was refused – which in a case this sensitive is insane in itself. I personally remember walking down the corridor on the fifth floor of Scotland Yard – the most important 1,000 square metres in all of British policing. Just ahead of me were two officers who were heavily involved in Duwayne's case. One of them put on this mocking accent and went, "Duwayne ... Doo-Wayne ... only a nigger would have a name like Doo-Wayne." They both laughed out loud, but it was bloody disgusting.

'And the drug corruption element is even worse. There was a particular detective constable who was actually in charge of Duwayne's safety. Years before, this detective had been sacked from the force – not disciplined, actually sacked. He'd then been reinstated by a commander who was also later alleged to be neck-deep in corruption, though none of the charges could make it stick. And why had he been sacked in the first place? Because he'd been seen receiving envelopes of cash from none other than Clifford Norris.

'This was the guy the Met put in charge of taking care of the main witness in this crucial case. It beggars belief. But, under-mining a key witness to protect a corrupt informant – that's what these people do. It has drugs corruption written all over it.'

Stephen Lawrence is a name that still reverberates all over Britain. The failures of his case rightly provoke almost universal disgust and outrage. What was not made clear at the time, however, was that this is exactly what the War on Drugs does to policing.

No one is claiming that racism in the police doesn't pre-date the drug war. And no one is claiming that senseless, brutal, tragic murders like that of Stephen Lawrence would not still occur without these failures of drug policy. But to consider what happened to Lawrence and his family, without looking at the corruption of drug-war policing, is to miss a vital thread. If you are disgusted by the failures of the Lawrence case – and you should be – then you are in part disgusted by failures of the War on Drugs.

Once again, we need to look at the drug war as a process of change over time. We have gone from the world of Lee Harris's Soho in the 1960s, with around 1,000 heroin addicts picking up their supplies from Boots, to a world where police corruption is endemic and cops use their networks of high-level informants to undermine and threaten each other.

The War on Drugs means corruption by definition. Look at Mexico; look at Brazil; look at Colombia. These are countries riddled with the corruption of a war that has been forced upon them – devastated by an American-led policy they did not freely choose.

The police in Britain do exceptional work – day in, day out, week after week. This is in no way an attack on their core principles. The British police have at least a claim to being the best in the world. But even they are not immune to the inevitable corruption that the drug war brings in its wake.

But there is a ray of hope here. The police are slowly recognising the erosion of moral purpose that the War on Drugs is inflicting on them and, significantly, some of the most effective and creative responses to these policies are now coming from within the police themselves.

11

Blood on Their Hands

The Here and Now

Ned's cannabis plants don't look particularly impressive. There are about 20 of them, none yet over a foot tall, sitting under powerful lights in a small thermal tent in the spare room of his house.

'They're only young,' he explains, 'the last crop I had was completely ruined by spider mites. Once they get into an enclosed space like a grow tent, there's no stopping the bloody things. So, for this lot I've had to use pesticides – but nothing is flowering yet, so I'm not spraying anything that people would ever actually smoke. I always use non-toxic stuff that's human-safe, kid-safe and bee-safe. Staying full organic is hard, but I only grow in soil, not on hydroponics, and I only use organic feeds. It's difficult and expensive to stay high-quality. It was a very steep learning curve.'

Ned is a self-confessed cannabis nerd. He talks about his plants with the geeky enthusiasm of a stamp collector or comic-book fanatic. He's also charmingly considerate – asking us if we're comfortable with him smoking a spliff while we chat, even though it's his house we're sitting in. He lights up and begins talking us through everything, from the genetic origins of his favourite cannabis strains and the ideal type of air filtration systems, to how he uses cannabis as a medicine and how he works so that others can as well.

'I smoke it to regulate sleep, pain, anxiety and depression – all of which I've suffered with over the years,' he begins. 'For me, it's more of a mental health thing. I don't like benzodiazepines, which is what would usually be prescribed. They make me feel like a zombie – even after three days, I'll be walking into the kitchen and not remembering why I've come in there.

'Cannabis isn't like that at all. It makes me feel better – I can't put it more simply. It's not about running away from your problems; it's just about having the mental space to deal with them. I've probably been using cannabis every day since I was 19, so about ten years now.

'The key thing is the strain you use. For instance, sleep has been a major issue for me since I was a kid, and the right strain of cannabis really helps with that. But if I smoke Gorilla Glue – which is what I'm smoking right now – before I go to bed then I'm too stimulated. That gets your mind moving too much. I'd use a totally different strain at night.

'I really believe in educating and helping other people to use cannabis for their own conditions. There are a lot of important networks out there now so that people can support each other and see what works. The internet has definitely been huge in bringing people together like that. Though, for me there was obviously a long step between being involved in activism to deciding that I want to supply people with cannabis.

'In my life, one of the most significant things I've ever done was helping one of my best friends, who had multiple brain tumours. He went undiagnosed for years, then he started having seizures and went into hospital.

'This was such a late diagnosis that they didn't even bother with chemotherapy. The doctors said there was nothing to be done except basic pain relief and anti-seizure medication. He was in this specialist unit – he couldn't speak, he couldn't move, he could barely open his fucking eyes. They wouldn't give him food or water, so he was being fed through tubes. They were just waiting for him to die.

'Then he had a tiny moment of clarity, and I asked him if he wanted me to get him some cannabis oil. He just nodded. So, I sourced a tincture from the community, and straight away you could see the tension in his body relax. He went into a natural sleep, not a medicated stupor. You can see when someone is whacked out on sedatives and when they're actually sleeping.

'Two days later the tubes were out and he was eating, and two days after that he was on his feet. Once they saw that improvement they sent him to a hospice. And from there he actually went home – which is very rare. I couldn't believe it. I'd helped a few older people through cancer with cannabis, but that was just a bit of pain relief. This was something else.

'Obviously the cannabis didn't cure him, but for his last few months it gave him a bit of himself back. He had several months more – living at his own home with his mum and dad, with dignity and quality of life. He died in his bed, with his girlfriend by his side, and his family all there. The last time I saw him, he was eating lobster, watching horse racing on telly with his dad.

'That's why I do this. When I was walking around the hospice, I saw so many people that I wanted to go up to and say, "I might be able to help you." But obviously you can't just burst into someone's room and offer them cannabis. Ultimately, this is what I believe the cannabis market should be like.'

Ned's enthusiasm is genuinely moving. But, in reality, that is not what the cannabis market is like. The majority of the cannabis trade is run by people like James, the Manchester bouncer-turned-weed-grower, and Alex, the 15-year-old Liverpool county-lines dealer who started selling at 13.

Ned himself is all too aware of the violent edge of the cannabis industry. He has encountered it first-hand.

'Back when I was first growing, there was a dealer I used to buy off occasionally. He used to get a lift down to my place with various mates of his, and they'd always come in for a smoke. Of course I asked him if all these people he was bringing round were cool – and of course he said he knew them all really well.

'But, a few months later – about midnight on a Friday – I'm just chilling at home with a mate, and I hear a tap on the door. I look out and see a guy in a hood. Usually people would call first, but I figure it must be somebody I know.

'The second I touch the latch – Bang! Three of them are through the door, all in balaclavas. I start hitting the lead guy – shouting for them to get the fuck out. But they all just started properly beating the shit out of me.

'Then, I just kind of shut down. He was choking me on the floor and I had this horrible vision that he was going to stab me – that I was just going to feel something slide into my ribs – so I just went limp.

'They went straight for the drugs. My MacBook was lying on the table, there were two Xbox 360s, two TVs, an iMac right there – but all they took was a few ounces of weed and some cash from my friend's wallet.

'Of course, if they only take the weed, then I can't call the police. Otherwise, I could file a report. The neighbour's kid saw the car they were driving and between that and a few other clues, we knew exactly who it was.

'I had horrible anxiety attacks after that, the night terrors kicked in. They knew I was growing, and could come back at any time. It wasn't a lot of sleep for me until I got out of that house. Nowadays people actually use drones with thermal cameras to figure out who's growing. The police use them to arrest people, and the thugs use them to rob people.

'To be honest, though, I'm still more scared of the police than I am of the criminals. If a guy kicks my door in and steals my weed, I can grow more – but the police will wreck your fucking life. And if the police are in the mood, they get rough too. I've had friends have had their doors kicked in by the police, and have got completely battered. That's how drug searches are.

'But – on the other hand – there was an incident recently where a PCSO came to our door and smelled weed, so he went to get a copper from their car. So, this cop comes down, says he wants to come in and tries to push through the door. But, my flatmate – who suffers from a very serious condition and uses a walking stick – just launches into this whole speech about how he's a medical user, how he has this very serious condition and how he saves the NHS thousands of pounds.

'And the cop actually backed down. At first he was aggressive – trying to ask questions about whether we were growing and stuff, but my flatmate just said, "I'm not discussing that with you." Eventually the guys just left. I've been petrified ever since. But we're moving out of this address soon anyway, and I reckon if they were going to do anything they would have done it by now. My feeling is that that copper felt like a bit of a dick when he walked away, like, "Shit, I've just hassled some guy with a walking stick."'

Ned occupies an incredibly confusing position. He grows cannabis to help other sick people and to make a bit of money. But he is caught between the gangsters on one side, and a police force that oscillates unpredictably between fierce prohibition and grudging tolerance of cannabis on the other.

This confusion is not unique. The position of cannabis in the UK is incredibly complex. It is by far the most widely used illegal drug in Britain – 2.1 million people smoked it in 2016, about 1 in 30 of the population. Devotees like Ned claim it is a harm-less way to relax, or even a beneficial medicine. Detractors cry that it's a psychosis-inducing gateway drug. Some police forces will arrest and prosecute users; others have stopped treating cannabis as a matter of priority altogether.

In fact, the picture is so diverse that, a lot of the time when people argue about cannabis, they can't even decide exactly what product they're arguing about. Much of the confusion comes from a single word: skunk.

In very basic terms, there are two main psychoactive agents in cannabis – tetrahydrocannabinol (THC) and cannabidiol (CBD). Essentially THC gets you high, euphoric and excited, while CBD offers a general sense of relaxation and well-being. It's thought that CBD can act as a 'shield' against the poten-tially harmful effects of THC – such as when excitement turns to agitation, and euphoria to paranoia.

In any given strain of cannabis, the balance between THC and CBD will go a long way to determining the effects on the user. Traditionally, the two main types of cannabis are sativa, which is higher in THC, and indica, which is higher in CBD.

Which brings us to skunk.

Technically, the word 'skunk' refers to a very specific strain of cannabis bred by the Californian David Watson, known as Sam the Skunkman, in the 1970s. Skunk #1 was a blend of Mexican sativa, Columbia Gold sativa and Afghan indica, distinguished by its high THC content – and, of course, its potent smell. Sam brought skunk to Europe in 1983, and it revolutionised the cannabis world. The plant flowered quickly, making it ideal for heavy yields, but most importantly it did well with the new tech-nologies that were emerging – such as growing plants indoors, under powerful lights.

Today, however, the word 'skunk' in the UK has become simply a catch-all term for any high-THC strain of cannabis.

These strains now completely dominate the market for street cannabis, and their potency keeps increasing year on year.

This is alarming because though there is no proven causal link between cannabis and psychosis, some evidence indicates that high-THC, low-CBD varieties are significantly more dangerous to mental health – particularly for younger users and those who might already have underlying issues. Unfortunately, the way the current market is structured, it is exactly these varieties that are most available – particularly to younger and more vulnerable users. Very few people even know what they are smoking.

This situation has become perfect fodder for the tabloids, leading to a moral panic churn of skunk horror stories over the past few years. However, talk to a connoisseur like Ned and a much more complex picture emerges.

'I read the press going on about Gorilla Glue and I just laugh,' he says with a grin, referring to a string of scare stories about that particular strain in 2017. 'It's reefer madness – they're just trying to get their social media clicks up. This is what the *Daily Mail* tried to do with the word "skunk" – to turn it into some terrifying nightmare thing.

'Different strains work for different people, and it's all about education.

'It's definitely possible that if you're mentally unstable or have certain issues in your life, it might not be a good idea for you to smoke high-THC cannabis. Personally, I have mental health difficulties, I smoke high-THC cannabis and I find it really helps. But that's just me, and I would never speak for anyone else.

'It is partly about the balance of THC and CBD, but there's so much more going on. Each strain has its own blend of terpenes, and a hundred other factors that make it unique. You can have two strains with similar THC contents, but completely different effects.

'Everyone is different, and different strains will work for different people at different times. I have hundreds of customers, and I generally don't see people with problems around using cannabis. I don't see people with lives falling apart, losing jobs and relationships and stuff.

'Personally, cannabis has helped me stop other bad habits. I gradually stopped using tobacco and alcohol. I used to love a drink, but it got to a point where it wasn't working for me. It was not making me feel well, and I was wasting time.

'A big moment for me was meeting the UK Cannabis Social Clubs, which are groups of people who are into cannabis as a knowledgeable thing – not just sitting around getting blasted. You can be the guy who knows all about great Scotch whisky and enjoys a drink, or you can be the one sitting on a park bench drinking Special Brew – they're both alcohol, but they're very different experiences.

'I started educating myself, and then I wanted to help educate others. There are so many people out there who don't realise they have a choice about what to consume, and healthy ways of consuming it.

'I want to help people have that choice – it's an education issue. People need to work out for themselves what works for them. This is something I care about. It's something I love, something that's really helped me – and it's allowed me to help some of my friends.'

The great crisis of the UK cannabis market – as it is currently structured – is that more people are not like Ned. Most users are denied the education and the opportunity to really know what it is they are smoking. Most people would struggle to find anything other than the high-THC street skunk that now completely dominates the UK trade.

This situation is almost entirely the result of operating an illegal, unregulated market. In 1986 the conservative scholar

Richard Cowan defined the 'iron law of prohibition': black markets always produce stronger and stronger products. Cocaine becomes crack; speed becomes crystal meth. In prohibition-era America people didn't brew beer – they made moonshine whiskey. Combined with a lack of education, the situation can spiral out of control. Research suggests that a majority of consumers would like a balanced THC/CBD product, but they find it impossible to get hold of.

At the time of writing, nine American states have opted for legalisation of cannabis – including California, with a population of 40 million and an economy bigger than Italy's. In the coming year, all eyes will be on Canada, as it becomes the first major economy to legally regulate cannabis on a national level – with the mandate of a general election.

The UK is lagging far behind these innovators. This is sad, considering Britain's historical role at the forefront of these movements – and it is costly. This is a multibillion-pound industry that the UK is letting slip away.

The cannabis market isn't going anywhere. The question is, who will dominate it – the connoisseurs or the gangsters? People like Ned, or people like those who robbed him?

In fact, the answer is likely to be neither.

The scene could come straight out of *Dragon's Den*. A woman wearing a smart-casual dress and microphone headset makes her pitch. She is slightly nervous, but masks it with that chirpy, skittish sort of positivity that people affect at business meetings. The pitch itself is delivered in fluent corporate-ese – revenue streams, growth marketing strategies, 10 per cent equity stakes, vibrant capital markets, second-round funding opportunities, etc. There are slides with pie charts and graphs.

When the woman is finished, the four men on the judging panel fire off a round of questions about her proposed business model, the audience applauds and the next hopeful entrepreneur is ushered onstage.

This could be any slick, well-financed investor roadshow in the world. What marks this event out, however, is that all the products under discussion are derived from cannabis. Products here are discussed in terms of 'revenue growth' and 'developing human capital' – some of these same products could land Ned, or indeed the gangsters who robbed him, in the back of a police car.

This is CannaTech, the leading conference for the global legal cannabis industry. Held at the Old Truman Brewery in London's East End, it's a slick operation. There are TED-Talk-style presentations, individual stalls for cutting-edge companies, an open bar and a buzzy international crowd of American, Canadian, Israeli and European business folk. This event is aimed specifically at potential investors in the emerging cannabis market. It is sold out, with each of the 400 or so attendees having paid £299 to hear about potential opportunities ahead of the game. The organisers take pains to remind the audience that this is a strictly non-smoking event. You can't score any weed here, but you can collect a lot of business cards.

CannaTech is the brainchild of Saul Kaye, an Israeli cannabis entrepreneur and founder of the company iCAN. We asked Saul about how this event came about, and what significance it might have on the global stage.

'My interest in this sector started from something very personal,' he begins. 'My background is as a pharmacist and my mother had Crohn's disease. She tried all the known therapies, which didn't work and were incredibly expensive. Cannabis worked better than anything else we found, and it wasn't expensive at all. This is a 70-year-old woman who's never smoked a day in her life, and this is a therapy that's helping her. That was the start. When you've seen – all around the world – mothers of very sick children and terminally ill patients demanding these treatments, it's very hard to ignore.'

Saul is clear that CannaTech is exclusively set up to deal with the medical uses of cannabis, which are separate from recreational use – even though the two obviously affect each other and are governed by related legislation.

'We wanted to move the conversation from legalisation to medicalisation,' he continues. 'It's about access to therapeutic products. If you've got a population of grandparents who are using cannabis because they have a prescription, then the stigma goes away pretty quickly. I think this will be the next step – cannabis is going to branch into fully recreational stuff, which is flower-based, and therapeutic cannabis, which is not going to have any flowers at all. People will stop smoking joints as a therapeutic solution; they'll take a patch, or a tablet, or an inhaler that is targeted at that specific condition.'

But CannaTech isn't actually set up to talk to consumers or patients. This is specifically about investment opportunities – and Saul is extraordinarily bullish about the industry's prospects. 'This industry is just starting out. In order to reach its potential it needs a billion dollars of investment. But, at the rate it's growing, it could be worth $50 billion over the next ten years – and that's only on current trends; it actually could be so much more.'

This confidence about cannabis as an opportunity for venture capital is echoed throughout the conference. Chuck Rifici of Nesta Holding Co., a large Canadian private equity firm moving into the cannabis industry, puts it very clearly during his talk: 'This is a product with a huge, already proven user base – regulations are changing in country after country – of course big capital wants to get into this space.'

When one thinks of legal cannabis today, the image is often of bearded artisanal growers in Colorado talking at length about their special bespoke strains. These are people a bit like Ned – the craft-beer geeks of the stoner universe. But this is not the future predicted by Rifici.

'This market is going to commoditise,' he continues, 'the last thing you'll want as an investor is some master grower with years of cannabis experience in his loft. What you want is the big commercial tomato farmer who knows how to save you three cents per kilo, because he's got that market efficiency.'

Amid all this frothy neoliberal excitement one does occasionally have to stop and remind oneself that cannabis is still actually illegal. Medical users like Ned and his flatmate still live in fear of having their doors kicked in at any moment.

With this in mind, it's somewhat odd that CannaTech chose to come to the UK, which is far behind many other European countries when it comes to access to medical marijuana. But then, CannaTech isn't actually primarily about cannabis – it's about money.

'London is still the financial hub of Europe, even with Brexit,' Saul Kaye insists. 'We're looking to educate an international investor base, so that by the time regulators do come round, the industry is already ready. By the looks of the conference selling out weeks in advance, I think we made the right choice in London.

'Also, the UK may be behind the times legislatively, but the biggest medical cannabis company in the world, GW Pharma, is British, and a lot of the key research is being done at British universities. The business world realises what's going on, most people on the street realise what's going on – the lawmakers just need to catch up. And regulation is good – we need regulation! I predict within 24 months medical cannabis will be available here as well. Once the right medical argument is made, there will be no logical reason to deny it.'

Back at CannaTech, the live pitch, *Dragon's Den*-style event winds up, and the crowd drifts off to a cocktail party that Nesta Holding Co. is laying on.

While there is an emphasis on positive ethical change amid all the money talk at CannaTech, one imagines that this is probably not what Ned and his friends would ideally like the emerging legal cannabis market to look like. It is certainly not what Smiles and the idealistic hippies of the 1970s had in mind. But then, as it stands now, the cannabis market is also run on utterly brutal capitalist principles, generally by men wielding machetes and shotguns – men like the ones who robbed Ned in his home. The guys in suits are certainly a step up from that.

CannaTech is very likely the way of the future, and the future rarely turns out how you once imagined it.

'I remember one party where I must have had sex with about 30 people,' says Denholm, a young gay man reminiscing about his chemsex days. 'There was this box of toys – and I'm not even that into sex toys – but off my face on m-cat I found myself gradually increasing and increasing the size. Then I woke up the next day, took another look and was like, "How the fuck did I get that in there?" I probably wouldn't have done that without the mephedrone.'

Chemsex is a central part of the contemporary British gay scene. Groups of men get together, often having met on Grindr, Scruff or another dating app, and have intense sex under the influence of drugs – particularly GHB, crystal meth and mephedrone. These days, mephedrone is used almost exclusively on the chemsex circuit, but for a few years between 2008 and 2010 it enjoyed wild popularity, redefining the entire UK party circuit and ultimately driving the government to try to ban all psychoactive substances. Mephedrone is a quintessential story of the contemporary War on Drugs.

The active agent in mephedrone is a form of cathinone. Humans have used cathinones to get high for thousands of years, notably in khat, the plant chewed for its mild stimulant effect throughout Yemen and East Africa. The exponentially stronger 'substituted cathinone' molecule in mephedrone was resynthesised in 2003 by the legendary Israeli underground chemist, Dr Zee, but the explosion in the drug's popularity in the late 2000s had a very different source – the War on Drugs itself.

In June 2008, Cambodian authorities seized and destroyed 33 tonnes of safrole, a key precursor chemical in MDMA. This was enough for around 245 million ecstasy pills, and had reverberations throughout the international drug market. In 2009 the purity of ecstasy sold in the UK plummeted from roughly 60 per cent to 22 per cent. In 2010, almost all the ecstasy seized in the UK contained no MDMA at all. At the same time, the quality of cocaine was running at record historical lows.

This set the scene for mephedrone – a drug described by most users as feeling like a mix of MDMA and coke, and which people could order cheaply and easily off the internet because it was completely legal. The government simply didn't know enough about this new chemical to have got round to banning it.

According to the clubber's bible *Mixmag*, in 2009 mephedrone was the fourth most popular drug in the UK, after cannabis, cocaine and ecstasy. It displaced the gloomy, dissociative ketamine, and it seemed like every club, house party and festival in Britain was awash with the stuff.

This presented a golden opportunity for amateur dealers. We spoke to Josh, who put himself through two years of university by selling mephedrone out of his flat in south London. 'Me and my mate used to buy it online in bulk from Nanjing, China for £3 a gram,' he recalls, 'then we'd just go from house party to house party and sell it for £15 a gram after hours, when people had run out and wanted a bit more. People just loved it – it started out as just other students in London, but soon it was guys coming in from the suburbs or Kent for a night out. It paid my rent for a year – always paying cash.

'Most people were okay and could do it in moderation – like anything else. But there was the occasional case where someone would be coming round every day. They'd lose shitloads of weight, and they ended up a fucking mess. Some people had to drop out of uni or repeat a year because of it. That was the dark side.'

Perhaps inevitably, the explosion of this new legal high had a knock-on effect throughout the rest of the drug world. Most noticeably there was an unprecedented drop in deaths from cocaine use. In fact, the only year since the Misuse of Drugs Act of 1971 in which cocaine deaths have actually fallen was 2009 – the year mephedrone was at its most popular. Cathinone is far less toxic than street cocaine, and because it was ordered direct from the factory, mephedrone was generally weighing in at 99.8 per cent pure, whereas the average for street-level coke was 20 per cent – with as many as 11 different adulterants.

Then the inevitable moral panic kicked in. It was as clear an example of manufactured tabloid hysteria as anything since Lee Harris first walked Anne Sharpley round Soho in 1964. The *Sun* led off with a lurid story about a 19-year-old who had supposedly ripped off his own scrotum under the influence of this new legal high. It later turned out the only source for this story had been a joke on an internet message board.

Next, a report picked up by the *Daily Mail*, *Sun*, *Telegraph* and *Metro* stated that 180 children had been off sick from a Leicestershire school after taking mephedrone. This was soon found to be completely false, with Leicestershire County Council insisting, 'those figures don't relate to any school in Leicestershire.'[88]

Then came the deaths of two Scunthorpe teenagers, Louis Wainwright and Nicholas Smith. The tragedy was immediately blamed on mephedrone and caused a huge uproar throughout the press. When the coroner's report was eventually issued, however, it was revealed that neither boy had taken mephedrone at all. Instead, both had died from ingesting alcohol, along with the heroin substitute methadone.

A few papers printed tiny retractions of these gross breaches of accuracy. Most went along with the standard rule that when it comes to drugs reporting, journalistic integrity need not apply.

Between March and April 2010, over 200 mephedrone stories appeared in the national press, the *Sun* leading the way with a loud campaign to get the drug banned.[89] In an impressive feat of fake news, the tabloids even managed to rebrand the drug with a catchy new name, 'Meow Meow' – a name no actual user ever really used prior to the press campaign.

On 16 April, the Labour government – looking to appear tough on drugs in an election year – banned mephedrone, classifying it as a Class B drug. Several members of the ACMD resigned in protest at what they saw as a kneejerk decision motivated by media and political pressure, rather than evidence. Mephedrone had only actually been mentioned on six death certificates, the majority in combination with other drugs.

Both the media hype and the resulting ban turned out to be great news for dealers like Josh. 'It was in the papers all the time, so of course people wanted to try it. They were doing our advertising,' he explains. 'But it was only when it became illegal that things got really good. We were reading the *Sun* and all the chat online. We knew it was going to become illegal, so we stocked up. After that we bumped it to £20 a gram, and started cutting it with baking soda. We didn't even have to go round the parties anymore, people started coming to us. I guess we made around 30k.'

* * *

To its credit, the ban did seem to convince most people to stop using mephedrone. They just started using cocaine again instead. The cocaine deaths that had gone down in 2009 began to climb back up, and have continued rising ever since.

In recent years the purity of both cocaine and ecstasy in the UK have shot up to record levels, but the one place mephedrone has maintained its popularity is the gay chemsex scene. When we ask Denholm, the chemsex enthusiast we spoke to earlier, why this drug in particular is so favoured for chemsex, he replies, 'There's a kind of relentlessness to mephedrone – a detached relentlessness. Whereas MDMA makes you lovely and friendly, drone makes you excited, but also detached from the world. Maybe it seems like a remedy to what lots of gay men feel … a kind of unlovability, being brought up with constant background homophobia. It's a way of escaping everything and just feeling sexy and elated.'

Many people enjoy chemsex safely as a part of gay life. But there are obvious dangers around overdose, problematic use and impaired sense of safe boundaries. However, among those who work on the frontlines, there is deep concern that the government's emphasis on law enforcement solutions only serves to drive vulnerable people further underground, discouraging them from actually seeking help.

David Stuart from the 56 Dean Street sexual health clinic in London, who originally coined the term chemsex and has worked on the issue for years, says: 'Chemsex is having a very significant impact on the gay community, as well as representing some significant public health challenges. Approximately 3,000 gay men access 56 Dean Street each month with the consequences of chemsex … Problematic drug use is a very troubling and upsetting mental health issue for many people. Though there are sometimes intersections with the criminal justice system, I will always see my patients as vulnerable people in need of compassionate support, and not as criminals in need of punishment.'

However, the main effect of the government ban on mephedrone – aside from lining the pockets of cocaine dealers – was a massive intensification of the chemical cat-and-mouse game that underground scientists had been playing with the authorities for years – making minute tweaks to chemical compounds, to create 'new' drugs before law enforcement had a chance to ban them.

This led to the explosion of so-called 'legal highs' – unregulated and often dangerous chemicals whose effects have never been properly studied. Sold under a range of euphemisms such as 'spice', 'bath salts', 'black mamba' or 'plant food', these new synthetic drugs have exploded in popularity since the mephedrone ban.

In response to this new crisis, the Conservative government passed the Psychoactive Substances (NPS) Act in 2016. This Act upturned centuries of legal tradition by pre-emptively banning any substance that 'by stimulating or depressing the person's central nervous system ... affects the person's mental functioning or emotional state.' Specific exceptions are made for food, drink, medicines and tobacco, but the Act means one must assume any substance is prohibited, unless one specifically knows otherwise.

Unfortunately, it seems that trying to ban imaginary substances has even less effect than trying to ban real ones. We spoke to Jane Slater of Anyone's Child, a group that brings together the families of those who have lost loved ones to the drug war.

'My sense is that there were two primary reasons the NPS Act came about. One was the media panic, and the other was the desire to decrease the visibility of the head shops that were perceived to increasingly be on every high street.

'Most of those head shops did shut down. But, in pushing these drugs out of sight, the Act pushed them onto the streets. At a stroke, the entire market for NPS was gifted 100 per cent to the criminal sector – which made it more dangerous and made the drugs get stronger.

'The concern is now particularly with the poorest and most vulnerable, particularly the street homeless. We're seeing an increase in harm to do with these drugs in that population, with more hospitalisations and call-outs for the emergency services. This is seriously being felt among the street homeless, and in prisons. There is no indication that overall use has decreased, but plenty to show that the incidence of harm has increased.

'We saw this ourselves in Bristol. Last year we worked with a local community group in Stokes Croft to put a mural up for one month, saying "Save Lives, Legalise Drugs." I was informed that over that month, there were three drug deaths, all involving spice, within 100 metres of our mural. We had to add the face of one of the people who died within a week of it being painted.'

The War on Drugs within the prison system itself has long been one of the darkest aspects of this conflict. With the emergence of spice and the other NPS chemicals, it has deepened into a serious crisis. Over half the prison population in the United Kingdom are there for drug-related offences – yet inside prisons the drug market is as fierce and violent as anything on the streets.

As with the progression in the cannabis market towards stronger and stronger strains, the growth of spice is a direct result of an unregulated market. Pushing these drugs out of sight will not decrease the harm they can cause. Six decades of history indicate that driving drugs underground only ever makes them more deadly.

* * *

In the chapter 'Epidemics', we met Lisa, the long-term addict who receives heroin on prescription. She told us how being given that prescription forever changed the course of her life – how it has allowed her to work, own her own flat and take care of her family.

She also told us that she now lives in constant terror of this prescription being taken away. 'When the new provider came in, they promised that no one's existing scripts would be affected. But, they've started trying to force me to reduce – totally against my will. Why would they do that? I'm functioning now, but if they force me off I really don't know what I'll do. I'm an old lady, and I'll have to go back to get my stuff on the street. I think it will kill me.'

Lisa's problem is not unique. It is part of a much bigger national story – a story that reflects wider changes in British society over the past eight years. This is a story of how a combination of politics and big business set about systematically attacking the remnants of the old British System.

In the 2000–1 financial year, the total income of the charity Crime Reduction Initiatives (CRI) was £2.1 million. By 2012, it had grown to £80.8 million – and by 2016 had hit £158 million.

This astronomical growth was achieved at a time when most of the charity sector was facing severe cutbacks. How did they do it?

The answer is that CRI – which specialises in substance misuse projects – capitalised on a radical strategic overhaul undertaken by the coalition government in 2010. Adopting a slick, corporate business model, they aggressively bid for contracts to provide drug treatment services formerly delivered by the NHS.

CRI weren't the only ones to spot this opportunity. Turning Point, Aquarius and Addaction are just a few of the charities that have taken on the methodology and style of the corporate sector – and done extremely well financially by taking over huge swathes of the British drug treatment system.

During the same period, drug deaths have massively increased. In fact, they have shot to record highs. There is, it seems, good money to be made in letting drug addicts die.

We spoke to Gus, who has worked in drug treatment for over 20 years – including a long stint at one of the charities mentioned above. He witnessed first-hand how the entire sector was transformed in this era.

'I was a drug worker, but also did a lot in business development,' he begins, 'so I really saw how these policies were implemented from the inside. All I can say is that 2010 really was the year of destruction.

'From 2010, Iain Duncan Smith at the Department of Work and Pensions really began demonising just about anyone on benefits – and drug users got it especially hard. They pushed this idea that people with drug and alcohol problems were just using that as an excuse to remain on benefits and not go to work. It was all part of Universal Credit and the scandals around the PIP assessments – forcing people off of disability benefits.

'Their main idea was to totally refocus all drug treatment onto "recovery". That means abstinence. And that means forcing people off their medication, whether they're ready or not. They even called their plan "the recovery roadmap".

'It was basically privatisation by the back door. Suddenly, all those charities changed their PR material to include the word "recovery" and started picking off the contracts. All of a sudden they weren't drug charities and drug workers – they were "recovery charities" and "recovery workers". It was pure marketing, nothing of substance.

'And the problem was that these charities are really run like businesses – they all massively underbid to get the contracts in place, cut costs to the bone and then can't actually deliver the service. It's just like what happened with Carillion – but with this, people die as a result.

'The standard caseload for a drug worker used to be around 30, maybe 40 in times of crisis. Now caseloads of 80 are routine – with no admin support. It automatically stops being about helping people, and becomes about box-ticking.

'What's really sad is that this has meant the complete loss of all the accumulated knowledge and experience that was there in the NHS services. There was unrivalled frontline knowledge; organisational knowledge; management experience – and they've thrown that all away. I've sat in meetings with commissioners and had them go, "Well, I've got drugs on my portfolio now, so I thought I'd come to this meeting because I really don't know anything about this." That's not a minority – that's most of the time.

'When I started, you needed serious training to deal with these complex cases. Now, with the charities, all you need is an NVQ3, and off you go. It just doesn't work.'

The coalition government's drive towards austerity was obviously not restricted solely to drug treatment. This period saw cuts and restructuring across the entire public sector, from the NHS to the armed forces. But, when it came to drug policy, the decisions being made went far beyond simple cost-cutting. This was ideological.

The government's recovery roadmap was a toxic mix of austerity spending cuts and a renewed commitment to moralising, American-style, abstinence-based 'recovery'. Evidence-based policymaking was aggressively undermined, and drug workers were once again expected to make their patients 'just say no' – by coercion if necessary.

'It was a complete attack on the British way of doing things, trying to force us to be more like over the Atlantic,' insists Gus. 'They started to spread this idea that people were being "parked in treatment". As if we just stuck them on methadone and left them to rot. This is a complete reverse of the truth – in a really perverse and insidious way.

'What drug treatment workers often talk about is "retaining" people in treatment. This is a good thing! It means that people are continuing to engage with treatment, and are stabilising their lives.

'But they twisted this into some sort of bad thing. As if the whole idea was to force people out – and retaining them, so they continue engaging with treatment, was actually a failure. It was so deceitful – it made me sick.

'They sold this idea that when people walked out the door, it automatically meant they'd stopped using drugs. In fact, people were being forced out before they were ready – so they were just going back to the streets. But now they were no longer engaging with treatment at all, because they've been forced out. So, their lives fall back into chaos – and often, they die.

'I'm not saying the system was perfect before. I'm sure there were a few people who could have used a nudge along. But the way it happened in 2010 was like scorched earth. It was inhuman.'

This is yet another replay of the intellectual divide between Harm Reduction and enforced abstinence; between evidence-based policy and moralising judgement; between the ideas that underpin the British System and American-style prohibition.

But it gets even more complex and murky. The history of public/private partnerships in Britain is Byzantine – and often riddled with incompetence, malfeasance and profiteering. Drug treatment is no different. The specific way that these contracts were structured encouraged a raft of perverse incentives and false economies.

'The contracts were a bad joke,' Gus continues. 'Each contract has a certain target for positive closures – i.e. getting people out of treatment. If the company misses that target, they will only get a certain percentage of the money for that contract.

'It's generally divided into alcohol, non-opiate drug use and opiate closures. The most money is always for opiate closures. The more positive closures they put on paper, the more money they get.

'So, this is a massive financial incentive to kick people out of treatment – whether or not they're ready. A manager will say to a worker, "I want three positive closures off you in the next six months." It's a completely arbitrary target – but that worker will get those closures, no matter what the consequences. This is something I have seen happening again and again. It's routine.

'Generally there's a clause so that the person has to stay out of treatment for six months. But if they force someone out, and the person comes back *after* six months – they can go through the whole charade again and get paid twice. It's a revolving door.

'Even worse is that difficult, complex cases just get refused. If someone is seen as unlikely to provide a positive closure, they'll just find a way to keep them out of treatment altogether. I've seen this frequently – and it's disgusting. These are the most vulnerable people who really need help. But the providers are all busy chasing the easy closure cases – the low-hanging fruit – so they get shut out.

'Obviously, drug problems often intersect with things like housing and mental health issues. Back in the day, we had specific facilities for dual diagnosis cases. That's all been cut away. Now, the idea is just to block difficult cases, and focus all the effort on forcing people into so-called positive closures.'

* * *

The man largely responsible for CRI's massive growth under the recovery roadmap was its chief executive, David Biddle. In a 2016 interview, Biddle spoke about the problems he saw in the old system: 'We wanted to get them in, but we forgot to get them out ... My joy in life is seeing people go through the door and not come back.'

One must assume that the joy Biddle is speaking of refers to cases where people truly do leave drug treatment and go on to a more fulfilling life. It would be unkind to suggest that it is because it's when people 'go through the door' that CRI get paid. But, with what the whistleblowing drug worker Gus has just related, the thought does flash through one's mind.

The most worrying result of these policies, though, has not been organisations milking the system. It's been people dying on the streets.

Just as CRI's income more than doubled over the years of the recovery roadmap, so did heroin-related deaths. In fact, the two rose in almost exact proportion. In 2012 there were 579 heroin-related deaths in the UK; by 2016 it had risen to 1,209. In 2017 – after seven years of these policies – drug deaths overtook road deaths for the first time in British history.

'They try and bury those statistics,' says Gus with a sigh. 'They try and say, "Oh, that's just older drug users dying of old age or poor health."

'It's total bullshit. If you look at the people who are dying, the largest cohort are people who are not in treatment – the people who are being kicked out. If you send someone back out onto the street with a lowered tolerance for the drug, you are seriously, seriously endangering their life.

'I don't even really blame the charities as such. I know there are some people in that sector doing really good work. The problem is how the entire government strategy was framed.

'I was a frontline drugs worker for years – I don't mess about. When you look at this massive increase in deaths, it's impossible not to say that Iain Duncan Smith at the DWP and Theresa May when she was at the Home Office have blood on their hands.'

There is, however, a glimmer of light for Lisa, and for all those caught up in the mess of the recovery roadmap. That glimmer of light comes from a perhaps unexpected source – the police.

What harsh recovery-based policies tend to do is to shift spending away from drug treatment – and straight onto law enforcement. When you force somebody off a methadone prescription that has helped stabilise their life, they more often than not go back to street heroin. They steal or become a user-dealer to pay for their habit, and the money they spend contributes to the gangster economy – and, ultimately, to corrupting the police. If they get arrested, it will cost £42,000 a year to keep them in prison. Perhaps coercing them out of treatment wasn't such a clever cost-saving measure, after all?

The police – who have also suffered savage cuts under Theresa May's run at the Home Office and as PM – seem to be getting tired of having to pick up the pieces of this botched, short-sighted drugs strategy. In desperation, they are rediscovering the British System.

In March 2017, Ron Hogg, the elected Police and Crime Commissioner for Durham, announced that his force would pursue a new policy of heroin-assisted therapy – to be paid for out of the police budget. His reasoning was a direct restatement of the principles underlying the British System. 'Controlling the supply of heroin by allowing doctors to prescribe it would reduce the flow of money to criminal gangs and destroy their power. It would also reduce the number of people committing crimes to fund their addiction, and save lives.'

Interviewed about the scheme in the *Northern Echo*, Hogg sticks strictly to the evidence:

> When I first stood for election, I said I would always support evidence-based strategy and ... there is a good solid basis of evidence for this. There was a study about six years ago which involved the same concept in Darlington, London and Brighton ... It showed that this allowed addicts to get back into recovery much more quickly and it reduced their offending. It reduced blood-borne diseases, and there was a reduction in the number of needles on the street.
>
> We did see a crime reduction, but just as important is getting people back into normal lifestyles. Each addict is a human being and is suffering tremendously because of that addiction ... It's not suitable for everyone. We're not considering putting 2,000 people on the scheme. It's very focused. It's a cost-effective use of police money.

Mike Barton, Detective Chief Constable of Durham Police, backed the scheme in more simple, copper's terms, 'The police are here to cut crime and this is a proven and effective way of doing it.'[90]

Ron Hogg has been at the forefront of many other progressive measures. He has encouraged safe injection facilities and instructed his officers not to target cannabis smokers and small-scale growers. He is leading the way, but he is not alone. Progressive steps are being taken by Arfon Jones, PCC for North Wales, and by forces in Surrey, Dorset, and Avon and Somerset. Most recently, West Midlands Police – the second largest force in the country – announced it would also be pursuing heroin-assisted therapy, and even recommended drug-testing facilities in the town centres to keep users safe.

What's even more encouraging is that there seems to be a response to this movement from within charity service providers as well. In 2016, David Biddle stepped down as chief executive of CRI – which rebranded itself as Change, Grow, Live (CGL). There seems to be a new generation rising through the ranks at CGL, and other service providers – a generation that sees some of the excesses and mistakes of the recent past. When West Midlands Police announced their Harm Reduction plans, they were immediately welcomed by CGL. They seem to understand which way the wind is blowing.

In a way, perhaps there is a nice circularity in the idea that it might just end up being the police themselves who call time on the British War on Drugs. Back in 1964, when Lee Harris was showing Anne Sharpley round Soho, drugs weren't seen as 'real police work'. Perhaps today's police are once again realising the need to prioritise crimes that are *mala in se*, rather than just *mala prohibita*. Perhaps modern police officers want to go back to putting their efforts into solving crimes that have a victim?

Perhaps there is even a vestigial sense of the Peelian Principles at work here? Maybe, as a collective, the police sense the damage that the drug war is doing to their bond with the community? Perhaps there is a swelling concern at the corruption that this war is sowing all the way through the ranks. Maybe the bobbies are beginning to realise that the War on Drugs is directly eroding their original moral purpose?

The best traditions of British policing are built on the principles of professionalism, fairness and the trust of the community. So, perhaps it is fitting that, in the end, it just might be the police themselves that save the British System.

12

We Can Do Better

Countless theories have been put forward to explain why people commit crime. Most fall into one of two main camps. Those on the political right tend to argue that some people are simply 'bad'. It is in their nature to be drawn to crime, and they will only be deterred by harsh punishment. Those on the left, however, insist that crime is a result of poverty, and if we could just alleviate economic and social hardship, then crime would fall.

Both are wrong.

The idea that most people who commit crime are inherently evil is an absurd, pernicious nonsense. The media constantly overplays stories of lurid, premeditated malevolence, but the number of authentic sociopaths who actively enjoy causing others pain is, in truth, vanishingly small. On the other hand, the very fact that crime often rises at exactly the historical points at which societies are getting richer and inequality is falling shows that explaining crime purely as a reaction to poverty is also inadequate.

To reveal what actually lies at the root of most criminal behaviour, the criminologist Tom Gash tells a fascinating story from Germany in the 1980s.

Throughout the late seventies, the big story in Germany had been motorcycle theft. Mopeds and scooters were soaring in popularity, and made the perfect target for thieves. By 1980, 150,000 motorcycles were being stolen per year. Insurance premiums were rising, the police seemed powerless and people were getting angry.

Then something happened. The rocketing increase in motorcycle thefts just seemed to stop – almost overnight. Then the numbers began to fall. By 1986 they were down to 54,000 – a third of where they had been just six years earlier.

There had been no revolution in policing methods, nor had any innovative new security system been introduced. What had happened was that an entirely different branch of government had introduced a very simple road safety regulation. They made motorcycle helmets compulsory.

Suddenly, if you were a potential thief and spotted an unattended scooter, you could no longer just hotwire it and hop on. You knew that within minutes you'd be stopped by the cops for not wearing a helmet – at which point they'd also check the ownership of the bike.

Would it have been that much effort for really dedicated thieves to think ahead and carry their helmets out with them? Probably not, and we're sure a few did just that. But for the vast majority, those few extra steps of forward planning were, in fact, too much. Motorcycle thefts dropped instantly – with no sudden uptick in other forms of crime.[91]

Crime is driven by opportunity. Cartoonish visions of 'inherent evil', or inevitable reactions to social conditions, are far too reductive. It is a subtle and complex picture. In a legal framework where easy profit can be made by breaking the law, the law will be broken. But adjust that framework correctly – often in subtle or surprising ways – and crime will fall.

This book has endeavoured to tell the story of how, over the past six decades of British life, a series of decisions has been taken that has created the greatest criminal opportunity in the history of this country. The War on Drugs has completely transformed the entire structure of criminality, policing and popular culture. In the process, it has made more criminals more money than anything else in history. When Francis Drake went off to plunder Spanish galleons in the 1500s, even he had to apply for a Letter of Marque from the Crown – and pay taxes when he got back.

But this story might also help to point the way to another path. It might help to show that another way has, in fact, already been practised on these shores. It might, in its own small way, help us see how we might do better.

We have seen how the world of Lee Harris's Soho in the 1960s, with a few hundred addicts picking up their gear at Boots, has metastasised into a brutally violent mega-industry stretching across the entire country.

We have seen how the destruction of the British System created a black market based on a pyramid scheme of addiction. We have seen how this left Britain defenceless when the heroin epidemics of the 1980s finally struck – sweeping up vulnerable characters like Danny and Lisa in their wake.

We have seen how those tiny embers of the British System that still burned, in the form of John Marks and the Merseyside Harm Reductionists, offered those vulnerable characters a tiny flicker of hope.

We have seen how racial politics and drug policy have been inextricably linked – from Alex Wheadle and his friends battered in the cells of Brixton police station to the corruption surrounding the murder of Stephen Lawrence.

We have seen how the astronomical profits of the drug trade have enabled the corruption of the criminal justice system, on a scale never before witnessed in this country. And we have seen how this tore apart the lives of people like Darren A., Kevin P. and Frank Matthews – the people who don't exist.

But, perhaps most of all, we have been able to see the British War on Drugs as a process of change over time. We have seen how one generation succeeded the next, how the drug war arms race has inexorably led to greater brutality and violence. We have seen how, with every fresh moral panic and knee-jerk political reaction, the situation spiralled further out of control.

We have seen this most clearly in the figures of Patrick, Will and Alex, the three generations of Liverpool drug dealers whose stories tell the progression of the drug war from small beginnings, through the gold rush and monopolisation of the 1990s, to the perfect storm we see today, with monopolisation and corruption at the high end, and nihilistic violence on the streets.

And what has this achieved? Has drug use been reduced?

From just over a thousand heroin addicts when the Misuse of Drugs Act finally eviscerated the British System, by the 1990s the number had reached 350,000.

There are 2.2 million cannabis consumers in the UK, or 1 in 30 of the population. When you exclude people under 14 years old, that number rises to 1 in 22. If the average household contains four people, you can estimate that, when you walk down the street, inside every seventh house someone will be smoking dope.

One in 24 people in Britain between the ages of 15 and 35 have used cocaine in the last 12 months. There are 900,000 regular users of MDMA.

In terms of its own stated aims, the prohibition of drugs is likely the most radically failed policy in modern history.

In 1993, when Neil Woods started working under cover, a 0.12-gram bag of heroin cost £10. It is exactly the same price today;

the only real difference is that the purity is higher. Compare this to the cost of a flat, a train ticket or a pint at the pub. Illicit drugs are about the only inflation-proof product available in this country – because supplies are never really interrupted.

No matter how the police and customs like to flash their seizures for the cameras, by any serious estimate they only ever pick up about 1 per cent of the drugs flowing into this country. For the gangsters, this is less of an operating cost than what most supermarkets allow for shoplifting. The National Crime Agency estimates that the drug trade in this country alone is worth £10.7 billion. It costs another £7 billion to police. Globally, the illicit drugs black market constitutes between one-tenth and one-eighth of all global trade.

There are a few cranks who argue that this abject failure is because the War on Drugs has never truly been fought. When you hear this guff, remember that over 50 per cent of the prison population in the UK are there for drug-related offences. That's well over 50,000 people at any given time. For comparison, total American casualties in the Vietnam War are estimated at 56,000.

At the same time, problematic heroin users – who make up under 0.2 per cent of the population – commit roughly 50 per cent of acquisitive crime. This is a war we are all caught up in. Even if you have never touched drugs in your life, when your house gets broken into, someone you know gets mugged or you see a story about police corruption on TV, you are very likely coming face to face with the failed War on Drugs.

But we can do better. We know we can do better because we have a vision of another way set before us in our own history. The humane, liberal and pragmatic principles that underpin the British System are still deeply embedded in our national culture.

We can do better. And to begin doing better, we need to talk about the way we talk about drugs.

* * *

In late 2017 we took part in a speaking event on 'The Media and the War on Drugs' with the veteran crime reporter, Duncan Campbell.

British papers learned how to report on drugs from the American 'yellow press' of William Randolph Hearst. This is where the pattern of sensationalism, racism and straight-up falsehood became established. And, as in the US, the original moral panics in Britain concerned the use of opium in the Chinese community. One of the earliest examples was the demonisation of the Chinese restauranteur and drug supplier, Billy Chang, in the 1920s.

We began our event by reading the audience some excerpts from the coverage of the Chang Scandal. We started with this, from Arthur Tietjen of the *Daily Mail*:

> Chang possesses a strangely macabre – some said hypnotic – power to persuade women to sniff cocaine. It may well have been that he did so as a member of the yellow race to degrade white women.

The *Daily Express*, meanwhile, took its readers on a tour of a 'dancing den', describing the clientele and the dealer respectively:

> the same old sickening crowd of undersized aliens, blue about the chin and greasy ... not the Chink of popular fiction, a cringing yellow man hiding his clasped hands in the wide sleeves of his embroidered gown.

This dealer apparently greets the room with

> that fixed Oriental smile which seems devoid of warmth and humanity ... who are these smiling yellow men?

* * *

We then read excerpts from the newspapers of the 1950s, when the British press followed the American by shifting their focus from the Chinese community and opium to the black community and cannabis.

The Times wrote that

> white girls who become friendly with West Indians are from time to time enticed to hemp smoking ... this is an aspect of the hemp problem – the possibility of its spreading among irresponsible white people – that causes greatest concern to the authorities.

while the *Express* warned that

> Coloured men who peddle reefers can meet susceptible teenagers at jazz clubs.

As we read each one of these excerpts out, we could see the audience actively wince. The utter shamelessness of this sort of prejudice seems almost incomprehensible to modern ears. As much as anger, the feeling in the room was one of collective embarrassment for anyone who could ever write those words.

Of course, the modern tabloid editor might argue that such coverage was merely a function of its time – that in those eras, such language was more accepted, and that things have now changed.

But, take a look at how much of the modern press speak about people who use drugs. Think of phrases like 'evil druggie' and 'junkie scum'. Think of adjectives like 'lazy', 'thieving', 'skiving', 'dirty', 'filthy', 'despicable' and all the others that are habitually hurled. People who use drugs are one of the last groups in society about whom one can say whatever one likes, no matter how vicious or blatantly untrue.

In a few years, the way the tabloids now talk about people who use drugs will be looked at in exactly the same way as how they once talked about black and Asian people. These writers and editors must now be put on notice. Times are changing, but their bylines will remain. Their children and grandchildren will read their words, and will look back on them with shame.

While there are journalists out there doing excellent, largely thankless work in accurately covering these issues, the tide of fake news in drugs reporting has never really abated. From Anne Sharpley and Ben Parkin's manipulative political play in 1964, to the vicious lies spread about HIV sufferers in the 1980s, to Kelvin MacKenzie's brazen admission that the *Sun* knowingly misreported the rave scene of the 1990s – all the way through to stories of teenagers ripping off their own scrotums, cribbed from jokes on internet forums, in the 2000s.

Multiple peer-reviewed studies have shown that roughly two-thirds of problematic heroin users are self-medicating as a result of childhood physical and sexual abuse. The War on Drugs is, to a great extent, a war on the survivors of such abuse. When you read the words 'junkie', 'druggie', 'filthy', etc. in a newspaper – know that it is abused children that are being shamed and demonised.

And this demonisation doesn't just apply to those who take drugs. Richard Peppiatt, the former *Daily Star* reporter, once publicly admitted, 'If a scientist announces their research has found ecstasy to be safer than alcohol, my job as a tabloid reporter is to portray this man as a quack.'

This mode of reporting ends careers and ruins lives. It also distorts policymaking in ways that are deeply destructive for the entire country.

It may sound as if we are disparaging the tabloid press as a whole. In fact, at their best, the tabloids can be a terrific force for good. They draw on the time-honoured British tradition of the pamphleteer – holding those who deem themselves our 'betters' to account, and doing so in a loud, scurrilous and often quite funny voice. This is an incredibly rich tradition with real value – the best in it should absolutely be celebrated.

But, where the press let that tradition down – where they victimise the most vulnerable, instead of challenging the powerful – then they should be held to account. We can do better. We can all do better.

The idea of 'British values' is a tricky concept. The very phrase is routinely twisted and stretched by politicians of all stripes until it describes everything and nothing. For every invention of parliamentary democracy and stiff-upper-lipped spirit of fair play, there is a Peterloo Massacre, a Mau Mau Rebellion and a Bengal Famine. This island's story is long, complex and contains multitudes.

Yet, considered carefully, without chauvinism or jingoism, there is value to be found in considering the meanings that 'British values' might hold for us – how we might find the best of ourselves in them, and the best of them in ourselves. We can do this by looking clear-eyed into our own history.

What the story told in this book shows is that – by any historically sensitive definition of British values – the War on Drugs is absolutely antithetical to them. For centuries, the British approach has been underpinned by a liberal, humane pragmatism. This was true from the Gin Crazes of the eighteenth century to John Marks's clinic on the streets of Widnes in the 1980s. There have, of course, been counterveiling, reactionary trends in British public life, and one must always be wary of overly Whiggish interpretations of history. It was, after all, the party of Oliver Cromwell that first tried to ban Christmas. But, at least in relation to the issues explored in this book, the British way has historically sprung from a rich heritage of pragmatic liberalism.

It wasn't called the International System. It wasn't called the Alternative System. It was called the *British System*. And it was called that for a reason. It is the same reason that Peel's Principles were developed in London, and nowhere else. It is the reason that when people throughout the world talk about Harm Reduction, they are talking about an idea born in Liverpool. Every home-grown British approach to these issues inclines towards this deep-rooted intellectual tradition, developed over centuries.

The moralising, abstinence-based model of prohibition by law enforcement is something that has been forced upon us. It is, in itself, an act of violence. One might have hoped that, with all Britain's long experience as imperialists, we might have noticed when imperialism was being done to us.

Whenever someone argues that prohibition is an effective form of law enforcement, or that it springs from any serious idea of British values, you can be certain that they understand little about either law enforcement or the very meaning of those values themselves.

It may also seem that throughout this book we have been very hard on the United States. This is not our intention. The USA is an inspiring, dynamic nation that has symbolised freedom and hope for millions, and whose founding principles are a testament to everything towards which humanity might aspire.

But the approach to drug policy that America has forced on the world has simply not worked. The American people themselves – particularly American people of colour – have suffered intensely as a result. In this, America can do better. We can all do better.

We began this book by asking the question *How has it come to this?* How has it come to the point where the police are forced to accept rampant corruption as simply inevitable? How has it come to the point of children forced to watch their mothers drink petrol over a £20 drug debt?

In tracing this question back through the history of this country, some of the answers we have found have been horrifying. When the Misuse of Drugs Act was passed in 1971, there were just over a thousand known addicts in Britain – and almost zero crime related to drug supply. Decades later there are 350,000 addicts, over half the prison population are inside for drug-related offences and the criminal justice system itself has been corrupted as never before in our history.

By far the heaviest burden has fallen on the most vulnerable in society. This is not just a failed policy – it is a failure in the duty of care that those who govern owe to the governed.

But threaded into this history is also the vision of another way. All we have to do is to dig into our own past, and have confidence in our own traditions. We stand at a historical crossroads. The idea of what it means to be British is being radically re-examined and redefined. This country's future role in the world is being determined.

In previous eras, Britain led the world in presenting an alternative to the prohibition model. Until now, this resistance has been a lost history. But it is a history in which Britain can and should take real pride. It is also an area in which – with a bit of courage – this country could lead the world once again.

The War on Drugs has failed. It has failed on the streets of the United States where it began. It has failed hideously in the carnage of Latin America and the poppy fields of Afghanistan. And it has failed in Britain.

The British War on Drugs is nowhere near the most violent theatre of this global conflict. But, as this story has shown, Britain has played a crucial role in its development. This is a history that the people of Britain should be aware of. It is a history from which the rest of the world might also be able to draw some valuable lessons. And it is a history that might present clues to developing a better way forward – a way perhaps more in keeping with the best of what we call British values. We can do better. We can all do better.

Acknowledgements

First and foremost we want to once again thank all those who took the time to speak to us. These are voices too long left out of the conversation, and this is their story.

Particular thanks to Jason Reed, Beccy Rawnsley, Max Daly, Sahar Ahmed, Darryl Bickler, Quentin Johns and Johann Hari for help with research, introductions and general support. Alex Miller, Jamie Clifton and all at Vice. Andrew Goodfellow, Laura Horsley and all at Ebury.

In writing this book we are building on the work of countless experts – far too many to list here, but we hope that readers will use this book as a springboard to further explore the crucial research being done in each of these fields.

In addition we would like to especially salute the tireless work of each of the following organisations, and to thank them for their continued support: Transform Drug Policy Foundation, Release, Volteface, David Nutt and the rest at Drugscience, HIT, Anyone's Child, The Loop, United Patient's Alliance, Virgin Unite, and Shaun Shelley of the University of Cape Town.

Special thanks to Carl Hart and Ethan Nadelmann for their invaluable insights, and to all the board and staff at LEAP USA.

And thanks to all of those showing courage and innovation in examining these issues. Like all of the great social transformations, there are countless unnamed heroes helping to sow the seeds of positive change.

Neil Woods would like to thank Lynette, Tanith, Gareth and his wider family for their ongoing support and love.

J.S. Rafaeli would like to thank his family for their constant and boundless love, inspiration and support. And, of course, Vera.

Notes

1. Morris, Nigel, 'Eden "Was On Purple Hearts During Suez Crisis"', *Independent*, 4 November 2006.
2. Wilson, Andrew, 'Mixing the Medicine: The unintended consequence of amphetamine control on the Northern Soul Scene', *Internet Journal of Criminology*, 7 February 2008.
3. Sharpley, Anne, 'I See Soho's Pep Pill Craze', *Evening Standard*, 3 February 1964.
4. The terms speed, pep pills and amphetamines are used interchangeably by users of this era. 'Cranking' refers to injecting.
5. Wilson, 'Mixing the Medicine'.
6. Leech, Kenneth, 'The Junkies' Doctors and the London Drug Scene in the 1960s: Some Remembered Fragments', in *Policing and Prescribing*, eds. David K. Whynes and Philip T. Bean (London: Macmillan, 1991), p.43.
7. Berridge, Victoria, 'The "British System" and its History, Myth and Reality', in *Heroin Addiction and the British System Volume 1: Origin and Evolution*, eds. John Strang and Michael Glossop (London: Routledge, 2005), p.13.

8. Bewley-Taylor, David, *The United States and International Drug Control, 1909–1997* (London: Continuum, 2001), p.18.

9. ibid, p.22.

10. ibid, p.20.

11. ibid, p.36.

12. Italics added.

13. ibid, p.23.

14. Hari, Johann, *Chasing the Scream: The First and Last Days of the War on Drugs* (London: Bloomsbury, 2015), loc.574.

15. For a full exploration of Anslinger and the War on Drugs, we very much recommend Johann Hari's book, *Chasing the Scream: The First and Last Days of the War on Drugs*.

16. Bewley-Taylor, *The United States and International Drug Control*, p.61.

17. His emphasis.

18. Lines, Rick, "Deliver us from evil? – The Single Convention on Narcotic Drugs, 50 years on', *International Journal on Human Rights and Drug Policy*, vol.1, 2010.

19. barbateboy, 'Scripping Drugs in Sixties London', Talking-Drugs, 3 April 2009.

20. Woodcock, Jasper, 'Obituary: Bing Spear', *Independent*, 19 July 1995.

21. Hallam, Chris, 'British System, American Century: A Short Case Study', Global Drug Policy Observatory, https://druglibrary.net/schaffer/Library/studies/dwda/staff7.htm.

22. May, Edgar, 'Dealing With Drug Abuse: A Report to the Ford Foundation', https:druglibrary.net/shaffer/Library/studies/dwda/staff7.htm.

23. ibid.

24. Spear, Bing, 'The Early Years of Britain's Drug Situation in Practice', in *Heroin Addiction and the British System Volume 1: Origin and Evolution*, eds. John Strang and Michael Glossop, (London: Routledge, 2005), p.22.

25. Woodcock, 'Obituary: Bing Spear'.
26. Mott, Joy, 'Crime and Heroin Use', in *Policing and Prescribing*, eds David K. Whynes and Philip T. Bean (London: Macmillan, 1991), p.78.
27. Spear, 'The Early Years of Britain's Drug Situation in Practice', p.23.
28. ibid, p.25.
29. ibid, p.25.
30. ibid, p.27.
31. ibid, p.31.
32. Leech, 'The Junkies' Doctors and the London Drug Scene in the 1960s.
33. barbateboy, 'Scripping Drugs in Sixties London'.
34. Leech, 'The Junkies' Doctors and the London Drug Scene in the 1960s'.
35. barbateboy, 'Scripping Drugs in Sixties London'.
36. Wells, Simon, *Butterfly on a Wheel. The Great Rolling Stones Drug Bust* (London: Omnibus Press, 2012), loc.1628–32.
37. http://history-is-made-at-night.blogspot.co.uk/2008/06/news-of-world-ufo-and-rolling-stones.html.
38. http://dangerousminds.net/comments/simon_wells_the_great_rolling_stones_drugs_bust.
39. Hallucinogens Subcommittee of the Advisory Committee on Drug Dependence (1968), Report on Cannabis (Wootton Report).
40. The *Daily Mirror*'s labelling of the report as 'A Conspiracy of the Drugged' is particularly telling.
41. HC Deb 11 March 1970 vol.797 c1349.
42. ibid.
43. ibid.
44. ibid.
45. ibid.

46. Wootton Report, p.81.
47. In practical terms, this theoretical reduction in sentencing cannabis possession would likely have made no difference to the sentencing guidelines judges received for simple possession of small amounts of cannabis. The 1965 Act was a cruder piece of legislation imposing a maximum sentence of ten years for all drug offences, with actual courtroom outcomes left to judges' discretion.
48. https://www.gov.uk/government/organisations/advisory-council-on-the-misuse-of-drugs/about.
49. Spear, 'The Early Years of Britain's Drug Situation in Practice', p.26.
50. Neal, Sarah, 'The Scarman Report, the Macpherson Report and the Media: How Newspapers Respond to Race-centred Social Policy Interventions', *Social Policy Interventions,* vol.32, 1, Cambridge University Press, 2003.
51. Leaf Fielding has written a good memoir called *To Live Outside The Law*, but was never quite in the 'inner circle' of the operation.
52. Smiles's real name is Alston Hughes – but he insists that only his mother calls him Alston.
53. Roberts, Andy, *Albion Dreaming* (Singapore: Marshall Cavendish, 2012), loc. 4610–11.
54. ibid, loc. 4085–8.
55. ibid, loc. 4695–8.
56. ibid, loc. 4610–11.
57. Bentley, Stephen, *Undercover: Operation Julie – The Inside Story* (Bentley Sabrine Books, 2017), loc. 1657–6.
58. ibid, loc. 1108–9.
59. ibid, loc. 1657–61.
60. ibid, loc. 90–7.
61. The rumours that Princess Margaret took Operation Julie acid, supplied through her friend Roddy Llewellyn, began

almost as soon as the busts went down. They have continued to this day, despite Llewellyn's fierce denials.

62. Bentley, *Undercover*, loc. 2128–30.
63. This was actually printed in the *Mirror* on 9 March 1977. It is a simple rehash of equally bogus scare stories that had circulated in the American 'yellow press' years earlier.
64. Roberts, *Albion Dreaming*, loc. 4998–9.
65. Bentley, *Undercover*, loc. 282–4.
66. Emphasis added.
67. Henman, Anthony, Lewis, Roger and Maylon, Tim, *Big Deal: The Politics of the Illicit Drugs Business* (London: Pluto Press, 1985), p.38.
68. Parker, Howard, 'Heroin Epidemics and Social Exclusion in the UK 1980–2000', in *Heroin Addiction and the British System Volume 1: Origin and Evolution*, eds. John Strang and Michael Glossop (London: Routledge, 2005), p.80.
69. ibid, p.83.
70. ibid, p.85.
71. Daly, Max, 'This Is What Happened to the "Trainspotting Generation" of Heroin Users', *VICE*, 18 January 2017.
72. Dr Marks sent us his original research, which is full of similarly impressive results.
73. Robertson, Roy J., 'The Arrival of HIV', in *Heroin Addiction and the British System Volume 1: Origin and Evolution*, eds. John Strang and Michael Glossop (London: Routledge, 2005), p.123.
74. http://www.gayinthe80s.com/2013/01/1984–85-media-aids-and-the-british-press.
75. 'The "explosion" that never happened; crack and cocaine use in Britain', http://findings.org.uk/PHP/dl.php?file=cocaine_treat.hot&s=ml.
76. ibid.
77. *Summer of Rave, 1989*, BBC documentary, dir. Anna Davies.

78. For a measure of British crime pre-and-post the War on Drugs: throughout their entire careers the Krays, perhaps the most celebrated pre-drug-war British gangsters, were only ever implicated in three murders.
79. Barnes, Tony, *Cocky* (Preston: Milo Books Ltd, 2011), loc.709–10.
80. Barnes, *Cocky*.
81. Johnson, Graham, *The Cartel: The Inside Story of Britain's Biggest Drugs Gang* (Edinburgh: Mainstream Publishing, 2012), loc. 2061–71.
82. *OESCE Guidebook: Intelligence-Led Policing*, Organisation for Security and Co-operation in Europe, https://www.osce.org/chairmanship/327476.
83. This was a major Met anti-corruption operation in the early 2000s. For more info on these issues, the book *Untouchables* by Michael Gillard and Laurie Flynn is highly recommended.
84. The member of the ops team mentioned here was also later implicated in the Ghost Squad corruption investigation.
85. *Observer*, 17 February 2002.
86. Barnes, *Cocky,* loc. 4145–8.
87. Ellison, Mark, *The Stephen Lawrence Independent Review: Possible corruption and the role of undercover policing in the Stephen Lawrence case — Summary of Findings* (London: HMSO, 2014).
88. Daly, Max. *Narcomania: A Journey Through Britain's Drug World* (London: Random House, 2012), loc. 3594–6.
89. Daly, *Narcomania* London, loc. 3585–8.
90. Conner-Hill, Rachel, 'Durham Police Plan to Supply Addicts with Heroin', *Northern Echo*, 5 March 2017.
91. Gash, Tom, *Criminal: The Truth About Why People Do Bad Things* (London: Allen Lane, 2016), p.1.